DATE DUE

UPI 261-2505   PRINTED IN U.S.A.

LETTERS
OF
J. M. BARRIE

BARRIE AT ADELPHI TERRACE HOUSE
From the painting by Peter Scott

LETTERS

OF

James Matthew

J. M. BARRIE

edited by

VIOLA MEYNELL

CHARLES SCRIBNER'S SONS
New York
1947

INTRODUCTION

BARRIE's letters of excuse would in themselves fill a volume—called Please Excuse Me. In one's dotage one might teach the children lisping at one's knee that the word *barrier* derived from the inaccessible Scottish playwright. His attitude to personal publicity was too constant not to have its set formula; it was always 'please excuse me'. To invent a new phrase each time would have been like saying good morning in different words every day.

But that volume is not this volume, though this may contain an example or two of that. This volume, if it were given a parallel name, would be Please Use Me. Like all people who have won eminence in any art, Barrie could have what friends he chose; he chose those therefore that he could rate highly. The beauty and talent that we all admire, mostly from afar, he admired, with susceptibility, at close quarters. Even stronger was his susceptibility to kindness, to whomever shown. A sensitive awareness to others' needs or ills was the quality in his friends that laid him flat; and in himself it was the quality that made him a walking embodiment of 'please use me'. Nothing in that line escaped him. 'Your first instinct is always to telegraph to Jones the nice thing Brown said about him to Robinson; you have sown a lot of happiness that way,' he writes to one correspondent, spying on a surreptitious habit. And here in these letters he may be found out in his own habit of delight to praise—and Barrie's praise was a very heart-felt brand. (The compiling of this book has been none the easier for that: people's modesty has put up many a formidable obstacle.)

The reader must expect to find this a very private collection of letters in the sense that they deal little with public affairs. Nor did his letter-writing include letters to the papers—that temptation of authors when reviewers trip up. Barrie is accused for instance of using, as Scotch, a word that is not Scotch: 'I wrote a brief letter to that paper,' he has recorded, 'saying that this word was not only good Scotch but was in frequent use in the Waverley novels. . . . I then put the letter

v

in my desk and went exultantly to bed. But there was something wrong and I could not sleep, and somewhere in the early hours I made up my mind to tear up that letter and never in my life to answer criticism. . . . Sometimes I must admit it has been rather a close thing. Several times I have indited a reply saying "Oh indeed!" or something stinging like that; but my post-box is at the far end of the street and there is also time for reflection when one is putting on one's muffler.' Since it was largely home affairs that employed his pen, lending themselves best to that 'Barrie touch' of his, he wrote with particular ease to women. When he knew a married couple it was to the wife he wrote most—even when the husband was Thomas Hardy.

A word about the handwriting in which these letters were written—and Barrie has himself many an illegible word to say on the subject. The narrative of his script is an eventful one, from the early days when Stevenson referred in a friendly way to its 'besotted ambiguity' to the time when he changed over to his left hand and, like Nelson, wrote better. In recalling his own journalistic days when he signed 'Anon', Barrie said: 'All the articles Anon sent to the *St James's Gazette* and elsewhere were in the same shaky scrawl, and oh it is ill to read. . . . In my schooldays I wrote the most beautiful copperplate; sometimes of an evening I still gaze at it with proud bewilderment. It went, I think, not gradually with over-writing, but suddenly like my smile. If the two ever meet in whatever Valhalla such things go to when they leave us, one would like to think that they quaff a goblet to "Anon". . . . About fifteen years ago a great change came over my hand-writing. I was saved by an attack of writer's cramp to which, once abhorred, I now make a reverential bow, though it is as ready as ever to pounce if thoughtlessly I take up the pen in my right hand. I had to learn to write with the left, not so irksome to me as it would be to most, for I am naturally left-handed (and still kick with the left foot). I now write as easily with this hand as once with the other, and if I take any pains the result is almost pleasing to the eye. The hope of my friends is that I shall never recover my facility with the other. Nevertheless, there is not the same joy in writing with the left hand as with the right. One thinks down the right arm, while the left is at best an amanuensis. The right has the happier nature, the left is naturally sinister.

I write things with the left, or to put the matter I think more correctly, it writes things with me that the right would have expressed more humanely. I never, so far as I can remember, wrote uncomfortable tales like *Dear Brutus* and *Mary Rose* till I crossed over to my other hand. I could not have written these, as they are, with my right hand any more than I could have written *Quality Street* with my left.' To Mrs Patrick Campbell he took the line, when the right hand was abandoned, that having written letters to her 'the hand that wrote them grandly destroyed its powers, as the true loyalist smashed his glass when he had drunk a royal health.' Eventually the right hand was cured and partially reverted to. 'I now write with whichever happens to be nearest the inkpot.' Perhaps the jests, when deciphered, cancelled out indignation.

Among lost or destroyed letters are those, unfortunately, to Stevenson and Meredith, and war-dispersal has meant the absence of some letters that should otherwise be here. But of these absent correspondents, not represented by Barrie's letters to them, many at least figure in his letters to other people.

The range of this collection is from 1884, when Barrie as a young man is applying for a post on the *Liverpool Post*, through the long years when comparative garrulity is left behind and he gives an increasingly concentrated and pointed version of himself, till the last letter he wrote on his deathbed in 1937 at the age of seventy-seven.

It has been thought best to present an uninterrupted idea of separate friendships as they occurred, and the letters belonging to them have therefore been grouped[1], to the detriment of a more general chronology. The reader will find that the formal beginning and ending of letters has often been omitted without signs to denote their absence, as have also, in some cases, the least interesting parts of letters. Where several letters follow to one correspondent, the address from which the letter is written should be understood to continue until a new address is given.

V. M.

---

[1] The star ★ is used to mark the beginning and end of such groups of letters.

To A. G. (later Sir ALEXANDER) JEANS, manager of the Liverpool Post and Echo

Greenbank, Dumfries, N.B. 21 December '84

Sir

In answer to your advertisement for an experienced sub-editor for a daily paper, I beg to submit my name for your consideration.

For the past two years I have been on the staff of the *Nottingham Daily Journal* where I acted as assistant-editor. The work expected of me there included leader-writing daily as well as much dramatic and literary criticism, and I had a share nightly in the practical subediting of the paper. My experience of sub-editing in all its branches is sound and thorough.

I left the *Journal* about a month ago owing to a change in its arrangements, but the proprietors were exceedingly sorry to part with me, and are ready and anxious to speak cordially in my favour.

I am in Scotland at present doing some interviews etc for the *Pall Mall Gazette* at the editor's request. For some months I have been one of the most frequent of the *Pall Mall Gazette's* occasional contributors, and articles of mine have also appeared in the *St James's Gazette* and other well-known London papers. I should like much to send you my scrap book with a large selection of printed specimens of my work.

I am 25 years of age and an M.A. of Edinburgh University.

For reference as to character and general capacities for filling the vacant post I refer you to the following gentlemen:—

Messrs Bradshaw, Proprietors, *Daily Journal*, Nottingham.

Professor Masson, The University, Edinburgh.

W. T. Stead, Esq., Editor, *Pall Mall Gazette*, London.

Rev. A. Whyte, D.D., Free St Georges, Edinburgh.

J. C. Ross, Esq., *The Times*, London.

C. E. Wilson, Esq., LL.D., H.M. Inspector of Schools, Edinburgh.

In conclusion I may say that should you consider my application favourably I would be untiring in my endeavours to justify the appointment. Any enquiries will be promptly attended to.

I am, Sir, your obedient servant, J. M. Barrie

[Mr Jeans, twenty-five years later, reminded Barrie of his application and invited him to send a message to the *Echo* on its twenty-fifth anniversary.]

Leinster Corner, Lancaster Gate, W. 10 June '09

I think I should feel flattered by your keeping that letter. I had forgotten it, and what amazes me about it is that I dared think I could sub-edit the paper. I wouldn't dare apply now.

But please excuse my not writing the line you speak of. I do wish the paper long continued success, but in this age of over-publicity I think writers should keep out of print when they can, and I try to live up to this.

I hope I wrote a better hand in 1884.

[Hilda Trevelyan, the 'Wendy' of 1907–8, let Mr Jeans's son, Mr Ronald Jeans, into the secret of an extra act to *Peter Pan* to be played for one performance only at the end of that season's run. Mr Ronald Jeans's notice—the only one—of the extra act, in the *Liverpool Post*, was sent to Barrie by his father.]

27 February '08

Thank you for the kind thought that made you send me your boy's writing about Peter Pan. He picked out the little things that pleased me I admit in the new scene. This is always the best compliment an author can get, and it's not a very common one.

I sometimes feel about Peter that there is a little inner circle who would know (as if it were a record of fact in which they had participated) the moment I went astray with him, and I certainly see your boy in that circle.

To T. L. GILMOUR, journalist, secretary to Lord Rosebery

Kirriemuir[1] [1887]

My dear Gilmour

. . . Have been to Kirk twice to-day (an old fellow-student preaching, cunning, a donkey) and thought out a title, *When a Man's Single*. Nothing fixed. Riach[2] would have had things

[1] Barrie's home-town.
[2] Alexander Riach, editor of the *Edinburgh Evening Dispatch*, where he welcomed frequent contributions from Barrie.

daily, but have so far only done two. The Free Assembly of next year the subject. Frightfully profane (see Thursday and Saturday). Great pains taken in the family to conceal authorship. . . .

133 Gloucester Road 15 February '96

My dr. Gilmour[1]

I meant to consult you about this last night. The fiends of the income tax are on me for what I am liable for. Do I pay income tax to them therefore from the year when I had a banking account (beyond that I don't know what my income was and don't want to know), or is there a limit of years beyond which they can't claim arrears?

Yours ever, Barrie Barnato

And what is this abt. taking the average for 3 years? Shd. each year be calculated that way, and if so how if the years before I had a banking account come into the calculation? Then how shd. I calculate '90 which was the year I began to bank?

★

To Mrs (afterwards Lady) QUILLER-COUCH, at Fowey, Cornwall

Kirriemuir, N.B. 3 April '92

Dear Mrs Couch

I have sent you a copy of my book because your big studio is a room I often think of with pleasure up here. Please take it. I don't know if you know how much I enjoyed myself at that corner fireplace. I am hoping Mr Couch is better: I saw a portrait of him smoking a cigar in the *Daily Graphic* which struck me as an uppish thing to do unless the intention was to make publishers think that literary hands (now the Copyright Bill is passed) do this regularly. And I have myself framed him from the *Bookman* all complete with a ring to hang him up by.

Lastly it will be a real gratification to him (and you) to know that his mysterious ailment has suggested a comedy or a novel to me. Seriously I want to hear whether he is better and I hope one of you will let me know.

Yours very sincerely, J. M. Barrie

[1] From 1885 until 1888, when Gilmour married, he and Barrie shared London chambers. Until 1890 Barrie had no banking-account, Gilmour acting as his informal banker.

3

To A. T. (afterwards Sir ARTHUR) QUILLER-COUCH ('Q'),
author, compiler of The Oxford Book of English Verse, *etc.*

Anchor Cottage, Shere, Surrey 26 June '92

My dear Couch

I am glad you are something better. Was beginning to fear otherwise as I could only trace you through the *Speaker*[1] where rather I could not trace you. I have had as it were to begin the world again since I saw you, for in the death of the man my sister was to marry the one great ambition of my life ends.[2] She is with me here, or rather what is left of her.

We came from Scotland a week ago. I have seen no one as yet. I see Barry Pain complaining to the press that his name is the same as mine. We may be here a month or so. After that I don't know. We may go to the sea. Is it possible to get rooms in your neighbourhood? My sister is not able to see a soul, but that would give me a chance of seeing you. She can't stay with friends. All the future is uncertain but this seems a possible thing. Let me know. With best regards to Mrs Couch,

Yours ever, J. M. Barrie

Garrick Club, W.C. 14 August '92

I am still at Shere and still meaning to go I know not where. At present I think it can't be Fowey, because I have some trivial business that sends me to London once a week. I often sit and look at Fowey in Bradshaw's map, which means that I have a hankering that way. I hope you are really better now, and doing more important work than I am at. I am writing plays to keep myself from thinking. I saw George Meredith the other day. He is better of a bad illness but more frail than when you were down. Have had some letters from Stevenson this summer. He can't endure *Tess* and says Hardy will need to do two novels as good as the old ones before he forgives this one. He also (Dagont!) refers me to a case Dishart v. Dishart as following the marriage of Babbie and Gavin. I see that you people don't know what love is. I want you to repeat this to Mrs Couch.

Yours ever, J. M. Barrie

[1]To which Quiller-Couch, as assistant editor, contributed largely.

[2]Barrie's youngest sister Maggie was to have been married in three weeks to James Winter, a young Free Church clergyman. Barrie had presented him with a horse to enable him to cover the distances in his scattered parish in Caithness. From this horse he was thrown and killed.

Kirriemuir 25 December '93

You are a low ruffian not to answer my letter, but I wish you a happy Christmas time all the same. If you will stay away from London you will miss much. I don't believe, for instance, that you know the new thing in shirt studs. For the sake of Mrs Couch I am remembering the fashionable colours and the new waists, and I have a novel blow delivered from the shoulder for the boy.

The *Delectable Duchy* is far and away the best fiction of the year. I enjoyed *Catriona* immensely though not quite equal I think to *Kidnapped*, but I would be much better satisfied with myself had I written your book. It is a good deal better than *Noughts and Crosses*. The 'new movement' (taradiddle dido) in fiction is sending all the clever young men off the lines I think but they'll get on the right track if they are much good. *Tess* was right, because it was Hardy's natural output. That is the whole thing surely. Blessed is the novelist who has no idea how he does it.

How does your book move on? I often think of it. Mine goes so slowly that it won't be ready for a year. The children won't grow up. The fact is that I find smoking an occupation in itself. I expect to be here for some time.

Have you read Zangwill's *Ghetto Tragedies*? He is improving immensely with each book, dropping smartness and vulgarity, and I believe in him. I see from the papers that I am in Switzerland with Maarten Maartens. Hope I'm enjoying myself.

3 January '94

It comes to this, that anything of the kind you cared to do is the kind of thing I could not possibly object to.[1] But I much question whether that is what is wanted. McClure's magazine dogs me as if it wanted my hand in marriage. There must be a mistake about Gilbert Parker. I only met him once (and liked him enormously), but remember no talk on any such matter. He wrote about interviewing me for this magazine, and I declined. Never shall man or maid interview me. Then Harold Frederic wanted to do a joint-author talk with me, a thing in which author (*a*) says 'When did you first feel genius springing up within you?' and author (*b*) (the owl) gravely

[1]A proposed article on Barrie.

5

tells him, and then (*a*) tells (*b*) which he considers his master-piece, etc., etc. I needn't tell you my answer to that.

Habits of life indeed! The low-minded might say that I have not even much habit of body. (That is 'graphic' and I expect the sort of thing wanted.) I like the magazine though. In appearance it is the prettiest on this or that side of the Atlantic, and has much better stuff in it than any of our sixpenny magazines. Also young McClure is a very nice fellow. If anything of the kind is ever done, it is certainly you I should like to do it. When I come to Fowey we can talk it over. Till then I leave the matter thus.

I wrote Andrew Lang and he answered. He is really very kindly, and I believe we have only to meet to be friends.

My mother is much better.

1 July '94

I could make a long letter of it but am shaky with a pen, though was holding a golf club firmly yesterday. My lungs are quite right again, and I have only to pick up strength now. Miss Ansell, who has an extraordinary stock of untrustworthy information on diseases of the human frame, knows all about quinsy and says she can sympathise in full. Yes, it is all true though it was in the papers,[1] and I am just recovering from the pleasure of having a letter on the subject—yours—which is not comic. Even so long ago as when I was going to you in Bedford Gardens I was beginning to hope that this would come about, and I am not in a position to deny, as the *Speaker* would say, that the obvious happiness of you two seemed to me a most enviable thing. We have worked hard to get married unbeknown to the lady journalists but vainly. In about a week it will be,—up here, so that we can go off together straight away, she to take charge. We go across the channel first for a month and fully mean to come your way soon thereafter. Vague talk of winter quarters, one idea to come to Fowey for month or two into rooms. I want Miss Ansell and your wife to be friends, and feel so sure they would be, and it would be a good place for me,—and consider the causeries we'd talk! We are both against London life for permanency.

Tell the Pippa[2] he knows nothing about it, and that she is

[1] His engagement to Mary Ansell.
[2] Bevil ('Pippa' or 'Piper'), the Quiller-Couchs' little son.

6

the kind he likes. Boxes well, but has to hold her tongue between her teeth.

The Boynes, Medstead, by Alresford, Hants 7 November '94
Being at present without any home in particular, liking your quarter of the world, eager to see yourselves, and itching to smash that there boy, we propose a descent on Fowey. This is to ask if you know of or can get to know of any rooms in the place that would be satisfactory to settle down in—probably for a month or two. The sort of thing we want would be two sitting-rooms, one of them such as I could work in and smoke in, and a good bedroom. An extra bedroom would be an advantage in case anyone came to see us. Also we have a dog[1] which needs a bit of garden ground to grow in, which he does a foot or so a night. Comfort and cleanliness is really all that is essential. We might come early next week so please let me hear by return.

Medstead [After leaving Fowey]
We have arrived. Glen was grand at first. Strutted about Par station like a gentleman in a fur coat but was bleary at Exeter and hangdog at Salisbury and limp as a rag thereafter. Has now recovered, and is going strong. Read a lot of news in the train. Crockett[2] has been interviewed in *British Weekly*. He rises at 4.30. *The Manxman* has been removed from some library because 'disgusting' and 'shameful'. Oh, my God.
Alack! We forgot to pack the tobacco and I'm living on cigars. My wife is writing to Mrs West to tell her to send it down to you. May it burn your tongue. Hope that chair is mended. Disgraceful not mended before. We go to London Monday.

Kirriemuir 26 March '95
Your bad news gave us a shock to-day and somehow the Pippa is the last quarter from which one would have expected bad news—it seemed so much a part of him to be well and full of spirits. You must have had a most painful time when he was at his worst and we sympathise with you both very deeply and feel some of the pain too. But that anxiety need not

[1]A St Bernard, first called Glen, later Porthos.
[2]The Rev. S. R. Crockett, Scottish author.

evidently trouble you any longer, and you have every reason to hope that he will soon be his own masterful self again. It seems often difficult to say what causes pneumonia, but I believe it is a fact—many people who have had it tell me so—that you are often stronger after it than ever before. It does not at all necessarily leave the lungs weak. You will soon see him lording it on the Parade again. He always seems to me as much a bit of the Parade as the grass wall, and I wish I were there again to be his very worst horse. We have not been having a very lively time either. As soon as I stepped on my native soil ten days ago the influenza snapped me up and though I am all right again, my wife and sister both have it now, and my mother is very frail. However all seem to be mild cases. We have not fixed the house yet, had to come north hurriedly, but unless something new turns up it will be the Chiltern Hills. I wasn't very happy in London, chiefly perhaps because I wasn't working, but it impressed me as a werry hollow place—and as for the clubs, after one look inside I conceived a desire to resign my membership, from which my wife enticed me. They are the most unprofitable places, and the only real club I know is your study when the lamp is lit and the top off the chair and the clock pointing to eleven P.M.

Meredith was in town and we dined with him. He had come to let the doctors work their will, but they found it unnecessary.

I have got no work done since I left Fowey from the various causes I mention. Glen is here and becomes very bushy. I wish you would let me hear how the Pippa gets on. He is my favourite boy in the wide wide world. With love from us both to you all,

Bally

133 Gloucester Road, S.W. 19 January '96
Almost do you persuade us. What we feel is that to go for ten days or so into such a celestial climate and then return to the cold and darkness of Gloucester Road would be to our hurt rather than our benefit. We don't want to be away longer than a fortnight, and two days each way would be spent on travelling. You are in different case as you will be away long enough to be set up. On the other hand it is immensely tempting, them there palms and roses and that banana. As for the billiard table, I know that billiard table. I should think

you would have a lovely time, and it is just possible we may fling discretion to the winds and come. We swither, as we say in the kailyard. It could not be for a fortnight or so, my play keeps me back, not my sister's affair which has come off all right.[1] It is a boy. What is a boy? as the one good page in 300 of a Bulwer Lytton says. I am heartily glad you like *Tommy*.[2] They begin with a very long instalment but must give much less hereafter. He goes to the kailyard presently and develops impishly, but you are supposed to like him against your better judgment. The Painted Lady's girl appears there and is an important character.

The *Westminster Gazette* has been inquiring at the libraries about what boys read and you, sir, have 199 votes, coming very near to Henty the Great. But it is curious. It must mean the *Spur* and *Dead Man's Rock* only,—so that these are the most popular boys' books of '95. Cassell's should take account of it. (Henty with scores of books is under 300.) Messrs Trollope, some-other-body and Barrie have *one* vote each. I should like to give my boy a sovering, poor lonely little chap.

Inform the Pippa that Glen has been behaving well and is at present lying in the hall in four positions. He would like werry much to be careering round the terrace of your hotel, with a stick in his mouth, Pippa hanging on. Well, there's no hope of his getting so far, and as for us, it's doubtful. But not impossible. Let us hear that the oranges have not gone bad on the under side and that the frost has not nipped the noses (roses). We might succumb. Mary has had a cold and so have I, and she sends you greetings from a long lie abed.

23 March '96

Ia finds me with mingled feelings—delight in the preface, which pleases me more than words can tell, and a good deal of indignation with the way the book is got up. I agree with you thoroughly, it is a triumph of tastelessness and really too bad. And to do the thing well is so easy. I don't know to what extent this may injure the sale. That it has some effect is undoubted. However Ia herself is a beautiful character and she will live it down. She is far away in front of any of your other women.

[1] Maggie had married William Winter, elder brother of the dead James.
[2] *Sentimental Tommy*, appearing serially in *Scribner's Magazine*.

9

We were in Paris a week and saw the dog Pippa mistook for Glen. It looked very cocky over that mistake. We were recalled by sad news. My sister's baby of whom I told you died suddenly, seven weeks old.

Crockett was with us for a week-end. 'His terms are'—'he sells'—'Watt says'—'his publishers say'—'his terms'—'his sale'— But otherwise he is all right and kindly and oh, he is happy. Met Hardy lately, he has taken a house for some months near here and tried to get me to talk about servants. Has dramatised *Tess*. When a man dramatises his troubles begin.

For some days I've been rolling about the floor more or less with indigestion. Am writing a little thing about my mother, which may make a small book though I meant it for a preface. I hope you'll go on with your long story now and get that shorter one in also. The 30,000 words story is really the freshest thing to do.

A painter who began a portrait of me years ago is at it again and I feel like flying the country to escape him.

We're going to Nicoll's[1] to-morrow. We had a ghastly passage across the channel and Mary still clings to the furniture as if it sea-sawed. Give your fair lady, as Crockett would say, my compliments and tell her I'm politer than ever.

21 November '96

I read your *Contemporary* article with vast pleasure and with a delight in the generosity that makes a critic of you. You are very ready in my case to take the will for the deed but you have found out some things about me and about the book that I thought were only known to myself. Well, I think I know some things about you and your books which are only known to the same two people. And it comes to this, that I would rather please you than any man I know. We had a roaring time in America and I wish I could drop in on you about nine P.M., put another log on the study fire and tell you all about it. The thing I am proudest of is that the reporters were much struck by the beauty of my *voice*. The only other person who loves my voice is (I need not tell you) Mrs Couch. She never admits it in words, but I guessed it from the first—from the way she smiled. The literary men were very good fellows. Cable[2] is the prince among them. The quaintest

[1] William Robertson Nicoll.
[2] George W. Cable, novelist and story-writer of Louisiana.

10

most lovable of human beings. We were some days with him and they are my best memory of America.

You should have seen Nicoll gloating over the bookstalls.

Is there any chance of your being in London? I wish there were, but not that you had to travel for the Pippa's sake. I hope he is lording it in the old triumphant way, and ready for a mawling at Bally's hands. Some day we may walk in on you and begin at once. One advantage of travelling in America is that it makes Fowey seem round the corner. We got back a week ago but have seen no one yet.

Glen is all right, and on our return could not make up his mind which of us to eat first—which was our saving.

3 December '96

The Stevenson Memorial committee at Edinburgh ask me to help them to try to get you to go there for the meeting on the 10th inst. Rosebery is to be in the chair and it is advisable we should do our best in the matter. Wherefore I who loathe platforms have consented to go. Also to speak, which I suppose is what they also want of you. I needn't go into details, as you will be hearing from themselves. They are trying to get Kipling also. It is a long journey and I know you feel about such things much as I do, but it is certain that if you can go you would be helping on the cause. I wouldn't propose it to you otherwise. Of course it would be gorgeous to me to be in Edinburgh on your first visit to the place. We would have great times. Let me know your decision. My wife is going. How about yours?

Edinburgh 11 December '96

I have sent you a *Scotsman* with report of the meeting. I really wish you had been here if only to hear the roars of welcome with which your name was greeted. They were the first out-burst from the crowd. You don't understand what a public you have here. It is comparatively limited but it is the public that will carry this memorial to success. The 'people' of course are as they always were indifferent to R.L.S. and think this confounded 'art' an absurdity. They were at the meeting because Lord R. was in the chair. There is a fierce enough local opposition to the thing, in influential circles, but they are afraid to speak out because his lordship is about. (I loathe snobbish-ness so much that I hate to write of it, but there it is.) The papers are really hating the movement but Rosebery sat on a newspaper article of yesterday morning advocating waiting 10 or 20 years, and they sneak behind him to-day. The cultured lot are very enthusiastic and the students and other poor men no less so. But there's no question that Rosebery has done it all, and I think courageously. He has his faults, but this is a real thing to his credit.

I thought the extracts the *Chronicle* gave us of your Poems and Ballads were very beautiful, incomparably more genuine poetry than Kipling's new book, which is amazing, wonderful, but to me not poetry at all. I don't care how much a man knows about machinery and sails, the one thing I want of a poet is beautiful thoughts (which means beautiful words also) and that you give me. However I had better 'hold my tongue' till I have read the book which is now lying waiting me at home. I should feel very miserable if I thought you were getting despondent about your books because they have not a great sale. Why, there is not any other young man *trying* to write, trying to think, attempting to look down into life at all. Go back to the *Dead Man's Rock* business and you will at once be in the running with the most popular men of the day. That is the kind of thing they are all doing. But go on doing your best and you have a reward which is the only real reward and as it seems to me the only thing that makes this calling of letters a manly one. And I tell you if you had heard what your name meant yesterday to the 1000 or so of students here, nearly all poor as mice, it could not but have touched you. The far more popular names passed without a sound, and no doubt it accounts for the papers giving your letter and omitting nearly all the others.

What you say of publishers is quite true. They are not advertising *Tommy* at all—absolute blank. Hodder and Stoughton must have spent ten times as much on the new book[1] already.

The only remarkable book I've seen by a newcomer is *Nancy Noon* (Fisher Unwin).[2] Mad, wrong-headed and all about brothels, etc. (never nasty) but I think a real arrival. I wish you would read it. I'll send it you if you have not.

[1] *Margaret Ogilvy.*
[2] A novel by Benjamin Swift.

12

I am glad you shook off the effects of the influenza so quickly. It was like the Pippa's cheek to escape the thing altogether. I mean the Skipper—as he informed me (with his head to the side) he is now called. *Eyes of the Sea* takes me as a title. I have thought for some time that the more of the sea you have in your books the better for all of us.

I have told Colvin your views on *St Ives*[1] and he is very pleased. He has not heard from Samoa yet, but expects word in a week or two, and will write you what they think on the subject. He does not think Osborne could do it, but they may think otherwise. As I understood, only one chapter would take place in Edinburgh and that a ball, and all action. No Scotch. There is a crossing to America in a balloon I think, etc., etc. All this to put in, but I fancy the scheme is in existence pretty fully drawn up. It is an unequal story I agree with you—beginning fine—cheapish plot creeping in but the death of the old man in this number A1. Colvin says there is one fine thing yet, but the rest not of his best.

I can't make out whether I have had influenza also. It may be only paint. If so I'm chockfull as if I had licked it off the stairs. One advantage, and a considerable one, of living in a furnished house is or should be that your wife is not seized with periodic frenzy for painting and papering. I'm dramatising the *Little Minister* or founding a play on it at all events. Oh, the re-reading of one's books. It is a grim ordeal.

Broadway, Worcestershire 20 April

Just got your letter which had to follow me here. I'm heartily glad you are to finish *St Ives;* it is the right thing to do. About the Assembly ball, I think I know the hall where they were held and am less confident that it is in Waterloo Place. The man to instruct you is Walter Blaikie, who will almost certainly be able to send you some old works on the subject. Wasn't it R. Chambers who did a book called *Old Edinburgh*? There are lots of such books and Blaikie is the very man, besides which it will be a pleasure to him to assist. I also think there will be illustrations of the Assembly rooms with costume figures, etc.

[1]Stevenson's story being unfinished when he died, 'Q' was to complete it from Stevenson's plan.

The same advice applies to site for balloon ascent. Good luck! a balloon. You will need to get at William Terriss Esquire to show how the thing should be done. As far as I remember Colvin's talk, the balloon goes down in mid-Atlantic, after which you will feel on safer *ground*. Haw haw!

Your own story sounds like the thing. Sandhills and a light-house are two things you can't help scoring with. Lighthouse is about the most dramatic object in the world—romance beats on it all day long. I'm finishing *Little Minister* play. We've come here for a week. A land of orchards, very beautiful and as English as anything could be. We bicycled (Oh, my ankles!) from Stratford—kept shouting every minute 'What a scene for Alfred Parsons!' when suddenly remembered that it *is* Alfred's own country and that he did last year the very road and orchard which we had specially fixed for him to do. Also discovered next day that he had been here same night (staying with Millet[1]) and gone off to lay out what you call Eve's garden.

There have been some big bargains going in the way of houses. The Navarros (Mary Anderson as was) have a glorious old farm-house, all over oak and ingle nooks with 10 acres of ground, £38 a year. A good deal to spend in putting it in order of course. Miss Maud Valerie White (musician) has another beauty, £20 a year, all Elizabethan.

I hope you will come on to London when you are in Cambridge. If you would stay with us we should be uncommonly delighted. Come along and bring the family and we shall invite the Queen in to meet the Pippa. It would be historic.

The reason my writing is worse than ever is that the table is werry low and the chair werry high so that I dive at the paper.

1 May '98

Yes, if you could arrange anything for Cable at Oxford it would be a comfort, particularly as he must go there at any rate. Also May 21 would suit well. He fires the first shot in this house on the 17th and I must arrange to have the dog out all day as nothing maddens Porthos so much as one person doing all the talking By the way Cable has a lecture on some literary subject which he gives instead of reading if preferred.

[1]Frank Millet, painter from New York, living at Broadway, Worcestershire.

14

He arrived on Wednesday and is delicious, goes into fits over the most unexpected things. The lamp posts in particular are a roaring delight to him and when he sees a pile of stones he asks if they are oyster shells. I have also to tell him how we build our houses and line them and keep out the damp and he takes my answers down in a note book. When he sees a soldier he mutters 'Well, well, there he goes, you don't say, oh, to think of it!' He calls half crowns two and a quarters and asks at the P.O. for two dime stamps, and oh, but I wish you were here just now. The sweetness, the dignity of him are things to revel in.

Our love to you both.

12 February '99

The most contemptible thing about the flu is its absurdly inadequate name. At the least it should begin with D. I hope I am too late to make the suggestion that you should try Christian Science on it. There can be nothing more exasperating, I should say, to a good sharp pain than your insisting blandly that it isn't there.

I am glad you have finished your story, it reminds me that after all one does at last get to the end. Oh, that final 'canter up the avenue'. They should see the author belabouring the brute.

I see the finish not so far off of my own, but it cracked somewhere about the middle and needs a deal of sticking plaster yet.

Do go on with the farce. I want to read it. And it may be worth Porthos's weight in gold. You never can tell. It all depends on the boy who brings our chops.

Porthos is much tickled at the Piping Pippa taking to whistling toons and wants to know how wide he stretches his legs when he does it.

That same dog has been down with the rheumatics and is very cocky about it.

Mary is quite well, but unfortunately it seems that she must have another of those operations again which depresses me though she makes light of it. We are hoping that buying the dining-room furniture will bring you up. It is a long time since we saw you now and we are always wanting to.

I have a real feeling of pride in you over this book,[1] which seems to me to be a beautiful work of art. Certainly I know of no boy's life in our fiction that pleases me as much. With the boy I include his parents. I am not sure that they are not the best in the book. I could have had a shot at the mother, but the father is altogether beyond me, men have seldom done the father well. I shall think of them as part of the sea every time I hear it. Those early days are the haunting part of the book to me, but the end at least is quite worthy of them and is obviously the end they really had. So far as Taffy goes I like his second part as well or nearly as well as the first, the girl I have less touch of now, she has shed her wings. But of course I see that this was in your scheme and that the one light pales as the other comes out. I wish you would come up so that we might have a talk over the book, it is the book I shall always think of you by, and the others are but prentice work in comparison. Mary read it in the magazine and has read it twice in the book.

That you should lose your mother just as the child came, I think teaches a great lesson in serenity. It is as if they had passed each other in their different voyages, the one coming in as the other went out. Can you not hear them hailing. And which voyages with most confidence, the dying or the child. We are never so confident between times, it seems all so easy at the beginning and the end.

Fay Felicia, you kept us waiting for that little skiff of yours; various people, madam, besides those you have taken up with were on the outlook for you and anxious about you and scanned the coast and were much relieved to see you step ashore. When you are really nice I mean to call you Dear Delicia but at other times I shall address you as fay felicia fiddle de da,—all, mark you, with little f's.

We are all well, except in the morning when we tremble so over the newspapers and what they may contain[2] that there is no keeping my tooth in. By the way another came out in Edinburgh, a real one, but I cut it with a penknife into the most fashionable shape, replaced it, knocked it in with a hairbrush, puttied it round, and it is 'doing well' though a bit

---

[1] *The Ship of Stars.*
[2] Regarding the Boer War.

16

sulky, the pride of the ingenious mechanic and the scorn of his domestic circle. Our warmest love to Mrs Couch and our godchild but Pippa needn't fear he's forgotten.

8 February 1900

. . . We are both as well as people can be who know that Buller has crossed the Tugela. I went to the House the opening night, a poor show. Balfour bewildered, neat, Bannerman lumpy, with his little joke—no rising to the occasion anywhere. . . .

27 December 1900

To wish a merry Christmas time—to wish the same to thee and thine. From this you will see that I am writing a pantomime. We have been mad enough to be inveigled thereinto and the result will be on view at this address on January 7. Drawing-room turned into a Hall by magic. We much and deeply deplore that the Piper cannot be present though he is now rather big. Our aim is to convulse the four year olds. I am Cowardy Custard, Mason[1] is Sleepyhead, and it is all as funny as that.

It is a long time now since we saw you and we hope you will descend on London again ere long. Your anthology is altogether delicious I think. Just when Craig is going at last, he comes upon it and stays another hour. I had the thin paper edition but the other is easier reading. It must be rather fine to have a book so well got up.

I have a small book and a play in my mind but not much on paper. The world will be younger in them than in *Tommy*.

Mary is at present trying on her fairy costume. She is a 'very-good-little-girl.' I tried on my trousers last night and have wanted to go into hiding ever since. Oh, that I had chosen the part of the Bear. I am glad that Fay Felicity will not see me. She could never love me any more. I am glad that Mrs Couch won't see me, though I hope she would love me even then. But I think I could make the Piper roar. *I take off twelve waistcoats*. Exit to rehearsal.

Leinster Corner, Lancaster Gate, W. 3 January '05

Yes, I do wish you could fix up some day for us to go to Winchester and be carted about by the Pippa. It is a thing I

[1]A. E. W. Mason, author and playwright, at one time Liberal M.P. for Coventry

17

should like uncommon and almost any time could be made to fit me. I thought that preface to Newbolt quite a beautiful thing, but I should like to feel, and you to feel, that 'we three' at Winchester would be pretty close connected also. It is sad that the six or eight hours between us should wall us off from each other so.

These *Peter Pan* rehearsals have given me a month's headache. I see plainly that one can't write plays and books alternately, or anything of that kind. One's ideas all get into the way of seeking for the one outlet, and so at present they form with me into acts. I never find myself wondering, should this be a story or a play. If it makes for the one, it couldn't to me make for the other. However I suppose if the right idea were to come for the book I should get back my old zest, and book or play it doesn't matter if one could do something good. How thankful we should be to feel when we sit down to the desk that we can work with some pleasure to ourselves. The great thing. And yet—if only we could dispose of that large assortment of second class ideas, for one first class idea.

I have no doubt you are right about that Sladen business. I have had two requests to join in the controversy from him and put them in the fire, presuming they were the usual newspaper trick. Dislike of papers and all their ways seems to grow on me. I fear they are a chief curse of the age and likely to become more so, despite the good men and true that are keeping the banner flying here and there. It seems a pity this little fiscal dodge is not exposed, if it hasn't been. I find I can't argue intelligently on Free Trade, though I'm still a devout upholder of it. I went to hear Mason and Sir Edward Grey at Coventry on it, and I thought they knew a deal about it at the meeting but was not so sure by supper time. Mason leads a light-hearted happy life. E. V. Lucas is the only man I've met of late years that I specially took to. You would like him. I end as I began by wishing I could see more of you. So do arrange the Winchester adventure. With love to Mrs Couch and the god-child and the P——.

9 January '06

What with your committees and things I believe you in Fowey are more in the world than I am in London. I am growing into a complete hermit bounded north south east and

18

west by my own petty little notions which I usually abandon in the middle not because they are actually bad but because they work out so dolefully second class. I have been having a bout of this depressing kind lately and little to show for it but a philosophic countenance. The glorious thing is not to know it's second class till it's finished. I think it's very good for you that you have these outside interests, they are a tonic. For a few hours lately I hesitated about standing for a seat—the Glasgow and Aberdeen universities—to see if I could get the tonic that way, but I soon fled. Henry Craik is standing and he once said I was badly dressed, but on the whole I couldn't decide that this was sufficient reason to contest his seat with him, all which is far from meaning that I'm not keen on the liberals coming in. What I should like is you to stand. I want somebody to represent me. Come and be my boy. Lord if I had a boy how I should back him up! I expect the Piper is now a formidable mysterious creature. I picture him a bit inscrutable to the common eye, hiding all sorts of fine things very sternly, for I can't doubt he is on the way to being a good man and true. I saw a good deal of him after all in the years that tell best what is to follow. I am going on Monday with E. V. Lucas (one of the few I see much of) to Coventry to Mason's election. He is loved all over the place and gets wound up by big meetings to great effect. I have been reading a bit of his next novel. His heroines (Mrs Couch will be interested at last) are always drawn from the lady he is then in love with, and by the time I see the proofs it is always all off but he keeps her in, and roars his great laugh when attention is drawn to the circumstances. He is as big a swell as ever, but his socks don't match and so all is well.

I am looking forward to the *Mayor of Troy*, and I think if you won't come to this place I shall soon take a run down to Fowey. One can't discuss ideas for plays by letter with any satisfaction and I want to talk with you long on that and many another subject. I think it's truth that you are what I miss mostly in London. It would have made a big difference to me if you had been here all these years. Your last book had one story which is quite the most diverting thing you have ever done. About the gentlemen in a state of nature whom they tried to catch in a net. I laughed aloud as I read and could have broken into cheers.

I think there is no doubt of the *idea* of the *Mayor of Troy* being right for stage treatment. I take the idea to be the apparently indispensable man disappearing as dead, and returning to find, so to speak, that he *is* dead. Among my notes I have an idea not dissimilar—A learned old fellow, scientific, wealthy, genial, full of kindness, much loved, simple, goes off for long voyage for health. That was first act. In second, years have elapsed. You see his relatives dining in his memory, drinking immortal memory, etc. His money has gone to them and to some hospital or other charitable object. His Life is complete (biography) but not yet published. They are feasting in adjoining room. He returns, glories in what he hears them saying about him, etc., chuckles and looks through MS biography. Then when reveals himself realises that in a sense he is a blow to them. Their worldly positions are injured, hospital money becomes his again, biography can't be published, etc. It puts him in an agony, and I know no more. The idea here is that the dead though loved and mourned (all are nice people) can't come back to be delighted in as the mourners think. It seemed too depressing for a play at all events, and though there is some grim truth in it, it doesn't seem to be all the truth. A happy ending if it could be contrived would probably be artistically the right ending. I am not sure how far these considerations apply to your idea, but I do think that in both cases it would be too painful to end in death. The kindliness in human nature seems to cry out against it.

On the other hand I do strongly believe in the return 'from the dead' as a strong dramatic motive. And possibly our two ideas might unite. I have a notion that my man who would have sympathy from the start is better for a play than yours, but that your period, manner of disappearance, etc., is better than mine. I wonder whether a subsidiary character could also return (servant?). Wife disgusted with him for return, he going to neighbours and demanding back the things of his she had given them as mementoes etc. They decline. Or possibly all might work into the one figure. If we could work out a scheme don't you think it would be good fun to do it together under an assumed name and really keeping it secret?

To return to the *Mayor* as a book, I think the latter portion fine and impressive. There is abundance of good stuff in the earlier portion but I do think you stand there looking at your people from an ironical (though kindly) point of view too persistently. It is an error I fancy I have often fallen into myself. The arrest of the actor is one of the funniest things I have read. You will have seen my political parody *Josephine* is out, but whether it will do is as yet open to doubt. I enjoyed writing it more than most things I've done of late, but for one thing a solemn burlesque calls for more from the audience than anything appealing to the feelings, and I daresay the irony is too prolonged. Nothing wearies more I believe than satire the moment it ceases to be attractive. It is such a confoundedly unloveable vehicle.

Let me know whether you find anything in my suggestion worth further discussion.

25 July '09

It was pleasant to see your hand again. I think the play is first rate and with your consent will advise Frohman to do it in his repertory. As you may know he is to convert the Duke of York's into a repertory theatre in February. The only difficulty I foresee is that it will be an expensive little piece to stage and the repertory business is a costly problem at the best. . . .

I'm glad you got some entertainment out of *What Every Woman Knows*. The first act I always thought really good and the second also as a whole (with the English ladies to spoil it a bit). The rest is rather of the theatre somehow ingenious enough but not dug out of myself. It isn't really the sort of man I am. I fancy I try to create an artificial world to myself because the one I really inhabit, and the only one I could do any good in, becomes too sombre. How doggedly my pen searches for gaiety. My last chuckle will be got from watching it. I miss you much and always. On the whole I've cared for you more than for any other of our calling. The Boy! To think he is leaving Winchester instead of putting on his pinafore. To-morrow he will be leaving Oxford. An English boy has almost too good a time. Who would grudge him it, and yet he knows too well that the best is past by the time he is three and twenty. Perhaps Oxford should be kept as a bait until we are fifty. I hope he is to have a happy and good life, and my love to all of you.

3, Adelphi Terrace House, Strand, W.C. 7 March '11

I am very glad to hear from you, always was and will be. I nearly went to Fowey lately to try to get rid of influenza, but I wasn't fit for so long a journey and went and wandered on the Brighton shores instead. I have not much concern now with literature and the drama, which both have flowed by me. I have in a sense a larger family than you now. Five boys whose father died four years ago and now their mother last summer, and I look after them, and it is my main reason for going on. The Llewelyn Davies boys. However, I do a little writing also and do it here, though mostly I am with them. I should be very glad to help in any sort of way with that play, there is no doubt about its being a fine subject but the difficulty is that it seems to lead to a grim end, and rather a queer view of life altogether. I have often thought of it in 3 acts and see the first two all right. The third seems to amount to this. No-one should come back, however much he was loved.[1] What I should like you to do is to draw up a scenario in quite a few words and let me have a think about it. Of course much the best would be if we could meet and talk things over. Couldn't you get up to town for a day or two—preferably not at a week-end as I am rather tied with the boys then. It would do me good to talk with you of that and other things.

I like to hear of the Boy and of Fay Felicia and often think of them.

[On January 2nd 1922 'Q' wrote to congratulate Barrie on receiving the Order of Merit. 'We had hoped it would be so (and the "we" includes your greatest admirer, aetat 21 now). There was great joy in this house to-day'.]

8 January '22

. . . Don't let us slip back into the idiotic condition of never seeing each other. What I should like to do is to come down to you for a little later in the year. There are corners in Fowey outside the home as well as in where I want to stand again looking at the Pippa, as he was and as he still stands out to me.[2] And I wish you would come here when in London. There is a room very much at your service.

[1] The future *Mary Rose* theme.
[2] He died of pneumonia in Germany soon after the Armistice.

22

I daresay you have heard that Fay and I pulled off our
rehearsal. It was a very pleasant time for me, and as I dis-
creetly watched how the proceedings affected her I was rather
elated to feel that she felt much as I used to feel in similar
circumstances in the days when I too was young. Before it
was over I could make good guesses at what her face was
going to say. And it is a dear attractive face too, and I don't
need to be told that you are happy of her. She fitted uncommonly into this room, and I wish I could see her often in it.
There is no marvel except the sons and daughters, and the
country is really all right as long as that goes on. She must
be to you like a continuance of good weather, and indeed I
felt that she was a continuance of our old friendship, which I
can assure you is as live a thing to me to-day as when you
were in Bedford Gardens or the day when we wandered around
at Fowey talking of R.L.S.'s departure from the scene. I am
taken aback by what you say of your eyes which have evidently
been a much more serious trouble to you than I had any idea
of. However Fay was able to give me a certain amount of
comfort on the subject, and if you do as you are told it seems
reasonable to expect some improvement. She was sublime in
her charity when she talked of you and your tobacco, and I
lit my pipe with a lighter heart. I wish she was my girl.

I do want to see you again on the old terms very much.
Fowey is very far away to me. Except when I go to Scotland
I never seem nowadays to go as far as Richmond Park. Don't
go to clubs or anything. A few years ago I was elected to
another club and went into it for the first time with a member
who said he knew I didn't go much to my other clubs but
hoped I would come oftener here, to which my reply, 'Dear
Sir, I *have* now been oftener here than to my other clubs'. It
was a very nice club but I have not been back. This is the spot
where I sleep best, which has long been a grand consideration
for me, and I am probably rather a coward about it. What
I hope will happen is that in this spring I suddenly send you
word that if you are there I am coming, but if I don't I still
wish you would let me know of a night or two next term at
Cambridge when you would have some freedom and we could
be together without my having to meet people.

My warm love to you all, and it won't be my fault if we don't
pull this off.

23

I am supposing you are now at Fowey and hope you are all having a good time together—if my affection for you all helps in any way it should be a very good time. Though I say all, don't think I am forgetting the fourth or that he was not often in my mind when I was at Jesus. The one regrettable thing about my visit is that we did not have a long evening alone together when we could have come closer to each other as I am sure we both wanted. And how tongue-tied was I when we were going to the station and at it. Yet I was full of affection for you then, and I can't tell you how sorry I am that you have this trouble with your eyes.

I could have made so much more of my time, but nevertheless it was to me the happiest visit I have paid anywhere for a very long time. Only next time let us have that evening alone. I wish so much I could prevail on you both to come for a few days to Stanway any time in August, bringing Fay with you. It is in Gloucestershire, about twelve miles from Cheltenham, a house I have had in summer for several years, and it would be an uncommon delight to me if you could do this. I want much to see my lady Q again and resume where we left off.

One of my boys, the youngest, is with me just now, and is taking me out to dine at his 'club' which is called the Kit Kat though he doesn't know why (nor care).

My love to you all.

Stanway, Cheltenham 12 August '26

Fay has just gone and I trust reaches you safely, but we here are all left lamenting. It is a joy to me to know that you have such a blessing about your home and that you are only half bereft though the Pippa as I still think of him had to go. It is not too much to say that she is universally loved in this house, and I can be sarcastic to her all day, which is the sort of girl for whom I have been looking for a long time. I salute the day you notified me that she wanted to see a rehearsal. She will tell all our news, especially about the Australian cricketers and how Macartney tamed and rode me. There has been nothing like it since the novels of Hawley Smart and Mr Smedley.

You send me such a very nice letter that it is hard for me to reply like a curmudgeon, and that indeed is why I have delayed, trying to urge myself to face the ordeal of public speech. But you see my horror of such things grows with the years, it is not the actual doing of it that so much disturbs me as the thought for weeks before that it is drawing n gh. Your lectures have saved you from getting into this morbid condition, as I suppose it is, but though I hate myself rather for writing thus I know I should go to bed appalled if I had accepted. So please excuse this dull dog. And smile kindly on the folly of your affectionate friend. All three of you please do that. The rest of your letter certainly holds out lovely prospects and I shall hope to get you to have me some other time when there are only ourselves (so to speak) in Fowey That little room and its books and outlook are to this day among my dearest and also most vivid memories, it has absolutely the face of a friend to me and might make me able to talk again or even write. I do hope this rest is truly being good for your eyes. I try mine a good deal o' nights reading Trollope in bed in small type and have now got to the pitch that if I pick up a book that does not conduct to Barchester I toss it contemptuously aside. I did write a long play to be done by eight children at Stanway last Christmas time but one of them[1] fell ill and had to be operated on instead. Now he's all right again and plays at operations unceasingly ('Nannie, bring me that potato peeler—I want to cut up mother') and we may do it at Easter. This is the proper way to write plays and you get superb actors. Programme enclosed. The performers age from four years upwards and they learn long parts as quickly as that peeler does for the potatoes.

11 May '30
Your letter means of course more to me than almost any others, I am dining with you to-night in Clareville Grove (wasn't it?). Or I am on my way to Fowey. A month or so ago I got hold of some old *Speakers* and you might say there we were, making friends, and those were bits of books we wrote while doing it. I think it is the truth to say that in these 40 years I have met no man that has meant as much to me.

[1]Simon Asquith.

I had a happy experience in my old home two years ago when I re-met the friend of my infancy and discovered that I was as much attached to him as ever. He is an iron-monger now and my oldest recollection is his running to my house (we were about 5) to tell me an old man we knew had cut his throat with a razor and if I came quick I should see the blood. And I did.

Well, well, my warm love to you all.

13 July '30

My installation as Chancellor of the University of Edinburgh is to take place there on Saturday, Oct. 25th, and I am writing informally, but with the authority of the Senatus, to ask you to grace the occasion by being present at 10 a.m. and receiving the honorary LL.D. degree, and very much hope that you will do us this favour.

The formal invitation cannot be issued till the Senatus meets in early Oct., till which time they wish no public announcement to be made.

['Q' wrote: 'To be sure I am proud! . . . Funny old world. Once, if I remember, Edinburgh was sticky about doing you justice. But this is fine. Thank you ever so much, my dear man. I prize the thought more even than the honour. But you know *that*.']

★

From Mrs DAVID BARRIE (MARGARET OGILVY) to her son, JAMES MATTHEW BARRIE

[As no letter from Barrie to his mother is in existence, this solitary survival from her to him is given,—written probably in 1892 when his sister Maggie, after the death of the man she was to marry, was living in Barrie's care.]

My dear beloved Jamie

My heart keeps blessing and thanking you, but no words can say my love. My heart fails words for my first birthday gift.

My dear beloved son, God bless you and prosper you. You are a precious God-given son to me, the light of my eyes, and my darling Maggie is safe with God and you till we meet.

Your loving Mother

14 Bryanston Street, W. 20 November '93

My dear Maartens

Ever since your letter arrived I have been swithering, as we say up north, whether to answer it in one way or the other. I have an uncommon desire to bear down upon you with Nicoll, and your warning that we should be alone is certainly an added attraction. I have about 500 things to say to you, some of them left over from our former meeting—a delightful memory it is to me—and others have shot up since then. However as it seems impossible for Nicoll to defer his visit I must come alone later if possible. Not work keeps me back, oh, no! But I can't get north to my mother until the middle of December and it would be a disappointment to her if I was off again in the beginning of January. Our home is reduced in membership now, and I like to be there a good deal. It is up there that I should like to receive you next time. And I should like to introduce Elias Lossell and some other people to some Thrums persons who as yet have only met on a shelf. Sad that characters in books should never meet, tho' as near as the two sides of a coin.

Which reads as if I had forgotten Lang's freak. But they do meet in a way when their authors meet, and the more we know of each other the better friends are they. Is there not something pleasant in that notion?

I wish you would write me sometimes and break down all barriers, so that we could truly talk to each other in an inconsequent way as if we were in your château or among my hand-looms. Stevenson is the only friend of this kind I have and we exchange thoughts that run to columns of the *Times* in length. He wails the dearth of books, but I have the luck to have missed some of the best until now. You will envy me when I tell you that I read the *Cloister and the Hearth* for the first time lately. Reade shares with Scott, I think, the supreme gift of narrative. He might have flung away some of his plots with advantage, but how good in a hundred ways! His women especially. Even his hobbies are a joy. Whenever a doctor is introduced, don't you hear the band striking up a lively air? A member of the Garrick told me he used to watch Reade writing his invectives there, and that the fiercer they were the sweeter his smile.

27

It interested me to see that Ascot R. Hope's *My Schoolboy Friends* was one of your boyish favourites. That is another bond of union between you and me. Do you know him? He goes to the Savile. Great talker who writes on his knee and thinks this his worst book. A good fellow, yet it is a mistake to meet those giants of our boyhood, we loved them so much.

I daresay you see the new books as much as I do—or more. I used to get my latest London news from a man in Bombay. The only novel of any note this season that I remember is *Catriona*. Beautiful stuff in it. All the boy and girl part is exquisite. The flaw seems to be that the central incident is of no interest,—I mean the effort to save an unknown figure behind a screen. But a grand thing surely.

I suppose you know Herman Melville's *Typee* and *Omoo*. If not, the mere telling you to get them is giving you a handsome present.

I am writing from my sister's in Hants. Your message to her gave me much pleasure. No one could understand me much who did not know what she has been to me all her life. To see her happily married is indeed a great happiness to me. I showed her your letter, and she asks me to say how much she would like to have you visit her.

I hope your wife's health is improving a little: I seem to know her. Indeed I mean I do. And to know you better from what I seem to know of her. I don't think of you alone, but of you two. And I hope to see you both—yet.

Ever yours, J. M. Barrie

Kirriemuir, N.B. 17 December '93

It is now some years since I set off to buy foreign writing paper but I always forget it until I am feeling for my latchkey again. Have an uneasy feeling that you will soon always know there is another letter from me when you hear the postman saying that there is half a franc to pay. Which reminds me of my schooldays, and a schoolmate who went to Paris and kept sending me French comic journals with translations of the jokes, for which I had to pay about a penny a word. I remember how horrible the postman's knock became to me, and that I at last appealed to the boy's friends to stop him. For the tragic thing was that I did not know his address.

You will see that I am a day further from you now. Had

to come home suddenly owing to the illness of my mother, and indeed we have had a fortnight of alarming days and nights, but she is much better again and so all's well with the world. Do you not often feel after these anxieties how childish our hopes and fears about smaller things—the new book, for instance—have been. Yet I suppose the pin-pricks continue to give exaggerated pleasure and pain to the end, a comic business. Now that I am here I shall stay for some time and hope to get to work again. This has interrupted everything and is the entire cause of the delay in answering your letter.

I was not sorry to leave London tho' I am always glad to sweep down on it for a time. Big as the place is, I don't think it has the effect of making you feel your own littleness, else could not you slave so hard in it. For they do slave in London, do they not? I have a sad habit of only looking on, and they shame me. The gospel of work, work till you drop often means that you are to live a life bounded on north-south-east-and-west by the mighty trifles of your own pen. As for the clubs, they are pleasant at intervals but it might fit in somewhere as an aphorism that nothing good ever came out of a club.

I wish I could have come with Nicoll to you. He is one of the few men I think I could travel with without wanting to push him over a cliff (without malice) and he is probably one of the few who would not want to push me over in the same friendly spirit. He and 'Q' have become great friends, which is a pleasure to me. Have you read 'Q's' *Delectable Duchy*? It is full of beautiful work, and I look forward to his long story with uncommon hopes. It is the long novel, where you can lose yourself for nights, that gives the most delight: with the short story I think it is more difficult to forget to be a critic. How delightful to enjoy oneself without in the least knowing why.

I had some native cloth from Stevenson lately, and an announcement that I had been elected a member of the Samoan Something Temperance Society, which has somewhat contradictory rules. Need not say who is president of the society. I have been looking at a map called 'Oceana' (which alone is enough to frighten one) and wondering if I shall ever get out to that Samoan group. At present I am like the pig that broke out and saw a cow, and then returned to the stye for life, confident that it had seen the world. But I don't know that I have even seen the cow yet.

About the photograph; in this house there is a garret, and in the garret a dozen boxes crammed with old letters, and among the letters a photograph here and there, but where! When delving for something else I sometimes come across my own face, and the next time I do so I'll send it to you. In the meantime, here is a modest thing in the shade done at the door of my sister's house the other day by a private camera, which has always proved so far a little frightened at its own handiwork! There are no garrets on the lake of Geneva, and even tho' there were, you have a wife, who will not let the rubbish accumulate; in other words you have no excuse for not sending me your photograph. I should like very much to have hers too. It would illustrate you to me.

There was an extraordinary gale here just before I came north. Wish I had seen it. Forests and hundreds of acres of trees laid low, not one tree in fifty left. The little wood where my little minister and Babbie made discoveries is all gone, went down in a few minutes. The trees can't be cleared away for years. She won't be able to dance there any more. No room for it. The squirrels will have to change their habits and ways of living, become another kind of animal.

Let this wish you a happy Christmas. It can clear the way for cards, if such things are in favour in Switzerland. Nicoll has two very attractive children, who are so excited about Xmas that they can't wait for it but send off their cards weeks before, which I think a much prettier custom than the other one. So I am taking an example from them.

★

To Miss CATHERINE POLLARD (*later Lady* ROBERTSON NICOLL)

133 Gloucester Road, S.W. 5 April '97

Dear Miss Pollard

I want at once to tell you of the immense pleasure which Dr Nicoll's news gives me,[1] and I hope you will forgive me therefore for writing. I am one of his closest friends, and it is naturally news of importance to me. And I hear it with real joy, as if some stroke of good luck had come to myself. It is a

[1] Of his engagement to Catherine Pollard.

poor word, luck, in such a connection but you understand. My wife and I look forward to knowing you as one wants to know not many people. Believe me, with heartiest congratulations and good wishes,

Yours very truly, J. M. Barrie

To WILLIAM (later Sir W.) ROBERTSON NICOLL, Free Church Minister, editor of the British Weekly, *writer*

Adelphi Terrace House 12 February '18

My dear Nicoll

Charlotte Bronte's *Vanity Fair*[1] will certainly be one of our choicest items in the Christies' Sale, and in the name of the Committee, including yourself, I thank you warmly. It is really very good of you to offer yourself up in this way and one may say 'If thus all!' But we seem to be doing well, especially in MSS. I sometimes feel it would be more entertaining to invent the things than to appeal for them (Lot 100—Four letters from Shakespeare to Lady Bacon showing that she wrote the plays &c.)

Yours ever, J. M. Barrie

9 January '21

Do you remember how, early in the life of the *British Weekly*, I wrote some papers for you on Scottish worthies, which were afterwards published as a little volume under the title 'An Edinburgh Eleven'? And how Dr W. G. Grace came across it and tossed it aside on discovering that not one of my eleven could bat or bowl? When I read that Dr Whyte[2] was dead I unearthed, with some difficulty, a copy of that volume to read what I had written of him so long ago, and to my bewilderment I find he was not one of the eleven, though his name occurs. How that came about I do not know—he might so well have been the captain, he or Masson,[3] for these were certainly to me the two great names in Edinburgh at that time. Perhaps he

[1]The copy of *Vanity Fair* presented by Thackeray to Charlotte Brontë, bought by Clement Shorter from Charlotte Brontë's husband, sold by Mr Shorter to Sir W. Robertson Nicoll for £100, and now presented by him to the Red Cross sale of which Barrie was Chairman.

[2]A Free Church minister of Edinburgh, famous as a preacher.

[3]David Masson, Professor of Rhetoric and English Literature at Edinburgh University.

seemed too near to me, and too dear, to be written about, for I had known him all my life, and sat at his feet from the beginning thereof, and always felt an awe of that leonine head. To know him was to know what the Covenanters were like in their most splendid hours. This may seem to lay too much stress on the sternness of him. He could be stern certainly, and then if you were its object you felt a gale of wind blowing that you were not likely to forget, but it was a face far more often lit up by delight in something fine that he had discovered; and wherever there were fine things he was the man to dig them up. He came to announce his discoveries with greater joy on his face than I think I have ever seen on the face of any other man. The fervour of his face, the beneficence of it, they will shine on like a lamp. His greatest genius lay in 'up-lift'. He uplifted more men and women than any other Scotsman of his time.

5 April '23

Often thinking of you, and a sudden desire to write comes over me. I hope all is well with you—not as well, one knows, as once it was, nor with me either, nor with any of our old friends for that matter, but I trust as well as may be. One thing that certainly has not changed in me, nor I am sure in you, is our old affection. In my mind I have many adventures with you still and embark once more on our lugger for U.S.A. Again I see us driven from place to place as your room became uninhabitable through the size of the Sunday editions in it, or we ran lest you be hauled before the magistrates for burning so many writing-tables with your cigarette-ends.

I have been writing practically nothing for a long time, leading a hermitish life on the whole—rather a reversion to my early days in London, when, however, as you knew, sometimes to your cost, I was better at pegging away.

To Mrs KIRKCALDY (*daughter of Sir WILLIAM ROBERTSON NICOLL*)

21 April '26

Yes, I am honoured and shall be delighted to be godfather to your baby girl. This linking of me with the baby's grandfather warms my heart, I assure you. Only a few days ago I stood at the gate of Bay Tree Lodge and looked in and sighed. May you and the babes bring all kinds of the best kind of happiness to each other.

To Lady ROBERTSON NICOLL

29 May '30

It was a nice thought of yours to send me the plaque. I shall always associate it with my happy visit to the Old Manse, now long ago. I don't need anything to remind me of all the kind things that were done for me at Bay Tree Lodge by W.R.N. of blessed memory.

★

To DAVID CHRISTIE MURRAY, author

Kirriemuir, N.B. 15 December '93

My dear Christie Murray

Your book (my book) followed me up here where I had to come unexpectedly two days after our dinner. It is delightful. I accept your challenge and do hereby undertake to talk to you at tremendous length, the first time we meet again, about the making of another novelist.[1] Not that he, worse luck, has had anything like such a varied experience. . . .

One thing I wonder at is what you say of acting. I would agree that everyone with imagination must find delight in the stage, but I cannot understand the author of *Aunt Rachel* having a desire—rather a passion—to exchange a greater art for a smaller one. It is not smaller, you hold. But surely it is, as the pianist is less than the composer.

I need not tell you again that it is a pride to me to have the dedication. The whole arrangement of this house has been altered to give the book its place of honour. The position of hundreds of books has been altered. The bringing of a small bookcase into a different room led to the alteration of heavy furniture in the other room, a sofa is where was a cupboard, flowerpots have been put aside, and red curtains have given place to green. I hope you are flourishing and with best regards to Mrs Murray,

Yours ever, J. M. Barrie

[1] Himself.

33

To J. J. CARRERAS, tobacconist

18 January '97

Dear Sir

In answer to your letter, it is your Craven Mixture—and no other—that I call Arcadia in *My Lady Nicotine*. I see no objection to your announcing this if you want to do so.

Yours truly, J. M. Barrie

To ROBERT McCOMB, of the Evening Telegraph, *Belfast*

183 Gloucester Road, S.W. 5 November '98

Dear Mr. McComb

I cannot advise you, in answer to your letter, to look on *My Lady Nicotine* as in any way autobiographical. Part of it indeed was written before I had ever smoked. With all good wishes,

Yours sincerely, J. M. Barrie

To the Rev. A. H. WATTS, then Vicar of Lenton, Nottingham

133 Gloucester Road, S.W. 27 February '97

Dear Sir

I thank you for your letter and wish you had a better subject for your lecture. I don't know of any personal article about myself that is not imaginary and largely erroneous. But there is really nothing to tell that would interest anyone. Yes, I was in Nottingham for a year and liked it well tho' I was known to scarce anyone. If you ever met an uncouth stranger wandering in the dark round the Castle ten or twelve years ago, his appearance unimpressive, a book in each pocket, and his thoughts three hundred miles due north, it might have been the subject of your lecture.

Believe me Yours truly J. M. Barrie

To WILLIAM WALLACE of Glasgow

133 Gloucester Road, S.W. 15 February '97

My dear Wallace

Many thanks for the copy of your Burns,[1] it is a fine edition

[1] The Chambers *Life and Work of Burns*, edited by William Wallace L.L.D., afterwards editor of the *Glasgow Herald*.

and I value it highly. I have read your estimate of Burns's character and genius with uncommon pleasure. As for the genius, that he is the great poetic glory of Scotland none I suppose would now seek to deny, but as for his character you seem to me to offer the truest conception of it I have ever read. He was a great soul who had to fight with himself all through, and to half win the battle, as you show so eloquently he did, was a great achievement. I remember Stevenson writing to me of some other writer 'The author may not be like his books—he *is* his books.' And Burns *is* his poems.

Yours very truly, J. M. Barrie

To MADAME DE NAVARRO (*Mary Anderson*), *actress*

[June '98]

Dear Lady[1]

I am naturally greatly elated by your letter, and the kind things you insinuate rather than express. What particularly delights me is the note of uneasiness which you are at such pains to hide, but which bobs out repeatedly, thro'out your bold defiance. The other day I showed my big dog to a child, and he kept saying, to give himself confidence, 'He won't bite me; he won't bite me; I'm not afraid of his biting me,' and it is obvious to the Allahakbarries that even in this manner do you approach me. They see also a wistfulness on your face as if, after having lorded it over mankind, you had at last met your match. Not, they say, that it will be your match. Hence the wistfulness of your face as the summer draws near. As one captain speaking to another, I would beg you not to let your team see that you are hopeless of their winning. It will only demoralise them *still further*.

I have no intention of changing my team this year. If I can get them I shall bring down last year's *winners* without alteration. Also I offered last year not to put on Doyle and Pawling to bowl unless you put in your cracks, and when the fatal day arrives I am willing to make a similar offer again.

Lastly, you say 'Be then like unto me.' If you would kindly tell me how it can be done I shall proceed to do it right away.

[1]The cricket-team which Barrie took this year to play Madame de Navarro's team at Broadway consisted of T. L. Gilmour, Conan Doyle, E. W. Horning, Bernard Partridge, E. T. Reed, Henry Ford, Owen Seaman, Sydney Pawling, Will Meredith, A. E. W. Mason and himself.

Don't think by this that I mean I want to lure your players on to my side. I mean I want to be like you in your nobler moments. Teach me your fascinating ways. Teach me to grow your face. Teach me how you manage to be born anew every morning. In short, I make you a sporting offer. Teach me all these things, and I will teach your team how to play cricket.

Awaiting your reply, yours ever, J. M. Barrie

★

To Mrs PATRICK CAMPBELL, actress
133 Gloucester Road, S.W. 6 November '98
Dear Mrs Campbell
I saw your Mélisande yesterday, and it gave me exquisite delight. It seemed to me that what you have been trying to do with your art for the last year or two rather lazily you have suddenly accomplished so triumphantly that the result is sheer beauty. The whole thing is a joy to look at, and listen to, and think about, and I can't resist the desire to tell you how it inspired me.

Yours sincerely, J. M. Barrie

Island of Harris, N.B. 7 September '12
Dear Stella
I thought when I saw your nice little monogram that it meant you no longer adored G.B.S., and that you had crossed the street again to me.[1] You see, I had watched you (a bitter smile on my face) popping in at his door instead of at mine. For the moment I am elated, though well I know that you will soon be off with me again and on with him. He and I live in the weather house with two doors, and you are the figure that smiles on us and turns up its nose at us alternately. However, I would rather see you going in at his door than not see you at all, and as you are on elastic I know that the farther you go with him the farther you will have to bound back. I wish I had not thought of this because it suddenly fills me with a scheme for a play called *The Weather House*. Will stop this letter presently to think scheme out, but as I see it just now I feel that G.B.S. and I must write alternate acts (according to which

[1] Bernard Shaw lived opposite to Barrie in Adelphi Terrace.

36

door you go in at). When I wrote that, I meant that we should each write the acts in which you were nice to him, but on reflection I am not sure that I would not prefer to write the scenes which took place across the way and leave him to write those of No. 3.

I have done no work here except a one act play, which striketh me as being no great shakes, for the Duke of York's, where a triple bill is to be done; I daresay I'll go on with the other, but why, oh, why don't you post, or, better, call on Frohman, as it goes to him if it's done? This place is very remote—nothing alive but salmon, deer, and whales, and I return to London in a fortnight, when I hope this comedy of the doors will begin again. Yours, J.M.B.

7 January '18

I am so sad that you should have this ordeal to go through,[1] and I wish I knew any way to comfort you. How much rather would you have had this sorrow than never had a son who would go to the war and die fighting gallantly for his country. How good that you have had a son who stood the supreme test of manhood. And in those three years he lived thirty of such lives as mine; he had in them the work he was so fitted to do superlatively well, all the joys that come to most lives that are spread over many years. He died in great honour. Surely you are a proud woman as well as a sad one.

I shall, of course, come to see you any time you want me.

[Mrs Campbell asked permission to print letters from Barrie in her book *My Life and Some Letters*.]

3 Adelphi Terrace House November '21

I am much elated to find that you have preserved for so long those two old letters of mine. Is the faint perfume that I fondly think comes from them really lavender? And if it is (I wish I hadn't thought of this) is it lavender meant for me, or were my little missives merely kept so near the beautiful G.B.S. budget that in time they stole some of the sweetness in which I am sure his lie wrapped?

This misgiving has come upon me suddenly, and I am rather dashed by it. My two little Benjamins are shrinking before my

[1]Mrs Campbell's son, Acting Lieutenant Commander Alan Campbell, 'Beo', was killed in action in France on 30th December. 1917.

eyes. All I see clearly now is the Shaw bundle, encircled by a pale blue ribbon. I doubt whether my pair were preserved intentionally. I daresay they got into his lot by mistake, and just fell out one day when the ribbon burst. Or an instinct of self-preservation had made them creep in there. They probably thought that sometime when you sat in the dusk with the G.B.S. bundle in your lap, you might inadvertently fondle them also.

All this is a bitter pill for me, who in the first thrill of seeing them again had hoped deliriously that you kept them because you could not part from them. I conceived you (mad fool that I was) carrying them everywhere in a gold bag attached to your wrist, constantly being late for dinner because you must have one more peep at them; climbing ladders for them when the house went on fire. I was proud to feel that (even though you could not read them) they were a solace to you when you were depressed and a big brother if you were almost reckless.

Another thing strikes me—that you preserved them to ask me to read them to you some day. I tell you flatly that I cannot read them. Even the 'Stella' seems to me (the more I look at it) to have an odd appearance. Hold it sideways and it is more like 'Beatrice'. Were you ever called Beatrice? A horrible sinking comes over me that these letters were never meant for you at all.

Even if they were, there is no proof nowadays that they were written by me, for the hand-writing is entirely different from that of this letter. I am trusting that my new superb penmanship is amazing you, even as you gaze at it through blinding tears. The explanation is that since the days of these two letters my right hand has gone on strike—writer's cramp—and I have had to learn to indite with the left. Perhaps these letters did it; the hand that wrote them then grandly destroyed its powers, as the true loyalist smashed his glass when he had drunk a royal health. At all events, we scarcely know the right hand nowadays—we pass the time of day and so on, but nothing more. At first the left was but an amanuensis. I dictated to it, but I had to think down the right arm.

But now the left is my staff. Also I find the person who writes with his left is quite another pair of shoes from the one who employs his right; he has other standards, sleeps differently, has novel views on the ontology of being, and is a more sinister character. Anything curious or uncomfortable about

38

the play of *Mary Rose* arises from its having been a product of the left hand. And now the question inevitably pops up: What justification has my left to give permission to publish letters written by that other fellow, my right? They don't agree about you at all (right says you make people love and writhe). They don't agree about me, they even hold contrary opinions as to what the letters are about. Left says that unless there is a cypher in the letters it can't understand why you want to print them. (By the way, as that is what this letter is about, you can print them if you like.) Left has the vaguest recollections of the doings, apparently referred to in the letters, when you visited me, in order to annoy the blue-eyed one[1] across the way. On the other hand, what memories do these doings recall to right, who is at present jogging me to let it get hold of a pen again! The pretty things it wishes to say to you! but left won't pass them on.

Ah me! You and G.B.S., and the days when I was a father to you both.

But enough of this. I can't pretend any more—not for long. Left likes you every whit as much as right does, as does the somewhat battered frame to which they are for the moment still attached. And we all send you our love, and wish for you the best kind of happiness and courage for any evil hour, and may the book be worthy of you.

To H. G. WELLS, author

                                133 Gloucester Road, S.W. 31 October '97
My dear Wells

Certain Personal Matters of my own have got in the way of my thanking you for the copy of your book[2] which I do very heartily. I'm glad you collected these papers for many of them are long lost friends of mine, and furthermore the 'Veteran Cricketer' which is new strikes me of a heap. Not by its merit (pooh) but because I have you now;—you have a secret desire to spank them to leg and lift beauties to the off, and you probably can't, and so you are qualified for my cricket team. Elected whether you grumble or not.

[1]Bernard Shaw.   [2]*Certain Personal Matters.*

Your Mars story is wonderful and I am confident that it will be the talk of everybody when it appears.

Yours very sincerely, J. M. Barrie

9 November '97

. . . But how I wish that instead of speaking to others about these early papers of yours I had written to yourself and so got to know you when that lung was bad and you needed cheering. At all events I am proud to know that *When a Man's Single* woke you up.

[1897-8]

There is something not short of the terrific about *The War of the Worlds* and nothing worthy of putting beside it of the same kind has appeared of recent times. Such is my candid opinion.

I wish you would let me see the play before you show it to the Haymarket or to any other Martian. I am vastly interested. Let us have that walk as soon as we can see it. I am like the man who began his essay on his favourite walk 'My favourite walk is when I do not have far to go to it.' No, I am not. In my schooldays I was famed for walking and our mathematical master, inspired thereby, propounded the problem 'If two boys walk from Dumfries to Carlisle, a distance of 33 miles, in eight-and-a-half hours, how long would one boy take to cover the same distance walking at the same pace?' It floored one youth repeatedly,—and he may be at it still.

7 June '98

I'm sorry about the play, but I have no doubt you know best.

Are you coming to my cricket match? It takes place on Saturday next the 11th at Broadway, Worcestershire, against a team of artists, etc. got up by Mrs de Navarro (Mary Anderson that was). We had a great time last year, and none of us can play. We are going down the previous day, for which she has arranged sports etc of a wild nature, a supper also at which there are great doings. Cricket on Saturday, return on Sunday. Our train leaves Paddington Friday morning at 9.50. Book second class to Evesham and bring evening dress.

Also we should be delighted if Mrs Wells could come with you. Send me a wire as I have rooms to engage. I go to Scotland for months immediately after.

23 October '98

I am cast down to hear you have had so trying a time and are

40

still in such a poor way. I wish you would let me know soon again whether you are picking up. I can't get the pity of it, that you should be in this condition, out of my head. My wife is ill also, otherwise I'd come down to see for myself, but she is getting better, and ere long I may insist on walking in on you whether you like it or not . . .

Leinster Corner, Lancaster Gate, W. 15 November ['04/5?]
I owe you for having directed me to *Said the Fisherman*. It is very fine—wonderful, and I think Marmaduke Pickthall will soon be known in the land. I shall write him.

Adelphi Terrace House 29 March '31
I have a feeling that the death of Arnold Bennett, which comes as a blow to all of us who write, will tell most hardly of all upon you who probably knew him best and so cared for him most. I never knew him very well but enough to think him one of the most lovable of men and among the most original; he was his own best work, so to speak, for though others have tried to make themselves there are few indeed who have made so good a job of it. And there is no doubt, I think, that *The Old Wives' Tale* is one of the really great novels of England. I have seen some good things written of him just now but have not noticed anyone speak of the beauty of some of his love passages. Either early in *Hilda Lessways* or toward the end of *Clayhanger* there is a love-scene in a Brighton boarding-house that I believe has not been beaten since *Romeo and Juliet*. Excuse my writing. I do feel for you.

30 November '33
Yes assuredly you may quote in your Autobiography the bit you say is in *When a Man's Single*. I am uncommon proud that anything I have written helped you however momentarily and I have a good mind to look up the passage and see what it is. But to re-read one's own works! All hail.

[In June, 1937, five days before Barrie's death, Wells wrote to him: 'I am very much distressed to see the report of your illness in the paper this afternoon. You and I have been in this old literary world together for I don't know how many years, fifty plus, and all through that time I've had nothing but an affectionate admiration for you, and nothing but friendliness and generosity from you'.]

★

To an Unknown Correspondent
                    Black Lake Cottage, Farnham, Surrey 23 July '02
Dear Madam
   It was very base of those children to kill the squirrels and I thank you sincerely for letting me know of it. I shall keep a look-out for them.

                                        Yours truly, J. M. Barrie

To the Editor, Motoring
                    Leinster Corner, Lancaster Gate, W. 8 May '03
Dear Sir
   I thank you for your letter but I do not care to be photographed, so kindly excuse me.

                                        Yours truly, J. M. Barrie

To an Unknown Applicant

                                                    23 May '03
Dear Madam
   I thank you for your letter, and I admired you playing when I saw you at a suburban theatre two or three months ago. But the part of Lady Mary is already assigned, and so there is nothing I can do just now.

                                        Yours sincerely, J. M. Barrie

To a Child

                                                    15 June '03
Dearest Madam
   Don't I know in my heart how true—as well as beautiful and good—your letter is!
   I am glad it is Wednesday to-morrow, because I always think very clearly on Wednesdays—and so about 3 o'clock in the afternoon I shall be able to make up my mind as to the conduct of Edward—whether he actually did kill Richard or only pretended to do it, as now seems more likely, and Richard is singing insolently at this moment on the second branch of the

acacia tree opposite your Terrace, the one that spreads out over the L.G.O. omnibuses and frightens the old ladies who are sitting on top. It would be so like Richard to choose that particular tree!

I hope you are ever so much better today, and I am, dearest Madam,

Your obedient servant, J. M. Barrie

To H. B. MARRIOTT WATSON, New Zealander living in London, journalist and novelist

31 March '04

My dear Watson

Let us say June 18, as that is the date they prefer and I shall try to get an XI for that day. The main fun of the thing, not to speak of the sentiment, would lie in their being the old team as much as possible, and the same with ours. I count upon yourself and will try to get Gilmour, Reid and Partridge—a really weak team.[1]

Yours ever, J. M. Barrie

To —— MURRY

21 December '05

Dear Mr Murry

Unfortunately I can throw no light on the ownership of that Bible, except that I am sure it never belonged to my mother. And I can't go into the past about our family because we were too humble people to know anything of our ancestors. Ogilvy was a very common name in our part as it is still.

Yours very truly, J. M. Barrie

★

To Captain ROBERT FALCON SCOTT, R.N., of the Antarctic

Leinster Corner, Lancaster Gate, W. 8 September '06

My dear Scott

I know the right boy so well that it is as if I had been waiting for your letter. He is the second son of Mrs Llewelyn Davies

[1] Playing Shere, Surrey.

43

(and so a grandson of du Maurier); from his earliest days he has seemed to all of us cut out for a sailor, he is really a fine intelligent quick boy with the open fearless face that attracts at first sight and in view of the future he already assumes a rolling gait. His people were meaning to try to get him a nomination for the exams next March (he is the right age) and so you can imagine how grateful they are to you. Mrs Davies sends you such messages that I decline to forward them. I enclose the paper filled in however.

Your invitation is really the only one I have had for years that I should much like to accept. I can't, I mustn't, I have been doing practically nothing for so long. But I know it means missing the thing I need most—to get into a new life for a bit. If you can ever renew this offer at another time it will be a serious matter indeed that will prevent my taking you at your word.

Altho', mind you, I would still rather let everything else go hang and enrol for the Antarctic. Everybody should do something once. I want to know what it is really like to be alive. I should probably double up the first day. So they say, but in my heart I beg to inform you I am not so sure. I chuckle with joy to hear all the old hankerings are coming back to you. I feel you have got to go again, and I too keep an eye open for the man with the dollars. It is one of the few things he can do with his money that *can't* do harm.

I hope you will be back in November. We all want to do that visit to the ship. Jack Davies must be added to the party. Pauline Chase made a large mouth when I told her of it, which is one of her ways of expressing pleasure. She was staying with us lately and when we got home my wife went into her bedroom and she sat up with her eyes shut and said 'My salary has been raised five pounds—they are very pleased with me[1]—it is not a dream,' and then went on sleeping.

Mason has got home from his Alp-climbing, and is to climb in the House for a month and then going to climb in India. My wife enjoyed her tour in France greatly. I was with the Davieses all the time by the sea and a week in Scotland. By the way it was Jack Davies who when his mother said 'You will be sick tomorrow' (he was stuffing at tea), replied cheerily 'I shall be sick tonight'. I put it in a play and gave him a halfpenny a

[1] As Peter in *Peter Pan*.

44

night during the run of the piece. They have all been trying to think out funny things for me ever since.

And so, good luck to you and the *Victorious*.

Yours ever, J. M. Barrie

11 March '07

. . . Jack is already beginning to wonder 'how young the youngest you could take would be'. Pauline and Co. are in Edinburgh now, and she is on the golf-club committee which gives a certain grand air to her communications. Mason is back from India. He seems to have been there and back in the time that I decide not to go to Clapham.

11 April '07

This line to say we have just got information that Jack Davies has passed his second exam also, so he will be going off soon to Osborne. He greatly enjoyed the excitement of being in London for the exam. He sat near Prince Edward and had a little talk with him, and was chiefly impressed by his watch. Mr Davies still remains much as he was.[1] I can say no more.

I suppose you have left Gibraltar now. Wherever you are may you have a good time.

Berkhamsted 1 May '07

I expect you have heard that Arthur Davies died nearly a fortnight ago. It came very peaceably. I am taking Jack down to Osborne tomorrow. Let me see you soon as you can.

To Miss KATHLEEN BRUCE, later Lady Scott

Leinster Corner 29 April '08

Dear Miss Bruce

I am enormously flattered, but I meant statuettes of other people.[2] I now know that you think me beautiful (I had long suspected it myself), but the general feeling is so much against us that we had best not put our lovely belief to the proof. This secret which we now share should bring us very close together,

---

[1]Arthur Llewelyn Davies, barrister, at the age of forty-four was stricken with a mortal illness.

[2]Barrie having admired Kathleen Bruce's sculpture was invited to sit to her.

however, and give us a subject of which one at least will never tire.   Yours very truly, J. M. Barrie

To Captain SCOTT

Lausanne 23 September '09

Your letter had to follow me about, hence delay. I shall be delighted to be godfather to the boy[1] and am very glad you asked me. May he be a great source of happiness to you both,— or let me say, please, to all three of us. Also I am very glad the expedition is to come off,[2] and it will be a real pleasure to me to subscribe. If there's anything else I can do, be sure I will. When I am back in London I'll write you and then let us have a talk about it.

To Lady SCOTT (*Kathleen Bruce*)

Adelphi Terrace House 11 April '13

I have been hoping all this time that there was some such letter for me from your husband,[3] and the joy with which I receive it is far greater than the pain. I am very proud of the wishes expressed in it, and I hope in time you will be able to say you were glad it was written. I know a hundred things he would like me to do for Peter, and I want out of love for his father to do them all. And I want to be such a friend to you as he wished. I should have wanted to be that had there been no such letter, and now I feel I have a right to ask you to give me the chance. I am longing to hear when I may see you.

10 July '13

Dear Kathleen

Something as brief and simple as this is what I think might follow the message to the public—

'Wilson and Burrows died first and Captain Scott enclosed

[1]Captain Scott and Kathleen Bruce had been married in September 1908, and Peter Scott was born in September 1909.

[2]Scott's expedition, in the *Terra Nova*, to the South Pole.

[3]Scott and his companions having perished in the Antarctic in the early part of 1912, among the letters found in his tent eight months later was one to Barrie: 'As a dying man, my dear friend, be good to my wife and child. Give the boy a chance in life if the State won't do it. He ought to have good stuff in him. I never met a man in my life whom I admired and loved more than you, but I could never show you how much your friendship meant to me, for you had much to give and I nothing.'

46

them in their sleeping bags. At some unknown time thereafter he removed the fur coat from his shoulders, bared his
chest, and, seated against the centre pole with his head
flung back and his eyes wide open, awaited death. We
know this because it was thus that the three were found when
the search-party looked into the tent six months afterwards.'
What do you think? Some of the words may not be quite
right but the brevity is.

23 Campden Hill Square 4 December '15
That was a notion born of a disgust with the pen in these days
of action, but I think it will come to nothing and I am thankful
to say I have writing that interests me a bit. It was some very
gradual change that turned me into a sedentary person which I
wasn't meant for. All my youth I was action incarnate. I used
to talk of these things with Con.[1] I was at the statue's unveiling by Arthur Balfour[2] and it is very fine. Went thence to
bed for some weeks. (To the people who wanted an MS or
something to sell at Sale I said No but they could have my
plaster when I was done with it.) I'm all right again but this
explains my disappearance from view and I am hoping to see
you and Peter soon. It was a nice feeling that made you keep
him away from the unveiling but I should have been rather
proud to have him cross-legged round my head that day.

Tillington, Petworth 2 January ['16]
I long to give the year at the top, but no good. Feel sure I'd
say 1915.
Greatly elated at having scored over the Penguin, looks as if
there was some life in the old man after all. So uplifted that
have begun a grand work.
I'm here on way to seaside with the boys.[3] When return we
must and shall meet. Rather needed someone Christmas eve.
Brown[4] and wife away, lit my own fire, (tell Peter out of Mrs
Brown's go-to-market straw basket), cooked dinner (eggs) and
so to bed (after I had made it).

[1]Captain Scott.
[2]The statue of Captain Scott in Waterloo Place, made by Lady Scott.
[3]Mrs Llewelyn Davies having died in 1910 at the age of forty-three, three
years after her husband, Barrie had adopted their five sons, George, Jack,
Peter, Michael and Nicholas.
[4]Man-servant.

47

Adelphi Terrace House 3 March '16 (?)

I am sorry to have kept this so long. Sorrier still not to have been in when Peter came. Brown says he delivered his message with masterly exactitude, though I don't think those were Brown's words. I am labouring rehearsing play, after which hope to descend on you both. The Zeppelin the French brought down near Verdun a fortnight ago fell almost into the garden of my hospital. They rushed out, but of the twenty-four on board only the cinders of one suggested a human being.

['16/17]

I think that quite splendid of you and one of the kindest things I have ever known of.[1]

I am not going to accept it because on the whole things will go on all right as they are, but I shall never forget it. One thing I do pride myself on, which is that before you proposed it I knew you were capable of proposing it. I think I know you well now and I have a mighty faith in you.

Nice language! but it's all true.

You would have liked to hear what the tall Peter[2] said of the small Peter.[3] I have never heard him so impressed (and he hadn't seen him signing his name at the Zoo).[4]

8 October

You have been very nice about Jack, and I have Peter here on sick leave and I have another cold ('contemptible little worry o colds'). I think this one came because a dog wagged its tail at me in passing, thus creating a draught, but I am all right again till another dog comes.

18 October '17

The only change in Lord Knutsford's advice[5] that I should like you to make is to substitute my name for his. If you have

---

[1]Lady Scott offered to take the boys when the nurse went to make munitions.
[2]Llewelyn Davies.
[3]Scott.
[4]Peter Scott was a fellow of the Zoo from babyhood and so signed to admit his friends on Sundays.
[5]Lord Knutsford had advised Lady Scott to appoint a guardian for Peter Scott in the case of her death, and offered to fill the position himself.

48

sufficient faith in me it is my earnest wish that you should do so. Or if you prefer it, at least please associate me with him in it. He can't love Peter more than I do, but he has the advantage of having the daughter, while I have no woman to work with me or to fall back upon should my end come before long. Experience teaches me that the one drawback in my tending my boys is that I have no female influence for them; the loss to them is very great and I must tell you this bluntly, as I think its value increases as the boy grows into a man. Of course the chances are great that you will live for scores of years after I am gone.

I should like to be the chosen man and consider it a mighty honour.

24 October '17

Lord Knutsford is quite right in saying that you and you alone must decide. Nevertheless it is plain to me that you would like some advice, so here goes,—it is very much from my heart. If it were just between him and me I would beg you to risk making it me, but it would not be wise to make it either of us without further arrangements in case of our death, and if he is the man the arrangement is already made because of the daughter, while I have no one. This is so important to Peter that I think I am quite out-weighed. But I should like you to say in your will, or whatever the paper is, that it would be a pleasure to you to think that I was looked upon as an uncle to Peter to whom he would come whenever he wanted. I should try to be a good uncle to him.

19 March '18

(I write with difficulty. A little lump that formed on my writing finger a century ago when I first began to be a quill-driver has now got loose, and I can't make up my mind whether to off with it or stick it on more firmly with glue.) It is splendid of you the way you have been exerting yourself on my behalf but the conclusion I have come to is that I would be no good at either French or Italian front and so ought not to adventure. If I can find a sufficient excuse to be in Paris[1] a few days while you are there, though, I will seize it, and then won't Peter and I make the French welkin ring! I shall bring a

[1]Lady Scott was working at the Consulate in Paris.

welkin with me in case you have run out of them. I expect there is a depressing enough side to your new experiences but Peter will blow it away, if sides can be blown,—a side of beef could certainly be blown nowadays. Do write me again when you have time. I should love to hear how it all goes.

To PETER SCOTT

9 April '18

My dear Peter

Your mother thinks I do not write clearly, but I expect this is jealousy. It is funny to think of your being at a French school, parlez-vous-ing with big guns firing and bells ringing and hooters hooting. What a lot you will have to tell me when we meet again. Michael and Nicholas are here just now, and to-morrow we are going to Wales for ten days. Michael won the competition at Eton for flinging the cricket ball farthest. Peter is where the fighting is heaviest, near Amiens. I think Brown will have to go and be a fighter now as he is under fifty. It will be queer if I am the only person left in London and have to cook the food and kill the cow and drive the bus. It will be rather difficult for me to be engine-driver and guard at the same time and also take the tickets and sweep the streets and sell balloons at the corner and hold up my hand like a policeman to stop the traffic every time a taxi comes along. Then I shall also have to be the person inside the taxi at the same time as I am sitting outside driving it, and if I run over anybody it will have to be myself, and I will have to take my own number and carry myself on a stretcher to the hospital, and I will need to be at both ends of the stretcher at once. Also I will have to hurry on in front of the stretcher so as to be door-keeper when the stretcher arrives, and how can I be the door-keeper when I have to be the doctor, and how can I be the doctor when I have to be the nurse? You see I am going to have a very busy time, and I expect that a letter from you would cheer me up. I will have to be the postman who delivers it.

Your loving Barrie

To Lady SCOTT (*Kathleen Bruce*)

2 Robert Street, Adelphi 10 August '19

I have been away and just got your letter. Very nice letter on

50

the whole though tending to skimpiness. I don't suppose I can get to you though I should like to uncommonly, and haven't given up hope. It depends on the movements of the boys and a man who has come over from New York to see me, and would have to be before Saturday on which day we go to Scotland. If it can be done I'll wire or ring you up and follow joyfully for a night.

Above is not my new address. I forget if I told you of my cunning device to print a wrong address for people I don't want to see. Another good thing I have done is to change my address in *Who's Who* (it used to be Kirriemuir N.B.) to c/o Scribner's, Fifth Avenue, New York. This all goes to show that there is more in me that meets your eye.

There can't be more in Peter than meets the eye.[1] There is the raw material for a conundrum in this. I went to the House of Commons to hear them on Labour the other night and talked so much about Peter that I shouldn't wonder though they asked a question about him in the House and divide on him in which case the ayes will have it.

To meet Colonel House again is a thing I much desire (with no third man there to do the talking for both of us). I believe (though the heavens might fall in) that I would dare tell him I was a bit disappointed in the President. Not that I don't believe in him still—I do—but I expected a greatness from him that would rise above all obstacles and make him the spokesman of humanity. It isn't a man to represent a nation that is needed so much as one who represents the best in all of them. In this I think he has failed—only failed in being a Lincoln— and I see no other body.

Why do you presume to use two notes of exclamation at the mere thought of my being American minister?? Observe I use two notes of interrogation. In the days when we had all so passionate a desire to do something for our country that was the one thing that in my secret heart I believed I could have done. And though in this country people care nothing for literary hands, in America they like them. What I devoutly hope in this matter is that Edward Grey goes, though I daresay there is no thought of anything of the kind. It would be quite a splendid thing for both countries.

Lavery painted the 'water-pageant' from my flat. Such a

[1]Because he wore so few clothes.

tiny unimpressive pageant. On the big river the little boats looked like paper things cut out by children. It should all have been held on the Round Pond.

Ping-pong has broken out in the flat with extraordinary violence since the boys returned and my arm ought to be in plaster.

The heat here is ghastly. You can hang your hat on it.

And so, Yours J. M. Barrie

I find I have addressed your envelope thus
My dear Kathleen
Worlingham Hall
Beccles.

I have a good mind to take out a patent for this. It would set a new and pretty fashion.

Adelphi Terrace House 28 September

I must write, sheer pleasure to write, and thank you for letter about Jack. I don't feel equal to King Constantine's brother. I enjoyed much your dining with me and hope you will come again and I shall ask the same people to join us.[1]

29 December '19

Thesiger would have been very good in the part I am sure, but it is cast and indeed the play is 'in rehearsal'. I think Thesiger one of the best actors of the day, and hope to have him in something of mine yet.

Grand poem from Peter—only surpassed by his pictures. I hope to see you both soon.

27 February '22

Ha! I hope to be, as you put it, 'walking by the House of Commons' (for about the first time in my life) at eleven on Friday,[2] but I ought to be rehearsing a play at that hour which they can't do without me, so that possibly I won't be able to get away. In any case you know how warm are my good wishes and that I do deeply hope for you both all the best kind of

---

[1] They had been alone.
[2] Lady Scott's marriage to Mr Hilton Young, afterwards Lord Kennet, in the crypt of the House of Commons.

happiness. Also may I bask in it at times. I am a bit concerned over what you say of Peter's measles and its complications. It would be sad if he had to go through an operation and I trust that won't be necessary, but even though it is he will surely soon be his great self again. I am very fond of him and proud of him and if anything of the kind takes place I trust to your letting me know so that I may see him and see too whether for a last time I can regain a little of the gaiety with youth I once had and that possibly might come back if I had a patient to deal with. My love to all the three of you.

To PETER SCOTT

21 January '23

My dear Scott

Poem excellent. Pictures superb. Go to top of class and stay there. I am expecting you in to tea tomorrow.

Yours, Barrie

To Mrs HILTON YOUNG (Kathleen Bruce)

Stanway, Winchcombe 4 August '23

Have just seen the good news in the paper[1] and congratulate the four of you warmly. May it bring you much happiness now and always.

Adelphi Terrace House 22 January '24

I am very sorry you did not bring Peter in, you would both have been welcome as flowers, but it is good that he has taken so rapturously to Oundle, which was pretty clearly the right place for him. I take off my hat to his words about my plays. Last night I had my first outing for ages, went to see the House of Commons in the throes—at least I expected it to be so, but they looked more like a jolly lot of scallywags.

15 April '26

It is uncommon delightful of you to ask me, but I suppose when August comes I shall be having a house of my own and people to tend which will make it impossible. It sounds very attractive all the same, and I must see more of Peter who seems to me to grow in all the best graces.

14 October '26

The 'Adventures among Birds'[2] is an engaging work and I am

[1] The birth of Wayland Hilton-Young.
[2] By Peter Scott and two other school-boys.

glad to have it. I have often envied Peter, and his sketches give me another jealous stab. When at school it was my ambition to become an artist but I always lost my paint box. I see now I might have done it without a paint box but it is too late. The book of your sculpture is fine. I hope to see you soon and probably will at the Speaker's function at which, as you are the lurer, I shall expect you to pay me marked special attention.

26 May '27

Seems to me Leinster Corner would be capital for you, especially if you could get the garage place at the back for a studio. It was where I had my workshop but I have an idea it doesn't go with the house now. As for the Adelphi I expect it will become a monster pile but nobody seems to know and I expect it will last out my time.

[Mr. and Mrs Hilton Young moved into Barrie's former house, Leinster Corner]

2 December '27

How nice of you to be concerned about that letter's semi-invalidism. But it is a month old and I am not only all right again but my doctor says that my throat in connivance with my nose has done something (I don't know what) of such surpassing grace that if I had my rights I should be in the *Lancet*. I don't feel equal at present to revisiting my old home though I hope you are to be very happy there, but I want to see that Peter, and a good plan would be if he came to me one forenoon in about a week's time and accompanied me to a *Peter Pan* rehearsal. All good fortune to your 'Bill' and may the East African affair[1] have happy results.

To PETER SCOTT

5 April '30

I have been down here for a fortnight (Brighton) and have ust had forwarded me a letter from your mother saying you are back. I am going back to London early in the week, and having heard a glorious rumour that you are growing rather

[1] A political mission to the African Colonies.

54

like your father I want very much to see you again. Could you come to lunch with me. . . .

To Lady HILTON YOUNG (Kathleen Bruce)

28 January '34

How do I like the picture?[1] Uncommonly well, thank you. I call it a noticeable success and hope you do also. Peter and I are rather big about it as I daresay his manner and an occasional dropped word have indicated to you. We were also agreed I think that the foreground should be toned down so as not to attract the eye and the pillows at the side made less dark, indeed of the cedar-wood colour which they are when in a stronger light. This would be playing a little with the light he had but I think justifiably. My shadow of course is not really mine but represents the intrusion of Miss Bergner.[2] Yes, I am proud of my godson.

To Lady KENNET (Kathleen Bruce)

24 May '37

I hope the Exhibition[3] will be as resounding a success as ever and wish I could be at the opening especially as George Trevelyan has the doing of it, but I am at present down with sciatica and other woes, so there must be a hated pause. Alas.

★

To BRAM STOKER, author

Divach Cottage, Drumnadrochet, N.B. 5 August '07

Dear Bram Stoker

Your letter has only now reached me in this delightful fastness. I am flattered by your proposal, but as it happens I dislike articles about myself, so shall be glad if you turn your pen to more worthy subjects. Hearty thanks all the same, and please let us meet sometimes in London, I for one should like it.

With kindest regards,

Yours sincerely, J. M. Barrie

[1] Peter Scott was painting Barrie seated at the open fireplace in his study at Adelphi Terrace.
[2] Miss Elisabeth Bergner bought the picture when it was finished.
[3] Peter Scott's pictures at Ackermann's Gallery.

55

To Lady ST HELIER

17 Stratton Street, W. 17 March '09

Dear Lady St Helier

Yes, indeed, as soon as you feel able to see anyone I shall be very glad to go round to you. I am very sorry you are not well, you are one of the kindest people I have ever known.

Yours sincerely, J. M. Barrie

Adelphi Terrace House 10 March '13

Dear Lady St Helier

I am myself again (tho' I wish I was lots of other people), and would be so glad if you would come in to tea some day about 4.30 . . .

Yours sincerely, J. M. Barrie

★

To D. H. AARON

9 February '13

Dear Sir

Thank you for a very pleasant letter. I suppose some day I will publish my plays. It ought to be done when one thinks them fine, however, which is not after one has re-read them in cold blood. Oddly enough the only one you don't mention, *Quality Street*, is to be printed in the autumn with pictures by Hugh Thomson.

Yours sincerely, J. M. Barrie

★

To HUGH THOMSON, illustrator

['13]

. . . The pictures are quite delightful. I love to think such work is done for a play of mine, and am quite sure *Quality Street* could not have found such another illustrator in broad England. My criticism is that Phoebe as the schoolmistress looks too young. I like you the better for this, and am in the plot with you. So don't you go and alter. I hope you will soon be better. Phoebe and Susan ought to give you some of the nice things said to Miss Livvy. 'I am very happy of you', as they would say.

To M. H. SPIELMANN, writer on art

Adelphi Terrace House ['20]

My dear Spielmann

I am glad to hear that you are writing a Memoir of Hugh Thomson. I have no contribution to send you of any value as I had, I think, only two glimpses of him personally, when he came to see me about his illustrations to two of my plays.

He was a man who drew affection at first sight, so unworldly, so diffident, you smiled over him and loved him as if he were one of his own delicious pictures. What the man was came out in his face and in all his modest attractive ways; it might be said of him that he was himself the best picture he ever made. His heart was the gentlest, the most humourous, and so was he. I delighted particularly in his pictures for *Quality Street*, and it is the figures he created that I see in that street now, with himself walking among them, understanding them better than the people of today, perhaps understood better by them.

Yours sincerely, J. M. Barrie

★

To HILDA TREVELYAN, actress

Adelphi Terrace House 12 February '11

My dear Hilda

I am very sorry you have lost your mother. She was a dear woman and I am sure she was blessed with a very good daughter. It must have been a fine thing to her to watch her girl fighting bravely and modestly, and foot by foot by sheer worthiness at last reaching your present position. Sometimes you must have cried and laughed together. In a sense it is now all over, but only in a sense, for just as some of you dies with her, some of her will live on with you. You can still commune together, and in time you will get much happiness from this. I don't need to tell you to be brave, for you have been it too long to change. You are always a pleasant thought to me, I respect you so much.

Always yours sincerely, J. M. Barrie

57

Thank you so much for the delicious nestful. They are Wendy in her nest, and you are Wendy, and there will never be another to touch you.

★

To LILLAH McCARTHY, actress

17 Stratton Street, W. 12 November '08

My dear Lillah

I expect you are feeling lonely with H. off on his travels, so this is me standing smoking at the door. 'The understudy left much to be desired, but his intentions seemed to be good'. See press.

I like to hear your voice round the door. It is a voice that sings so true in my ears. I am putting it in my pipe and it smokes well. Sometime I expect you will be Lady Macbething in the repertory theatre, and I will say to the enthusiasts 'Ah but you should have seen her when I was smoking at the door'. Goodnight, and may I be round again soon.

Yours ever, J.M.B.

Adelphi Terrace House 15 November '12

May you have a great success tonight[1] and indeed I thought it assured when I heard you speak those beautiful speeches last night. I don't see how they could be spoken better, with a finer art or less artifice.

17 April '17

I saw you in *Half an Hour* tonight, and was proud of you. You gave quite a splendid performance and looked adorable. Bravo indeed. This sort of thing heartens an author.

13 June '18

I am glad to have your letter, and though you don't say how long you are to be at Lulworth I suppose this will find you. I don't suppose you know how long you are to stay yourself. From the point of view of health it ought to do you a lot of

[1]As Viola at the Savoy Theatre.

good and it is good to hear of you bathing etc., but mentally it must be trying, the days long however courageously you fill them in, and if one is sad I don't think that any comfort is to be got from the throb of ocean. I don't agree with you that you are no fighter, for you have fought valiantly. It is true that you have no disposition to fight, but when needs must you can fight and you have done it, and the manner of your doing it has certainly won high admiration from me. Don't think I have not often been aware how sad you were when you were presenting a bright face. These are days of such universal suffering that it is the common lot and we are all part of a darkened world. One face should help another, and if ever there was a time for being kind it is now. Just go on trying to be kind, as is natural to you, and you will get some serenity from it. The great thing is that you should be invigorated by your holiday and then get back to interesting work. There is little enough of it going just now, but you made such an impression in this last piece that I can't doubt you will soon reap the benefit. I must say I was amused by your offering yourself for the *aide-de-camp* job, but I quite think you could have done it. I rather admire these wild impulses. Let me know about the next one, and what you are doing and when coming back.

★

To R. GOLDING BRIGHT, theatrical agent
Adelphi Terrace House 13 March '12
Dear Golding
Herewith receipt. As for the three weeks not played, I would rather let Mr Stoll off paying them, as tho' it isn't business I don't like to take money in the circumstances, and the only person I may blame is myself for weakly assenting, against my better judgment and your advice, to include my piece. I rather applaud Mr Stoll for being the first music-hall manager to try anything in the theatre, hopeless as the scheme was. I am sorry tho' to feel the play itself is damaged. I expect it was made to play in about twice the time it ought—but I should have gone to rehearsals, so there I am again.
Yours, J.M.B.
Put it pleasantly to Mr Stoll, as best not to do such things by halves.

Lately Mr Pinker wrote offering me £2,000 in advance of royalties for *P. Pan* in cinematograph. This can't be, but it has struck me since—what about certain of my other things? Suppose you communicate with him.

22 May

Received with thanks your cheque for £96 11 for amateur rights as in statement. This promptitude will astonish you but I don't mean to affirm that it implies I am turning over a new leaf. I think it comes of the excitement of my having at last gone to the Derby. I won a gold (or brass) watch at the first throw.

7 May '14

I think Miss Terry appearing in a film play merely would be poor. Better would be something in nature of 'A Quarter of an Hour with Ellen Terry.' Something recalling her great parts, her lovely movements etc.—a record of her. Conceivably she might be seen dreaming of her parts and we see the dreams— Portia, Ophelia, Olivia, etc.—and if a man sufficiently like Sir Henry could be got to play opposite to her. The film perhaps could show her as these people in same picture—all meeting as it were (and crowning the sleeper).

6 June '16

I have not heard from Miss Adams yet about the *Professor's Love Story*, and suggest to you that your New York representative should take up the matter of Arliss doing it, explaining that this is subject to Miss Adams not doing it. I don't see how she can, with *Cinderella* in future and *Little Minister* doing regularly still between £2,000 and £3,000 weekly. I get grand cables for a film play from Mary Pickford!

9 March '17

Much obliged to you for the arrangements about film and I think it very good for me that you so to speak asserted my rights in this way, but now that is done I'd like you to tell them that as it's their first film and I'm interested in them and we all get on so well together at Bushey I want the thing rearranged thus, that £100 of the £150 should go to them and £50 to me, that the copyright of film should be theirs, that they can lease it or do as they like with it as long as I get my third, and that if the thing went into bankruptcy I would only weep with them.

In short a pleasant friendly arrangement. But I repeat I'm glad you made the other proposals.

5 December '17

Herewith I return scenario[1]. I think it very well done. I've made a few alterations in titles. Here are a few other suggestions

(1) We might see Ernest flinging bottle into sea.

(2) When Mary and Tweeny fight they could have a real encounter as of two amazons who knew now how to attack and defend.

(3) (More important.) I think we should see more of Mary's athletic powers on island. Why not show her actually swimming after the buck, taking a header, going down waterfall, etc. Also Catherine wading or, better, crossing a stream on a rope (hands over head) and Agatha climbing high tree.

(4) When Mary tells how nowadays she goes upstairs four at a time we might have a picture of it.

(5) After 'not even from you can I listen to a word against England,' we might see Crichton and Mary reflecting island memories. (We see one of the island pictures and Mary waiting on Crichton. Then we return to Hall and get final picture as it is.)

I'm really very pleased and should like to see some of the pictures being done.

30 January '18

As for filming of *Sentimental Tommy* and *Tommy and Grizel*, they are eligible therefor. Only a big offer would tempt me however, but if one is made I'd consider it. I wouldn't suggest any figures, it would have to come from them.

9 October '18

I should be delighted to have *Crichton* done at Haymarket with Eadie as Crichton. He is ideal, don't you think, for binging out the two sides of the character.

4 December '18

P. Pan film I'm not having done at present. Was offered £20,000 in Paris the other day, advance sum!

29 September ['20]

Ainley has found a boy whom he thinks highly of as a possible

[1] Of *Admirable Crichton*

61

Peter. I have sometimes hankered after that, and as the photographs he sent me are promising I've agreed to wait a fortnight until I can see the boy. Of course if he is decided on, it would affect the Wendy and other boys—mean their all being children, so nothing definite can be done at present about such parts. Ainley also says he would like to play Mr Darling as well as Hook—as du Maurier used to do. I'm doubled up with lumbago. Will see if I can find a copy of *Mary Rose* when I can stoop.

16 January '21

As to Miss Adams, all you need say to Dillingham is that there is no one for whom I should like to write a play so much, but I am not doing any play at all just now. However she knows all this herself.

28 May '22

I should say £50 a week from Coliseum for *Pantaloon*. Mme Karsavina had already spoken to me about it and I had said I'd let her have it for nothing (idiot!) but best you should work the thing and afterwards I'd give her a present of it, less your percentage.

About *Little Minister*, Dean came in about it and I said I thought Miss Albanesi the right person and asked him to communicate with you.

22 July '22

All right about Dean doing *The Will*. Keep to the £50 if business is over £1,200. If it is under that, will let them off with something quite small. As for *Rosalind* I should prefer it to be played first. This is the right place for a one-act piece, and I want you to make a stipulation that *The Will* is played first also. Dean was in to speak of it and *Minister*. I am going over *Minister* in my usual way, and when I've done that let us discuss cast. In meantime I should be glad if Rosina Filippi was got for the French maid. Of course not if she is too expensive, but I have her in my mind's eye.

9 April '23

Mr Vedrenne writes me that you have told him I was substituting something else for the very brief suffrage bit in Act III[1]. If so you have quite misunderstood. All I wanted the

[1] Of *What Every Woman Knows*.

62

prompt-copy for was to put in little verbal alterations from the printed version. The suffrage must stand, for though there is so little of it, it is an integral part of the play. It only 'dates' the play to the extent of showing the action takes place a few years ago and I think it should give opportunities for the society-ladies to wear dresses that will be more interesting than absolute present-day—probably those long tight skirts (of which I see myself making some play.)

16 February '26

All right, they can adapt *Half an Hour* to the French stage if they wish to and you can guard its being properly produced. It is one of my things that I have very little interest in, truth to tell.

22 March '27

All right about *Quality Street* in Yugo Slavia and *Dear Brutus* in Holland. *The Old Lady* at the Comédie Française is very interesting.

2 October '28

Yes, I think that an excellent idea—Charles Laughton for Crichton. I saw him in *Alibi* some months ago, and was much struck by him. My original idea for the part, as I may have told you, was Charles Hawtrey.

28 April '29

Very glad you like the idea of going on helping the Hospital in *P. Pan's* affairs. I haven't heard yet whether the legal deed has been completed[1] but it is only a form and I suggested to the Secty. of the Hospital that he should see you. Explain to him how it is all worked so far as the performing rights are concerned.

About Scandinavian rights, you will have to trust your own judgment I fear. Now that the Hospital is in charge the money becomes more important, and advance payments.

[1]Barrie had decided to give to the Great Ormond Street Hospital for Sick Children the perpetual rights in *Peter Pan*, still earning at least £2,000 a year at that time.

Adelphi Terrace House 19 April '12

My dear Scribner

I have an uneasy feeling—I have had it before—that I never acknowledged your last cheque, £378 . 18 . 4 royalties up to date on *Peter and Wendy*. I am glad you are coming over this summer, and hope to see as much of you as you can spare time for.

I don't know whether you publish Masefield's work but I think him easily our best young man. Another good one is Compton Mackenzie, author of *Carnival*. I should like to see these under your banner.   Yours ever, J. M. Barrie

16 September '15

If you had been with me last Wednesday night you could have watched the Zeppelin and the guns firing at it—as if from a private box. It was a dark night with a few stars, and the Zeppelin stood out very clearly in the searchlights. The firing went on for 20 minutes or so—many guns to the minute, mostly falling short but a few very close, and gradually it got out of range. London seemed very still, a dog could be heard barking far away; it was very eerie waiting. What must it have felt like to be up there! I went into the streets after; there was no panic but rather a crowding to see a wonderful sight. It was about a mile from here that the damage was done, a good few houses largely destroyed and 20 people killed and twice that badly hurt. The figures published of killed and wounded on these occasions have always been the truth (despite rumours) and it is remarkable they are so small. That night one bomb dropped in middle of Queen Square in Bloomsbury (the nicest old square there) smashed about 2000 windows, yet not one person was damaged there. The windows just fell in or out—effect of the bombs on the air I suppose.

I fancy the view of sensible people here on the American situation is that if you think we are to win you should keep out of it, but if you think we are to lose you should for your own sakes come in. We think we are to win! I suppose we should like best that you withdraw your ambassador to Germany, which would assuredly be a big thing for us. Wilson is evidently a true leader, however, and so far as I can see you should be thankful you have him.

I have been reading O. Henry lately. Very delightful. I would have given something to know him. He was a genuine 'swell,' as Henley used to put it. Can't you get his Life, which I see is being prepared? Aumonier has written the best short stories I've seen of late, especially one called, I think, 'Old Friends.'

26 October '17
Belatedly to acknowledge your cheque for £236 . 14 . 5 as according to statement, and with special thanks for what you say of *The Little Minister*. I wish those days of your visit could be resumed. In the meantime you have now like us to face a long war with stout hearts. On the whole we can say that they are not vain or boastful hearts; and I feel sure that the vast majority on both sides of the Atlantic are seeking the freedom of the world and not merely of the bits of it to which they happen to belong. We should do everything in our power to make the German people also believe this. I can understand with what feelings you watch those who are dear to you buckling on their armour. I hope if any of them come to London you will ask them to come and see me. One of the effects of the war is the friendliness everywhere.

I have moved to the flat above my old one, as it has some advantages, including a wonderful view of the river, especially when the searchlights sweep the sky. Hardy was staying with me lately and he and Wells and Shaw and Arnold Bennett and I sat one night watching the strange spectacle. It is an exposed spot, tho', and after raids I always find shrapnel on the roof. Callers who don't find me in might have better luck if they tried the cellar.

15 November '19
Received with thanks your cheque for £1240 . 17 . 7 as in statement. Very good I think. Your other statement is pretty grim, I mean about the printers' strike holding up the magazine. However, the turmoil in all our countries must be taken as the result of the war, and we must take it with the feeling that people who got thro' the war can face anything else without blanching.

No foundation for any report that I meditate crossing the

Atlantic. Nor that I had anything whatever to do with *The Young Visiters* beyond writing the preface. It is printed word for word as originally shown me. I think I say this in preface, and I rather resent people's not accepting my word. The whole affair has been something of a trial for me, as hordes of parents here keep sending me their children's works, and now they are doing it from America. I have to employ a secretary.

Stanway 20 September '25

I am here once more and glad to have your letter though your presence would have been still more welcome. Fifty years have you been at it! How do the fleeting years roll by, as Simon, aged six, said yesterday when recalling the past in a little play I wrote for his birthday. We here join with Princetown, etc., etc. in a cup to the continued glory of the house of Scribner, and acclaim you a Freeman and Burgess of Stanway. For myself I can say gratefully that I have had a mighty pleasant connection with you, and Scribner's is a name that will always roll pleasantly on my tongue.

I am very interested in what you say of America and Europe. I suppose I have been less in politics than most people and never must it be divulged how seldom I have used the privilege of voting at elections. Anyone can floor me by saying 'The whole thing of course depends on the amount of oil in Asia Minor', or 'What did Joe Chamberlain say to Algeria in 1887?' or 'How about the gold standard?' Nevertheless, though secretly aware of my incompetence, I do look on with interest, and once or twice I have said a good thing about international finance without letting on that I have boned it from Alexander Dana Noyes, who fascinates and bewilders me every month. As to U.S.A. and her position to-day I form my views for myself and I think she is doing the wise and sensible thing these days. At all events if I were President it would be along those lines I would seek to guide my countrymen and I have little doubt that if I sought to guide them otherwise I should soon cease to be President. It is your good fortune (one might find a better word) and ours that you have once again sent us a fine Ambassador. I had a long walk and talk with him the other day (and am hoping to get him down here), and certainly fell a victim to his charms. A great entertainment to watch the wit creeping into his face to have a peep at you and see what

66

you are made of. It is remarkable what a series of first-rate men you have managed to send us this fifty years. Well, Houghton is going to rank among the best, most sane, shrewd and good.

There is an author here whose work I have known for a short time only, though she has produced several novels, who seems to me so notable that I want to press upon you strongly her high claims, especially if (as is probable) she is not yet published in America. She is Mary Webb. She is so good that her time must come; she is more the woman-Hardy than anyone else, and I believe it would be a feather in the cap of any firm to have her on its lists.

Speaking of Hardy, he is in great fettle (at 85) and much interested in the production of his play on *Tess*. I am expecting the Galsworthys here next week. By all means publish a volume of my plays similar to Galsworthy's if you think it a good plan. I should like Lyon Phelps to write introductions but probably he wouldn't think it worth while. Anyone you like.

To CHARLES TURLEY SMITH, author

['Charles Turley' wrote chiefly boys' books. He was a member of Barrie's 'Allahakbarrie' ('God help us') cricket-team. He lived in Cornwall. See *Dear Turley* (Frederick Muller.)]

Adelphi Terrace House 10 July '11

My dear Charlie

'I am always glad to see your writing tho' I cannot read it.' This is a quotation, and not meant for what I say of yours but what you probably say of mine. I saw it as the beginning of a letter addressed long ago to James Payn.

I have so many letters to write that it comes to my not writing the ones I want to write. This far from meaning that you are not often in my thoughts, and I was very glad to have your letter the other day. I have been visiting at Campden Hill[1] for a longish time owing to one thing and another. For one, Jack had his operation in May that kept him from joining his ship for a time. The 60 of his Term are all about Canada just now in a cruiser for six months before they become middies.

[1]At the house where Sylvia Llewelyn Davies had lived before she died, still at this time the home of her five sons.

He sends me graphic letters. I have been teaching Michael to bicycle, running up and down the quieter thoroughfares of Campden Hill and feeling what it must be like at the end of a Marathon race. Have also taken him to a garden in St. John's Wood where an expert teaches fly fishing on a lawn.

I saw a little of the Eton and Harrow match, but Harrow were so slovenly in the field it was poor sport. Pity George didn't get in but I expect he will next year. Peter is bowling very promisingly also.

We are going for seven weeks or so beginning of August to Scourie in the west of Sutherland. 630 miles rail, then a drive 44 miles. The nearest small town is farther than from here to Paris in time. Nothing to do but fish, which however is what they want.

Now that Miss Corelli and Ranger Gull have appeared among you I shall expect to see an improvement in your style.

You don't say whether you are working much but I hope all is well with you, body and soul. I have nearly finished my P. Pan book.

We might play draughts by correspondence so as not to get rusty at it.

Yours affectionately, J. M. B.

10 May '13

Many thanks for the bluebells and a squeeze of the hand for every one you plucked. Still more for the affection that made you know how sad I would be about Michael gone to school. He is very lonely there at present, and I am foolishly taken up about it. It rather broke me up seeing him crying and trying to whistle at the same time.

I wish you could manage to come to us in Scotland this year —August and September. Few things could now give me so much pleasure as to know you mean to do this. *I would rather have you than any one.* And I do hope you'll come to Milne's wedding whenever it is, entirely in the hope that you will stay with me—the longer the better. I feel I want you badly just now.

Have been thinking a lot about you lately, and how much you mean to me. You can't think what a success you are to my mind. I would like the boys to know this and why, by knowing you well.

Checkendon Court, near Reading 25 May '13

I have thought a good deal lately of how Frank Millet's[1] death must have saddened you. One saw very little about him on the ship but I suppose there is no one known to either of us of whom we could feel more certain that he was coming out strong in those tragic moments. We used to discuss whom we should prefer to be wrecked with. Here was a man one would choose to be on a liner with when it was going down. Tho' I had seen nothing of him for years I have always had this same feeling about him, that he was brave and true and loyal.

What are you doing yourself now and how are you, and is there any chance of your getting up to me in Scotland for the summer? We shall be in the wild Hebrides. It's a place Lindsey found for me and I should be immensely glad if you could come. I think the E. V. Lucases will be there, and I'll try hard for Lindsey who captivated the boys. Also Mason is coming.

Mason, E. V. and I saw Australians v. M.C.C. Australians looked much the better lot!

3 Adelphi Terrace House 3 July '13

! ! ! This is my reply to you about the baronetcy,[2] and I rather flatter myself you are grinding your teeth because you did not think of such a good way of referring thereto yourself.

Nicholas was good on the subject. I had told him the night before to look in the papers next morning for surprising news, and he was up betimes and searched the cricket columns from end to end.

4 July '13

The test match had its features—Hobbs, Rhodes, Macartney. But ——— was dreadful beyond words, he was just a stick shoving the ball back. My best memory is Barnes bowling. He took no wickets but it was the most 'classic' sight I have seen since Richardson. What do I mean by classic? Well thus I feel the Greeks would have bowled.

Not certain if George is to be at Lords. Nobody has been chosen yet except the three who played last year. But he seems to be liking, and is doing well at, Winchester.

[1] He went down in the *Titanic*.
[2] In the Birthday Honours List of June 14, 1913, Barrie's name was among the new baronets.

69

Just a word to say what you will like to know, that George was killed instantaneously. It was in a night attack. I had a letter from him two days after I knew he was dead. This is now the common lot. I feel painfully for Peter between whom and George there was a devotion not perhaps very common among brothers. He is at Sheerness. Jack's destroyer goes to the Dardanelles in a few days.

11 July [1916]

You may have seen that E. V.'s brother Percival, who some-times played cricket with us, was killed in the 'push.' He had George's revolver and field glasses, which are again without an owner. In a recent letter to E. V. he said he didn't see how one could escape. Peter is out there in the thick of it. Life is forlorn despite the gaiety of the newspaper press.

I expect your agricultural work is a real good successful job.

15 July '17

Have been across and back again and find your letter. I had some success. I got Peter to myself for two days.

Perhaps the strangest thing I saw was from the Messines ridge. A German aeroplane suddenly emerged from a cloud and went for our six balloons. Four of them went in flames, but we saw the balloonists all descend safely by parachute—a beautiful sight. The only time I was in any danger was searching for George's grave, which I found. Of all these things when I see you.

Edgerston, Nr. Jedburgh, Roxburghshire 30 August '17

I'm glad you wrote me about it and I enclose two guineas with uncommon pleasure. I am up here with Michael and Nico—the last house next to the English border. Three German escaped prisoners are lurking about and Nico is looking forward to being compelled to exchange clothes with them some day when they catch him fishing. He is then to Sherlock them. We had Jack and his inamorata a few days. You see how time passes. He may soon be married.

My love to you.

70

Adelphi Terrace House 6 October '17

You evidently have your trials and I guess they're worse than you make out. I wish you would get some leave and make straight for this flat, the cellars could be worked up into good accommodation for a dambrod[1] championship and we could pick out as antagonists the most unlikely looking ones of the wild fowl that there do congregate of an evening. After a raid it is quaint to see people emerging like worms from their holes to search the Terrace for bits of shrapnel. Some on my roof every evening last week.

I have Jack's wife staying with me for the moment. He is in the hospital at Portsmouth and not at all well at present. She is very nice and attractive, I'm happy to say.

E. V. is in Devon doing some writing for war work. Audrey has joined her mother in Paris. I'm rehearsing a play—about people who think they could make so much more of life if they got a second chance. I like the subject but the treatment is a bit sketchy.

11 March '18

And so you were 50 lately, and know so little of yourself that you feel 'you have lived so long and done so little'. I have known many men, and very few indeed who in my opinion have done so well with their half century. You have helped others more than any one I know, and there are hosts in various classes who bless your name. In fact you are probably No. 1 of the Smiths.

A sad tale that you tell of the boy. Not 15, it makes one shiver. We jog along here, not very gaily. Peter has just gone back from a fortnight's leave. Michael is editing the *Eton Chronicle* and contributing leaders and poems galore.

2 Robert Street, Adelphi 19 March '18

The primroses give me enormous pleasure. They stand on this table in four happy little bowls, and smiling at me every time I look up. The courage of flowers in these days to go on just as usual!

10 May '18

It is very exasperating the way the authorities treat you and not much comfort to know that it is so more or less all round.

[1]Draughts.

71

I suppose Maurice has some answer to the Govt.'s statement. The debate in the House seemed to me ignoble on both sides.

Painful news—Nico goes into 'tails' to-morrow. I begged him to go into one at a time so that I could get used to the idea.

Peter was all right a week ago and still in the thick of it. Freyberg[1] writes me how he had been fighting for seven days on end and adds 'It is very beautiful.' He is nevertheless a most humane man.

Voormezcele near Ypres where there is so much fighting is where George is buried. I know the ground very well.

Adelphi Terrace House 15 October '22

If you were to expose that extra rib to me I feel sure I could blow it away, such is the force just now of my cough. This means that I am on the way to emerging, triumphant but broken, out of another of my bronchial outbursts. I hope you will find some more scientific or at least painless way of separating from your rib if it is really there. I suppose they do know things from X-rays, but my throat was once done and I used with complete success to show the photograph as a scene in the Alps.

Mrs Lucas and Audrey are coming to me for a week next Sunday on their way to Melton Mowbray where they are to run a shop of antiques. I trust you will get on well with the book and hope you'll bring it here to the flat when finished.

20 December '22

The calendar lies on my table ready to spring into life on January the oneth. Many thanks. I see you have been having more than your share of troubles still, and I hope you will soon be able to get going again strong at the book. I have been having electricity forced into me, which makes me feel quite champagny for half an hour but I question longer effects.

Nicholas is back and we have gone to some rehearsals of *Peter Pan*, which is rather bleached bones to me in these twilight days. I am to be at Stanway for Christmas to New Year, and it will be good to be where there are children. May the best come to you in the New Year.

[1]Major-General Bernard Freyberg, V.C.

11 February '23

Very delighted to have you here whenever suits you. I must search out the draught board. I think you had black last.

I looked in at Lavery's studio to-day and found him painting Cosgrave the Irish president with two detectives in the hall. They rose simultaneously as I took my pipe from my pocket. I am overjoyed at the thought of having you here so soon.

14 January '24

I seem now to be quite well thank you and am not afraid of the immediate future despite the newspapers. I find Miss Bondfield lives next door and I don't turn a hair. That's the kind I am. Have read a good deal of Sheila Kaye-Smith lately. Excellent, and an honour to the Smiths. Your pride in no Smith ever having been hanged was short-lived, as I daresay you saw correspondents writing from all quarters to tell of innumerable Smiths who have departed in this way. Great joy to me if I am the first to let you know of this.

Red Redmaynes scored with the woman being the bad egg. I knew she was but didn't think any author would have the courage to admit it.

My love to you.

16 September '24

The great news (which I hope will leave you breathless for a space) is that three weeks or less ago I played in one of Nicholas's matches at Stanway. Even that is news as I have not played anywhere since before the war. But it is not the astounding news. The Stanway XI (which has been quite swagger this year) were our opponents and on being put on to bowl I did the Hat Trick in my fourth over, one of my victims being the cock of the walk. One bowled, two stumped, Bridgeman being the stumps. What a glory for you and all Allahakbarries. I ought to be one of the Big Five in *Wisden*. In the same match Worthington (who was 12th man for Eton in Nico's year) made 139 not out, including about eight sixes and 16 fours. No, I am not going to America, but obviously I ought to be packing for Australia.

Lady Cynthia[1] and her husband are going to-morrow to Mullion Cove Hotel, probably for a fortnight, and will look you up.

My love.

[1] Asquith.

73

This is very sad news indeed. I wired you yesterday, but Cury it seems is not on the telegraphic wires so the telegram was returned. It must be a painful blow to you, and in a sense I am sure from your letter that you are taking it too much to heart. To an extent it must be a little like an experience of my own of some seventeen years ago when a friend ended his life in this way. I daresay they are unlike in an important matter as mine had taken money (a good deal of it mine). Well, I thought then, and think now, that he was the dearest of men, with just one black spot in him, as a human body may be perfectly healthy, all but for one atom. Your case is probably quite different, and from what you say I gather he was just badgered by having to do things in the accepted way in which they must be done in a business concern. There is no doubt that they must be done thus, and that any governing body which does not insist on the old fashioned coming up to date is failing in its duty to those whom it represents. As for yourself I know very well that you must have been kind and loving to him as no other man probably that I know could have been. It is the kind of thing that seems much bigger in a small community than in a big one where, so to speak, we often brush shoulders with the like. The main purpose of this letter is to beg of you very seriously to let it have no effect *at present* on your future. As to that, decide later when you have got a little further away from it. I almost demand this of you as your friend, very troubled about you. What I think you should do at present is to avoid all decisions and as soon as you can possibly get away come up here and stay with me for a bit, and let us consider the matter in all its aspects. The warmest of welcomes awaits you.

26 September '25

My maledictions on the rain that kept you from getting here. It has rained mostly ever since, but that is less material. I had just got back from the remote Highlands where the talk was so exclusively sporting that though I carried but a walking stick (purloined) I feel now I was all day landing the salmon and gaily putting bullets into the deer. We had one exciting day with—the cows. I may tell you that up there they are terrific. They had been separated from their calves a few days before and the glens were full of their moanings and stampings.

On this day I was watching a fisherman when the cows got beyond all control and swam the river—a roaring torrent in which no man could live—a 100 or more of them, then formed in battle array and thundered down the glen after their calves which were some miles away. I leapt into a tree.

The Stanway time was darkened by a bad accident to my sister who fell on a slippery floor and broke her leg. She lay there four weeks before she could be got to her home in an ambulance, and it will be long at the best before she can go about again though the doctors consider all is doing well.

I want to know what you are doing besides this extra work for Lucas. I have done a school story (Eton) for an annual. Lady Cynthia is editing *The Flying Carpet*. Rather poaching on your preserves! A good annual with contributions from Hardy, Belloc, de la Mare, Milne, Chesterton, etc. I hope you are keeping better. I'm pretty right.

1 October '25

I consider that in your choice of test teams Champain and you cover yourselves with ignominy, though *you* may be dragged out while *he* is sunk from sight. As 'one who knows' (my name in this matter) there are four certainties, Hobbs, Sutcliffe, Tate, Macaulay. He omits Sutcliffe altogether, and you gingerly include him at the end. The man who stood out beyond all in Australia in the tests. Why have you this ill-will to him? What is behind it?

We must have an amateur captain I suppose, so I grant you Carr. That is all the 'certs'. Strudwick may still be the best wicket-keeper. I give you Holmes, Woolley and Kilner—not Fender nor Sandham (Fender courageous but he couldn't get those blokes out and Sandham doesn't seem to have Test qualities.) I hanker after Hammond or Hallows, but we must have two bowlers—chosen from Larwood, Root, Parker.

This knocks out Hendren and Hearne, as having proved themselves not great Test men, but it only *guesses* their substitutes *may* be better.

On paper we can't make a superior team to the Test XI that were in Australia except for one man, Macaulay, who certainly adds something definite. I feel like risking Larwood (especially if he changes his name to Harwood—must have another H.).

(To be continued.)   The only One Who Knows

16th or 17th suits me equally for your arrival, but I hope you'll manage more than 'two or three days.' All hail. Am oiling the draughts.

You seem to have been having a rotten bad time, and I am so sorry. Flu of any kind is bad enough by itself, and accompanied by laryngitis must be doleful in the extreme. And of course a mental depression is their brother, and in such a family it is hard to hold out. I wish I was there to cheer you, if only by eating your eggs. I am (I say it with proper shame) rather well at present and leading an extraordinarily placid existence, especially after going to bed where I read Thackeray by the hour, not because I am especially a Thackeray man but the books are so long and I read so slowly that I feel when I begin on one that all my arrangements are complete for the spring. Have you seen the articles on the Tests that are appearing in papers by Clem Hill and Noble? Clement has a judicious and pleasant pen but Noble boundereth a bit, and maketh it more necessary that we should disturb the invader. If our 'tail' was one that lashed we might make some use of it. They are trusting a lot to that tail, and we must admit that the kangaroo hath it not. I have agreed to go to a press luncheon to them a day or two after they arrive,[1] and if possible will cast the Evil Eye upon them. I see Parkin has said that if Mailey and Grimmett were in League Cricket here they would never be heard of. This is the stuff to give them. I expect it is not so far from the truth too. The problem is

[1]Barrie's speech on this occasion began 'How much sweeter those sounds [of cheers as he rose] would be to me if I had got them for lifting Mr Mailey over the ropes. If I were to say one-tenth of what I could say about cricket, especially about my own prowess at it, there would be no more play to-day. Once more I buckle on my pads. I stride to the wicket. I take a look round to see how Mr Collins has set his field—and, oh horrible! I see Mr Gregory waiting in the slips. What can he be waiting for? Mr Gregory is now joined in the slips by Mr Hendry and Mr Mailey. Three to one! I don't know what they think they look like, with their arms stretched out imploringly, but to me they look as if they were proposing simultaneously to the same lady . . . I suppose I am the only man in the room who knows what is to be the constitution of the English eleven. I am afraid I must tell Mr Collins that this year there is no hope for his gallant but unfortunate company. Our team is mostly new, and is at present hidden away in cellars. Our fast bowler is W. K. Thunder, who has never been known to smile except when he hears Mr Gregory referred to as a *fast* bowler. Of our batsmen I shall merely indicate their quality by saying that Hobbs is to be 11th man.'

how to get them promptly into League cricket, and to find Gregory already there. This is all intended to encourage your hopes. Since reading Noble I have a fine confidence that we shall pull it off. Oxford should recover now that Holmes has passed his exam. How he got that wicket deponent knoweth not. He should now be able to open any oyster. I am alone in London for the Easter holidays, and will go out into the silent streets to-morrow as the only man therein. Creepy. I do hope you will get better soon and to have a line from you on this to me very important subject.

8 June '26

That seems unfair of you to have an extra rib, but not only that, to keep it up your sleeve as it is apparently in your arm. Your bowling arm? If so you might lend it to Tate. Evidently it is no use to you and I do hope the medicine men will dispose of its power for harm. I am very glad Mrs Millet is so much better. Please, my love to her. I went yesterday to England *v.* The Rest and was very bored. Hobbs had no gaiety, but, my word, he played like a true master of the game and his placing made all others comparatively clodpoles. They seemed nearly all to be paralysed. Duleep's catch was a line of poetry tho'. Larwood I expect will be a swell ere long. I suppose Root will play instead of Allen. It will be quaint if the rest win. High time Carr proved his choice.

24 July '26

I hope you are feeling pretty right again, though I am none so sure and would like a bill of your health. I thought there had been Test cricket, as it has been a good day here until evening. What is needed is not more time for matches but a fleet of aeroplanes to rush the combatants about England in search of a dry spot where they could alight and toss at once. I conclude from the composition of the English XI that the idea was for a draw, leaving the final match to decide. It should then be composed of the eleven who can stick in longest waiting for the loose ball. I was hoping Carr would win the toss to-day and put the Australians in again—a pretty sure way to getting into *Wisden* for ever.

I am going to Stanway about August 4 for a month and as the Australians are to be playing Glo'ster at Cheltenham, 7,

9 and 10th, several of them will probably be staying with us and they'll all come over on Sunday. Does not this tempt you to come for a few days? I wish it would.

7 March '27

Wisden's has arrived and was received with 21 guns, if that is the correct number for a royal reception. He is now playing a triangle match here with Trollope and Winston's 'How I won the War,' and the one who has done best for the day is the one I take to bed with me. There is good scoring going on all round and so far no one is out. I am now once more alone in the flat as Peter has found rooms out Kensington way. Brown[1] paid me a visit the other day and is now a farmer with large moustache and probably, except in London, straw in mouth. I had Mrs Lucas a few days trying to recover from a devastating cough. E. V. is back and I expect to see him to-night at a little club dinner. I ardently hope you are pretty well, which so it leaves me at present.

11 May '27

Blue-bells still nodding fragrantly on my table but beginning to look like topers after a night out. Sic transit, but they have been very lovely, and I thank you much.

You seem to have been having a rotten time, though, and as far as the influenza goes (and it does go a long way) I have been keeping you company. Better again however. All London seems to be stirred into briskness—people walking more jauntily—a feeling in the air that we are not played out—by the new Body-in-a-box murder. The evening papers ought to head their articles 'Brighter London.'

Judging by results, that 'smaller ball' is what the Allahak-barries needed throughout their career.

The play went well. Simon[2] (in amazement over the unexpectedly grand performance of another child of seven) 'And she only knows the names of two counties!'

9 November '27

I could have warned you against trying to dig up rose-trees if you had consulted me in time. When I was about 5 or 6

[1]Ex-servant.
[2]Asquith.

another lad and I set off to dig up a goose-berry bush in his people's garden, and with (I think) the first blow of the spade I split his lip. He clutched his lip and ran into his house. I threw down the spade (oh, to have to tell it) and ran for my home and announced that I had 'deaded' him. Lip had to be sewn up, I abandoned spades. But you see it was not my lip I maltreated while it is your own arm you have damaged. I hope at any rate it will soon be better and that you will now join my side on the great spade question.

Come along here and I'll invent a cure. I have a lot of medicines, effect of them unknown, but by taking them all you can weather any storm.

12 January '30

I am glad the hot water bottle promises to settle down into a useful career. As for the haughty ones who scout them, as the years roll on we shall forgive them. I hear there is now a way of pouring heat on to beds by electricity. We may come to that. Your general condition seems now to be what my nation call 'there about it' and 'nothing to boast of and nothing to complain of', which on the whole is not so bad, though I am in even better fettle. As for war books I am kept busy reading Peter's.[1] One of them is at present the serial in the *Daily Mail*, and another just coming out. *Her Privates We* is a fine study of the common man. They speak coarsely but that is how they did speak, no doubt, and it is really an ennobling affair.

Test matches seem to have broken out with violence. India can't expect equal rights till she has test matches.

2 March '30

Avaunt. This is addressed to myself for not having thanked you for *Wisden* ere this. You must take as compliment however that if I'd seen it in a shop window before it reached me I'd have sent you promptly enough a letter of remonstrance. It now makes a nice solid weapon for throwing at stone-wallers. Though their test team is so much younger than ours they are probably still slower.

14 September '30

Yes, rather, I went to see *The Left Hander*, it has a special appeal to me now that I write left handed and always bowled

[1]Peter Llewelyn Davies, now a publisher.

79

left as you have no doubt good cause to remember though I don't believe you do. We talked those old days over again at the Navarros the other day, and there were several priests there with whom I made an unintentional hit by saying (perhaps brazenly) that I had once made two fours and a five, and I found afterwards that they thought I said I had made 245 and now are telling everyone about my prowess, so when next you sit between two priests do be careful and don't give me away.

That dinner with the Australians was quite enjoyable and I said in my remarks that I hoped when Woodfull was sitting in his cabin on the way home nursing the Ashes he sometimes would wonder whether he should not have given a handful of them to Gloucestershire. I have since had a letter from Bradman asking me to write a preface to his forthcoming book but am not doing it. Thus you see I now move in highish circles. I am all right at present and had a good time at Stanway and wish you had not that tired feeling.

I think *Angel Pavement* very good.

19 February '31

Wisden's has at last come and I sat far into last night with him, which is my best thanks for him—or if there are better I send them also. I gather that you are now a bit better, and for that, after all, I thank you still more. I seem fairly right myself too. As for S.A. cricket, it seems plain that we need to send our best possible elevens there, and a numerous reserve as they get so wounded. Peebles and Voce seem to promise well for the future. I feel sorry for Chapman who has everything in his favour except the score-sheet. I agree with you about *Morning Tide*—a fine thing. I understand that (like Burns) Gunn is an excise man. I have not seen *The Three Brothers*. I note that Lindrum is firing you to emulation with the ivories. This I regret. The dambrod is your game.

21 April '31

I am so sorry you have been having troubles and made unhappy by them. Times seem to bring them nowadays more than ever before, at least so I too find—as one grows older they are perhaps harder to bear, or at any rate bring a longer sadness. I do hope yours will become smaller. I was in the country lately, and trees hardly in bud, while driving back through Hyde Park in a taxi I found them well-advanced, and as for flowers, the ground was so gay with them that I felt I should be sending samples to you instead of you to me. However they were probably mostly stuck in the night before. I wish cricketers would put on a few extra garments and take to the field if only in the interests of newspaper-readers.

6 May '31

Your servant warmly appreciates the blue-bells, and speaking thereof is also glad to know that you got into warm pants to pluck them. Do you know that the saying (perhaps Scottish) 'Ne'er cast a clout till May be out' refers not to the month but to the tree? You don't say how you are, which I hope means all is fairly well. I have a very frequent weariness in the legs but otherwise am well to do. If you had not that wireless to spoil my cricket messages I'd have felt impelled to send you a telegram with the result of Glos'ter v. Surrey.[1] Lyon is a nailor for audacious cricket and will evidently compel some other counties to follow suit. Some day he will start with the second innings. This young Hardstuff at 17 must look on Bradman as quite an old chap.

20 September '31

I have been gallivanting in Scotland, hence delay in getting letters. I have seen no one in the inner world of politics, but fear that things may soon be much worse than they are at present. The balancing of the Budget is evidently only a first step. It is also difficult to believe that the present Government can become sufficiently harmonious to bring in a tariff, and mortal eyes cannot predict what might be the result of an election, though I presume that the Conservatives would come in—to face a hard fight. The tariff may be the thing that is needed, but disillusionment must come to the many who seem to think that prosperity must follow it next day. Your team is a happier subject, and I agree with you that all you mention should cross the seas, if Hobbs be willing. I would keep Farrimond for 2nd wicket-keeper and put Ames first. The

[1]Barrie had been accustomed to telegraphing Test and County cricket scores to his friend in Cornwall.

extra people should perhaps be Robins, Peebles, Bowes and I have a hankering after Chapman as probably a better captain than Jardine—heartier and more able to cheer his men. Three fast bowlers is probably wrong for Austr. wickets, but I don't think Robins and Peebles can be left out. Did I tell you of my being at the Canterbury week and hobnobbing with the Kent and Somerset men? The Somerset hard hitter whose name I forget for the moment had only one over, as follows— 1 (really a miss) 6 (into a wood), 6 (into the town) 0 (but it was nearly 12), 6 (into the cathedral), and next bowled neck and crop by Freeman. If budgets could only be balanced in this way!

Do try and get away and come up. I won't give you my Economy Burgundy (S. Africa) which tastes too like blacking.

10 October '31

I am very glad the larynx and pharynx have decided to behave better. A doctor's mandate, perhaps, in political language. The excitement over the election seems to have died down here—at any rate I notice that the evening paper placards have given it up and gone back to 'Disappearance of a one-eyed girl', etc. However, there will be rowdyism anon and to spare. It is obvious I think that Protection must now get its head for a full trial though whether a successful one none can tell. Vote for larynx or pharynx—you cannot have both. (Oh, can't you, *C. T. S.*)

Yes, Earle was the man I saw smiting them. I forget if I told you of a schoolboy at Stanway who asked me to write my name in his autograph book. It had various coloured pages and he told me to write on a yellow one. Afterwards I found the book on a table and found written in it 'Pink pages specially reserved for cricketers only.' Oh, my pharynx, O, my larynx!

4 December '32

What warfare in Australia! We have certainly made a big start but I think people are far too confident in looking on the match as already won against such stout opponents and the weather and the 4th innings. Larwood's three wickets after lunch was in the grand style and I hope to have good news for you to-morrow. Ditto about McCabe. I sent him a cable: 'Glorious performance by the night-lights-boy'—a reference to my having told him here that he was so young I understood he could not sleep without a night-light. I think both teams made a mistake in not having an extra bowler. The A's should have included Ironmonger. It all seems mysterious about Bradman and sad too. Whatever it is it may have been his reason for all that earlier correspondence about other engagements. Evidently several of their best funk Larwood, but they will reconstruct their team if necessary in their game way and learn how to deal with such bowling. In the meantime Jardine seems to be very capable and it's funny about his cap. I think he should reserve Larwood entirely for tests, and Voce as much as possible. That curious treatment of the ground to spoil shock tactics may have spoilt Allen—and also the fuss about his boots. Hendren says he never disturbed the ground here. I am assuming that our bowling is all legitimate. Armstrong writes unpleasantly about it, but that does not move me. What a team we could have had with Duleep and Robins and another bowler!

27 March '33

Many thanks indeed for adorning this room once again. I have put in a new system of lighting which is just in time to greet them by night as well as day. Your east winds of venom disturb me though, for here we are basking day after day in weather that obviously thinks the month is July. To-day I had to shout to Frank[1] for my summer jacket.

It is an odd coincidence your query about Lord Cecil (as he now is) because his nephew or cousin (I am not sure which), Algernon Cecil, is staying with me here at the flat at present. His wife, Lady Gwendolen, died very sadly a few weeks ago and was a great friend of mine, and he is here for a week or two, as all I can do to help him a little. I told him of the Nansen matter,[2] and he has written Lord Cecil telling him my blunt opinion of you. We are both sure Lord C. will do everything he can to help you, and what you now do is to write to him and explain.

I knew Nansen slightly myself. I remember taking him to

---

[1] Frank Thurston, successor to Brown.
[2] C. T. Smith was writing a book called *Nansen of Norway*.

a box to see *The Admirable Crichton,* and how when I told him
that the company were playing it to him alone (as was the case)
he responded grandly and cheered them till the audience
recognised him and cheered him. A splendid fellow with eyes
that were like holes in his head. A gift from the snow I daresay.
That seems to have been my only meeting with him. I think
my friend Gilmour whose father-in-law was Secretary of the
Royal Geographical Society knew him better and I'll find
out if he has anything worth communicating to you.

5 August '34

I haven't actually seen any cricket but follow the movements
in the press. I don't think you will be able to wangle Robins
into your side for the Test, but the bowling of Allen to-day
should give them to think. Odd about Hammond who after
all is our best. Woodfull (take note) is coming out strong again.
Bradman has been staying at my surgeon, Shields's, cottage
in the Burnham Beeches. I saw a long letter from him the other
day which was one of the nicest and warmest I have ever seen
from a young man.

21 March '35

Wisden's came all right, and many thanks to you. I, also,
find I can't go through it with the zest of yore nor do I thrill
over our rather lamentable experiences against Hedley
Constantine and Co. Very sorry surely that Wyatt had his
skull cracked, but alas again. More concerned that the bramble
got at your ear so efficiently when you were engaged on the
kindly primrose venture. These last four days have been almost
gorgeously sunny here and I hope the same with you. Nothing
to be heard in London now but hammers and nails preparing
the Jubilee which I suppose is our way of replying to Hitler
and not a bad way.

5 February '36

I seem to be quite well again. It seems almost strange with
so many passing away. About a month ago I was at a little
dining club where Kipling and Owen Seaman were. Owen
I only waved to as he was at the other end of a long table but
Kipling was beside me and we had a good talk. I know how
you must be feeling about Owen. It was my first thought when

I saw the bad news. He was lovable and straight and kind—as soundly good a man as one is likely to know. At present I am unhappy about my sister, who is in a nursing home here and so ill (heart) that the doctors say she is just fading away in a long sleep. My last near relative and inexpressibly dear to me. You will understand all these things should bring you and me closer together, but indeed we are as close in love I think as two old friends can be.

23 February '36

It is now nearly a fortnight since my sister died, and I am not sure whether I let you know, for I have been in a poor way, she meant so much to me. She had no pain during the whole illness, and during the week at the end was nearly always asleep and in this really rather serene state passed away. I was not able to be at the funeral but am fairly well again and even working hard at my play rehearsals[1] though they are not what I think of. This is just a bare letter to tell you—you can fill in the rest.

13 October '36

You seem to be having a bad time in bed with your throat and I am very sorry. I cough away interminably but somehow the throat seems to be listless about it, and I am in fair fettle. I'll be occupied a bit now with the resumed rehearsals of my play.

If the Rest has beaten the 1st 11 in Australia to-day it will be an excess of the grotesque like the counties here against the Indians. I think two equal teams (outside the glorious uncertainty) for the tests would be as they stand except that Bradman plays for Britain and Hammond for Australia. They are undoubtedly the two champions but B. is the certainty and if we gave him 150 not to play (for two innings) it would be quite worth our while. We seem weakest in our two opening batsmen, whoever they turn out to be. Our best XI might have batsmen, all but the last man, either Farnes or Copson, who are no good with the bat nor on the field. Or we could play neither of them and have a complete batting and fielding side. What does your throat think of that?

[1] *The Boy David.*

85

19 October '36

Committee formed here to make you vigorous again as quickly as possible. Members present J. M. B., Mrs Stanley,[1] Frank Thurston. Moved, seconded and agreed unanimously, that a member be sent at once to Fortnum & Mason. After statement by Mrs S. stating that she was the one for the job, especially good at bachelors, proposed by J. M. B., seconded by F. T., that she be the member. She sets forth in her black merino in an hour and Fortnum & Mason will doubtless do the rest.

Signed with significant crosses

J. M. B. X   F. T. X   M. S. X X

18 March '37

Just a line to thank you for *Wisden's* and to report progress. The Sciatica, etc., are still going pretty grim at times, but at other hours I feel well and am getting a lot of 'treatment', and at times indeed there are about as many hot water bottles in my bed as runs on an English test score sheet.

24 April '37

My letters get into such confusion that you must be very bewildered and wondering if I exist at all. In a nutshell the truth is that I have for a long time been ill, but not talking about it, and have the best possible attendance at the flat with doctor, nurse, etc., and seem to be slowly getting better. Mrs Lucas is a great deal here and if you write to her at the above she is sure to tell you how I am getting on. I assure you I am nothing worse than sluggish and too sleepy headed, and a bit old.

★

To Mrs E. V. LUCAS

Hotel Meurice, Rue de Rivoli, Paris 31 July '15

My dear Elizabeth

9.30 is the hour, and I have just finished dining alone, Edward being out having an orgy with his relatives. Melon, lobster, turkey,—I am not boasting; I was wishing all the time I could pass the dishes to you, and oh dear, I was reflecting

[1]Housekeeper.

(1) (as Michael would say), how tongue-tied of me not to have told you how lovely it was to me the way you were devoting yourself to our little attempt to do good at Bettancourt[1] and (2) what a difference knowing you has made in my life. The latter (selfishly perhaps) is what I have thought of most, and suddenly I felt compelled to drink to the health of Hewlett, who first presented us. We might have met later without him, but it is a strange world, and who knows? so here is to him, and to his spouse, if she had a share. My life would have been so much gloomier without you. I would go off feeling happy, really happy, if I could be sure that all was well at Bettancourt, but those bad throats make me anxious. I do trust all is to be well. If it is not, the doctor must take strong steps, and you must submit. Outside that shadow all seemed to me very real and good, and I had the firm conviction that you really were doing something in a small way for mankind. Helping to build up the people of the future. It is like a tree we have planted which will bring forth good fruit long after the German invasion is but a memory. I say 'we' but it is really you who are doing it, and I love to see you doing it so efficiently and modestly. That wisest of the Greek sayings (which I must have quoted to you before now as I am constantly thinking of it) that if we would love our fellow-beings we must not expect too much of them, holds true, but I do expect a lot of you, and in this matter you have come nobly to the grapple.

It took all morning to get passports put right even tho' we were helped all the way by Sir H. Lee's services, and I pity the weary ones who had to do without him. In the afternoon I got your things. I hope the chain reaches you all right. Perhaps something old would have been nicer. We are on same floor but *au gauche* instead of *au droit*, and so *bon nuit* or *bonne nuit*, and how good life is to all of us when there are such as you in it.

Yours, J. M. B.

Adelphi Terrace House 29 January '18
Michael's letter to Audrey[2] has told you of our adventures

---

[1] A large château near Révigny where Barrie had set up, in the charge of Mrs Lucas, a hospital for the war-victim children of Rheims and its neighbourhood.
[2] Lucas.

at Tillington where we had a very happy time, and M. discovered an old shop at Petworth and triumphantly bought a soap-dish for his room here. That room is not finished yet, indeed three rooms are still in confusion which will give you some idea of the difficulties with workmen nowadays.[1] I have got into the study now, however, and at last the chimney behaves and certainly it is a very attractive room, and the little kitchen off it is good too. I had begun to feel in my bones tho' that it was all too fine a flat for me and that for my lonely purposes all I really needed was this room and the bedroom. Brown could have done for me so, and I had quite planned letting the rest with its own door. However the way has been cleared by trouble at Campden Hill. Mary is going sometime in February. This means Michael and Nicholas making this their home, as my idea is to put caretakers into Campden Hill for a little and then store the furniture and dispose of the lease. Of course it is a great thing to me to look to having M. and N. here tho' they are so much away. A sad thing is that Michael is now 17½ and in a year or less is eligible for the army. The depression of it all! I shy at thinking of it but it has no doubt a great deal to do with the gloom in which one seems to get enveloped. Then I don't seem to care to write even to you. But I'm often wondering how you are getting on and wishing you could come in.

The beauteous ladies you speak of are not to be seen much cooking my bloater, and I'm not positive whether they tire of me or I of them. You will have heard of the Red Cross work we are doing, of which E.V. is doing a great deal more than I am, but still it gives me a good deal of work. I promised them the MS. of *P. Pan* and then could not find a single page of it. However, there is plenty more. A good many authors appealed to for MSS. reply that their wives, etc., won't let them. The great box-load I have, and nobody to care! But this is gloom again, and heaven knows I have much to be thankful for still. We had alarums and excursions in the air last night and the casualties are mostly close at hand. I suppose I ought not to put it more clearly.

My love and write soon and I will too.

---

[1] Barrie was moving into the larger flat above his own.

I emerge out of my big chimney to write to you. I was sitting there with a Charlotte Brontë in my hands (when I read her I think mostly of Emily) and there was a gale on the roof; it is probably not windy at all down below but with the slightest provocation the chimneys overhead in their whirring cowls go as devilish as the witches in Macbeth, whom they also rather resemble in appearance. I hope, however, it is a sufficiently dirty night as the sailors say to keep the air-raiders at bay.

My fire behaves handsomely now and the logs—three footers —do go a-roaring; the smell of them ushers you into the room like a nice farm-hand. I wish, heaven knows, that it *would* usher you into the room. Sometimes as I sit there I have a queer feeling that I am downstairs in the brown chair and this is someone else up here. Down stairs seems to belong to those Victorian days before the war and it is queer to have lived in them without knowing what was coming. I shall go in some day when the door is open and see if I am there. And the desk in the corner and the two sofas at right angles, which I have since been told were celebrated as the two most uncomfortable sofas in London. I have got rid of one of them but the other and the desk will see me thro'.

As I had to do without you this time and scorned to put anyone in your place the decoration of this room is perforce all my own. I feel rather like the prentices of old who had to turn out one passable piece of work to show they could do it before getting their diplomas, or whatever corresponded thereto, and then never attempted another. At all events I feel this must serve for me. The woodwork is very restful to the eyes (and the eyes are getting werry bad at type they didn't use to boggle at—I'll be doddering in sight sound and limb by the time you come back having forgotten your native tongue). It is just stained sufficiently to look as if we had been together for one decade. The floor is matting, with rugs by Michael Llewelyn Davies, Esq., and I think you would like the curtains which are grey with a red braiding that when Brown is in the mood he wilfully shows, as a lady might flick her skirt to show her pretty petticoat. There are no pictures beyond tiny ones, the books and wood crying out against our experiments therewith. They turn up their noses at furniture also, and there's nothing new but one soft chair, also by the aforesaid M. L. D. You sink into it, at least it is there for you to do so.

We have coverings for the chairs and sofa in the grey of the curtains, and on them are to be cushions when we can enter a shop for the purpose. Naught else but in the fireplace two old settles and piles of firewood which in these days have the look (and bearing) of masterpieces by Benvenuto Cellini.

I had an odd thought today about the war that might come to something, but it seems to call for a poet. That in the dead quietness that comes after the carnage the one thing those lying on the ground must be wondering is whether they are alive or dead. Out there the veil that separates the survivors and the killed must be getting very thin, and those on the one side of it very much jumbled up with those on the other. One can see them asking each other which side of the veil they are on, not afraid that they may be dead so much as surviving. And then the veil thickening a little and the two lots going their different ways. You could even see some going with the wrong lot, a dead man with the living, a living man with the dead. Perhaps it is of this stuff that ghosts are made. These be rather headachy thoughts.

I expect the lot on the other side had as many Germans as British, and that they all went off together quite unconscious that they had ever been enemies.

To avenge the fallen! That is the stupidest cry of the war. What can the fallen think of us if they hear it.

Audrey would be amused with the subject Michael had to write a poem about in the *Eton Chronicle*—not had to but greedily pounced on it. Three house-masters, including his own, were summoned by an officious special constable to appear at Slough under the Defence of the Realm Act for not pulling down their blinds. Delight of the boys! Opportunity for M. L. D.!

Now goodnight. It's midnight so I don't expect the maroons to sound. They use rockets that go off like a gun and then spread red stars in the sky. Beautiful enough. I'm not off to bed yet. Resume *Shirley* by the fire and mix you up with Emily, whom you are not unlike.

3 July '18

Nearly four years of it now. I think it was four years ago to-night that my cinema supper took place, a good many of them

90

gone since then. We were bright enough that night. One gets used to all new conditions but we go off on different lines and in four years are out of hailing distance of where we should otherwise have been. Universal destruction probably deprives us of so much life in the same way as the death of an individual dear to us does.

I was entertained to hear of the Americans calling Audrey 'marm'. Had often read of marms but never believed I should have the luck to know one. It is almost like saying I know a real cowboy. It's very interesting what you say about the serenity of Paris. I had been told so and scarcely believed it. You are so near things that we can't guess here at what your feelings are. More breathless than ours, tho' indeed I hold my breath waiting for the next big stroke. The Americans are now pouring in wonderfully.

Michael and Nicholas have both had slight attacks of influenza but I hope to hear tomorrow that they are out again. Whether it is Spanish or not I don't know, but it is all over the place again. I am wondering whether Audrey will get across as it seems very difficult but if she does I'll love to see her. The three little plays did very well especially *Well Remembered Voice* which has made quite a stir.

I have had Jack and his wife for the last fortnight—they went off today and were as devoted as ever and a complete world to themselves.

I went to a big dinner as it seemed a rather historic affair. It was at George Curzon's to meet the P.M. and the Colonial pioneers and there must have been about 100 people, mostly men. I sat between Lloyd George and John Morley. It was the most democratic gathering, an England of the future rather than of the past.

I expect Brown will be called up before long, which will be a deprivation to me, but very hard on Mrs Brown if he has to go out of London. Her heart still gives him constant anxious nights. A letter from Turley says he was to be medically examined today. Gerald du Maurier goes into the guards directly. And so it goes on.

Tomdoun Hotel, Glengarry, Inverness-shire 9 August '18
No word from you yet, and I do hope all is going well at the Château. I had a budget of letters from Brown today and

hoped to find one from you in it. Seemed to see you writing it in the evening in the library, but it hasn't come. This place seems worlds away from the Marne but in a sense it has the mark of the war on it too, for it is a lonely land. All the highlands of Scotland are denuded of their young men, there are scarcely any tourists, and we have this big hotel to ourselves—indeed we seem to be almost the only people in Glengarry.

I had to knit my teeth to come away at all and it is uphill work to make the days pass.

Michael feels the dreariness and the sadness of it too and we flounder about my lochs and streams with an effort. I am out with them all day, carrying the coats. We may try some other place soon, so London is still my best address. Tomorrow we are going where we were the summer of Arthur's[1] death. It is 30 miles away.

I enjoyed having Audrey with me and would have liked to have her up here too but Edward naturally couldn't spare her. I'll try to stay in Scotland four weeks, but we may make tracks south before then. Michael would like me to take him to the château but I suppose better not. I liked that woman who called you the 'beautiful girl'. She was a woman of discrimination. I think of you as peculiarly French, moving about the château as a very fine lady. I always thought you that, but certainly never more so than in the château, with all its discomforts and hardships. I think you affect the children in that way too, and that that memory of you will live on with them. Something fine and rare in a squalid time. Now I'm off to read *War and Peace* in bed.

Adelphi Terrace House 17 January '19
I have no doubt you are much in need of your change and am very glad you are to get it. It sounds attractive too. Why not let your flat to the Peace Conference and secure a competency! Gilmour is there in form. They must with their satellites have control of Paris. I gave a grand party in the study—cocktails by the united strength of the Savoy but everything cooked here; when the time came and indeed all thro' the festivities I was wanting to go and shut myself up in my bedroom. Upon me descended gloom. I can only hope it did not seem as sombre to the guests as to the host. It is high time you were back to

[1]Arthur Llewelyn Davies, the boys' father.

92

drive away my dark spirits, you do it better than anyone else. The guests were: Lord Milne, Galsworthy, Belloc, Gilmour, Hawkins, Walter Raleigh, E.V., G. du Maurier, Freyberg, Mason, Wellesley, Wells, Admiral Sims.

Michael went off today to Oxford and Christchurch full of suppressed excitement. He has a very nice panelled sitting room, with furniture that would make you shiver. He hopes to be able to put in pieces from Campden Hill in place of it. Freyberg has been staying here for the last fortnight also and got on very well with the boys.

Nicholas just come in and calling for billiards.

13 February '19

It is like a whiff from a better world to have your letter. I don't so much mean because you have sun and we have snow, but you seem to have got hidden away in a real place of rest while here there is heavy rumbling of storm. I believe the strikes are owing to the 'classes' not realising that life has really changed for evermore in its externals at least. It is not higher wages grudgingly given that will settle the unrest. There must be a 'league of classes', rich and poor to work together sympathetically and putting their cards firmly on the table. The workmen must have access to the business they are in, know all that is happening to it, get a fair wage and then be paid once a year in shares in the business. Co-operation of a real kind, leading to emulation and also to faith in each other. And so on. Easy to talk.

What I meant to say was that you deserve your ease and I hope you will be able to bask in it to the full. It must be rather lovely to have Audrey developing under your eyes. So soon they fly away at the best, but there are sudden moments when they are children again.

After the long wait the Campden Hill Square house really is let to Speed the artist, and all the furniture is to go to storage next week. It's rather grim work for me as I have no one to help me but Brown, and I shall be glad and sad when it is over. A few things are coming here, and Michael has now at Oxford the small dining room chairs and a sofa and the sideboard from the dining room.

Peter is demobilised and has been in twice.

I was at Eton to-day and joined Nico in great fettle with a

pair of skates. You can tell Audrey of Michael's coming adventure for next Sunday. There is it seems at Oxford a dean's daughter of the not very striking name of Mary Cook whose awful attractions are such that she cannot appear in the streets (such is the excitement of undergrads) except guarded by dogs and strong men. Michael is to have tea with her on Sunday. Whether chuckers-out are placed behind the chairs deponent sayeth not.

Nothing about myself, but I am pretty gloomy. Can't get hold of an idea to write of that really engrosses me. When I am working I am all right. Write soon. It cheers me up immensely.

Miss Adams not well, hasn't been playing for months and won't before autumn. It makes a mighty difference in my income!

20 May '19

I suppose your wanderings have taken you to Paris by this time so I write to *rue Duret* on the chance. I'll be precious glad to see you when you get back here and miss you many a time and much. Audrey, as I daresay you know, I see sometimes, and tomorrow I'm taking her to the Russian ballet with my sister. I haven't planned anything about summer holidays yet, but I hope you and she will come to us when we go anywhere. Michael's recess comes long before Nico's now, but as it's the Long Vacation he will have August and September as well. I was at Oxford yesterday, and it was as lovely as any

> Magic casements opening on to foam
> Of perilous seas in fairy lands forlorn.

which someone said (Wordsworth?) are the loveliest lines in English verse. Yet tho' he likes it all M. says he could conceive nothing more delightful than to wake up and find there was another half at Eton. That last year takes an extraordinary grip of them.

My sister and husband are with me just now. I had the Welsh Lewises[1] last week—searching for Welsh people much of the time. Mr. L. reminds me in this way of my uncle who used to wander London looking for faces from Motherwell, N.B.—and found them too! We went to the theatre, and what interested Mr. L. was whether the actors were married and how many children they had. Very simple and lovable.

[1] See letters beginning on page 120.

2 Robert Street, Adelphi 12 August '19

I am very sorry Cornwall has a depressing effect on you. I expect that you have kept going so long that nothing to do is a labour. If that is it it should get less at any rate. And oh, if you knew what the heat in London is now you would feel that the billows and the breezes make amend for anything. I have never known anything like it and the only moments of comfort are when you, sticky, get into a bath. We are getting off on Saturday, and the address is Edgerston, by Jedburgh, N.B., where I'll hope soon to hear from you. We travel by night, so we won't have the baking sun, but we arrive at 6 a.m. and then have a long drive.

The 'water pageant' was the mildest and tiniest affair. Small boats 50 yards behind each other and dwarfed by any ordinary river barge. They looked like paper things made by children. It should have been held on the Round Pond.

No secretary at present as Lady Cynthia expects her baby in about a week.

Astounding offers from cinema people, and yet when you calculate the taxes hardly worth bowing to. Audrey will be impressed to hear that Mary Pickford has been at me strong again.

After talking of it for years I got a field-glass today, and strangely enough there was a terrific fire down the river this evening. I don't know what it amounts to yet, but I have never seen such a blaze.

I have been 'entertaining' an American, Mr Hayman, from the Frohman Co., and he took me to Hampton Court yesterday to dine on Tag's Island. It was against this island that my houseboat used to lie when the surroundings were very different.

There was an American girl with Hayman who confided to me that I was the first nobleman she had ever met. *Leaf from a nobleman's diary:* Today Brown measured me with a tape and went off to buy me a suit of reach-me-downs. This because my tailor says impossible for six weeks.

Adelphi Terrace House 1 August '20

I hope you and Audrey are having a great time and a good deal of sunshine. You must have been chased out of England on Friday by the rain. I got dripped between here and the

Strand and had to come back to change. How I wish I had an Audrey to trot about to *plages* with. Not that there are or can be more than one of her.

The news? (1) M. comes back from Scotland and N. from camp on Thursday and Friday next, and we go north on the night of the 11th. (2) Cynthia and husband have gone now—to the Wemyss's house. (3) The long curtain in this room blowing thro' the open doorway was ignited by a spark from a chimney and half burned before we noticed. Shows another way fires may occur. (4) The Margot diary is still the talk of London.

I'm rehearsing Leon Quartermaine in Loraine's part in *Mary Rose* and think he will be much better. If you are back, Monday, 9th, we might all go together. I met Compton Mackenzie, light trousers, grey silk hat, doggedly foppish, manner to match, face not matching, interesting suffering face. Now you can go down to the *plage* and bathe.

17 October '20

I am so glad to have your letter and to hear you found so much that was good in S. Jean to buy. I wish I could suddenly appear round a corner, and hope I would have been considered one good thing more. Life becomes somewhat different when there is nothing to be expected round the corner.

I am supposing you have got back to Audrey and Paris and are engaged on that troublesome business of finding a spot for yourself.

It was nice of you to have that talk with Michael and I have no doubt that for the time at least it had a steadying effect. All sorts of things do set him 'furiously to think' and they seem to burn out like a piece of paper. He is at present I think really working well at Oxford and has at any rate spasms of happiness out of it, but one never knows of the morrow. I think few have suffered from the loss of a mother as he has done.

You will know we have a miners' strike on here, and the vital question is whether the railwaymen, etc., will come out in their support. I always hang on to the side of the working man as long as I can, but the miners are not being wise. On the other hand they behaved honourably in giving a long notice, and at present there is not much bitterness on either side. That will come of course if it lasts.

Nico will be having Long Leave in a fortnight,—so quickly do terms pass, but the strike might interfere even with that. He writes me nice letters.

It is settled now between the Frohman Co. and Miss Adams that she does not play Mary Rose. Sad to me, but I can see they couldn't hit it off together.

I hope you will get some work of a kind that interests you and is not very strenuous, for I feel all you are fit for at present is to be taken care of and made much of and kept in the sunny side. It would really be better if you could find a post for me as I am very well and can't get going at anything.

27 February '21

Everyone seems to have colds just now except me, but yours is the one I most hope has gone. Not a very elegant sentence but from the heart. I have been twice to Brighton for a few days looking after Freyberg, who has had another bad time. When I left him the first time he was weak as a rat, but when I went back I found him on the pier trying for the world's record at punching the ball (and I think achieving it). No place is quite so like itself as Brighton, especially at the Royal Albion, but the air maketh amends. E.V. was there also, fit again, and escorting us to that little oyster shop.

It is good to hear that Audrey is getting on so well, and I look forward yet to hearing her ask for a second helping of something. I have Nicholas this weekend for Long Leave, so the flat is merry and bright again. Michael will be back soon, but contemplates a reading-party with another undergrad in Dorset, and that will be much better for him than London. He is working hard and really enjoying his life at Oxford for the present at least. He has the oddest way of alternating between extraordinary reserve and surprising intimacy. No medium. In his room at Oxford lately he suddenly unbosomed himself marvellously. One has to wait for those times, but they are worth while when they come.

You will see the marriage of Lord Milner to Lady Edward Cecil. She was in the other day to sit with Freyberg, to whom she gave her son's things when he was killed. I used to know her long ago at Meredith's birthday dinners. She was a Maxse. I'm giving a dinner myself on Friday to say goodbye to the American Ambassador, whom I have a great liking for.

97

Ladies also. An odd situation arises. I am writing a one-act play in which all the company are seated at dinner,[1] and I'm also planning the real dinner, and I quite mix up who is to be at which. Not a bad subject for an article. John William Davis and Mrs Davis, Lady Cynthia and husband, Squire Bancroft, E.V., Walter Raleigh, Lady Dufferin, Raymond Asquith's wife etc. are I think the real party, but perhaps they are the other one.

Mary Rose came to an end last night after 400 performances, which is about my longest. It would have gone much longer in normal times, and still be playing to a big profit if cost was as it used to be before the war. The provincial companies are doing extremely well.

Now to a restaurant with Nico, as it is Sunday night.

19 April '21

Just been saddened by news from Wales of the death of Mr Lewis.[2] He had an attack of influenza a few weeks ago and complications set in, ending thus. I don't think there can ever have been a more attached happy family circle than that, he was a fine and lovable man. It must be a painfully stricken family.

You will know from my note to Audrey that Michael joined the Defence forces, and is for the time being at Wimbledon, a full fledged private of the London Scottish, with kilt expected daily. They joined for a possible 90 days, but I think will soon be disbanded. Awful weather for sleeping on the ground in tents, but he is up here for a few hours' leave and certainly looks the better for it. Nico also is here, and I took him for the week-end to Lady Dufferin's at Reigate, where she has a house for the moment. E.V. was invited, but the strikes prevented him. I am supposing that he is going over to Paris this week, to start Audrey on her American journey. I hope that will be a success, and that you won't feel too lonely without her. I should like to come over before long, and see if I can't brighten you up a little. You must have some fits of depression and the world seem very drab. At any rate the summer days should be a help.

Lady Cynthia is sitting at her desk and sends you her love.

[1] *Shall We Join the Ladies?*
[2] Hugh Lewis, his Welsh friend. (See page 127.)

98

How would it be if I came over on Friday the 30th for the week-end? That seems from what you say to be a time that would suit you and I shall be so glad to see you and hear you again. Tho' I write little you are very much in my thoughts. I seem to have got into a listlessness that makes it very difficult for me to take any initiative, and sometimes feel that if I get into a train by myself I might without thinking get out at some place on the way and drift from view. However I suppose I can get to Paris all right once I start, and you will be there to warm my heart. Also I'll try to do all I can to warm yours. I think you have shown extraordinary courage thro' these long months of often too hard work and, I fear me, too much loneliness.

Our time at Stanway was the best I think we could have had, and there was so much for Nicholas to do that he was mostly happy. He is sometimes overwhelmed by what he has lost and is a touching boy at such times. He is away at present at a boy's house, and goes back to Eton on Wednesday where he is now in Pop, etc., and a very important person.

Cynthia is still at Stanway. I am dining with E.V. to-morrow to meet Charlie Chaplin. *Quality Street* is doing enormous business but I have not seen it.

Freyberg is back from New Zealand and is staying with me at present. Let me know about my visit.

To AUDREY LUCAS

3 December '21

My dear Audrey

To wish you a very happy Christmas. I send my wishes off in good time as I am not sure how long they take to journey to California. There are many things in this flat that remember you well, chairs, pictures, books (even the lift was asking after you the other day) and they all send the season's greetings and will be glad when you return.

It is of course a very different flat from what it was until the 19th of May.[1] All the world is different to me now. Michael

[1] On May 19th Michael Llewelyn Davies, with another undergraduate, had been drowned while bathing outside Oxford.

99

was pretty much my world. I can still care for those who cared for him, and you are one of them.

I don't suppose I have much in the way of news. Nicholas walked in unexpectedly today—he is off to the Eton missions in the east end for two days. Such a great strong fellow—in the football list in the *Eton Chronicle* he is officially stated to weigh 12 st. 5 lbs. You will fatten a great deal under Californian skies before you turn the scale at that! He is a terrific gun at school now and little boys tremble as he strolls by (with an eye on them to see that they tremble). He has a great friend who is much concerned because his father is not bright enough. He consults Nico about how to brighten father. The odd thing is that the father (who is a member of the Government) is quite celebrated for his brightness. The boy stayed with us in summer, and I told him on his departure that I expected a very fine letter of thanks for my hospitality. He took it solemnly, and I had a grand letter from him, and Nico had one at the same time asking him to wire how the letter had been received. He is very argumentative and clever and the other boys delight in putting him up to arguing with the masters until those poor souls tear their hair.

One night this week, about two in the morning, the embankment suddenly lit up as if lightning had come to stay. In time it dawned on me that the cinema must be at work so out I went and found them doing *London Nights*. I was taken (with a crowd) drinking coffee at a stall, and I'm told I figured therein in a picture in the *Daily Mirror*.

No, I never 'went west' in U.S.A. San Francisco must be memorable. Tho' you don't get much of it in R.L.S.'s letters there is a good deal about it in one of the volumes of travel—I think it must be in the 'Emigrant' book. Your experiences of the negro porters and waiters are very amusing. I shall certainly get one here to put your hat in a paper bag.

You will have heard long ago about my visit to Paris. I had a letter from your mother to-day saying she is soon off to Italy, which will be a lovely change for her. Also she gives me your change of address. Your father rang and hammered on the door last Wednesday night and I never heard him!

To Mrs LUCAS   18 May '22

It seems I hope rather dreadful to you that I have been so long in writing for indeed it seems so to myself, but I often as it were do drop you a line in my thoughts to which you reply from the couch in the fireplace. I wish you were there now and often wish it, and to hear the bell ring and Audrey come in with all her bravery on. It was good to have you and I look forward to the next time. I am glad you found me at a time when I was working, I seem to work so little nowadays and am so much happier when I do. Cynthia tells me she wrote you about the St Andrew's affair,[1] so all I'll say about it is my mind ceased to trouble about it once I got there—the students warmed me up and we understood each other, for which I am thankful. I think the chief reason I felt at home was that I was again among rather poor people, to whom I truly belong.

The St Andrew's Principal and his wife have been in London and stayed with me a few days, and I expect Cynthia and Beb next week for a time.

Do you know that this day a year ago Michael was alive and as well as any of us and that next day he was dead. That is really why I am writing to you to-day. I feel that he is at Oxford to-day in his rooms and that tomorrow he is going out to be drowned, and doesn't know it. I spoke about courage as you know at St Andrew's, but it does seem to me often as if there was something rather monstrous in my still being here. Peter is coming tomorrow to stay the night and will be everything that is kind.

The chairs, etc., are covered and the curtains up, all looking very nice and worthy of the attention you gave them. Write soon.

18 June '22

Chief news is Freyberg's wedding, of which you may have seen. I acted as best man. It was in a sunny church on top of a hill and we managed to keep the press at bay.

I went for Whitsun for five days to Sheringham on Norfolk coast with a large company—Arthur Balfour, Lord and Lady Wemyss, Cynthia and Beb, Lord d'Abernon, Lady Desborough.

Michael's birthday was on Friday. His two sonnets were in the *Eton College Chronicle* that day and in the *Times* today.

Often thinking of you and the joy of having you here and of your coming back.

[1]His rectorial address.   101

[From a Margate Hotel] 12 June, '23

. . . . All going well, last evening he[1] dressed in brown, shaved (which he thought made a lot of difference) and we dined in the great room, celebrating the event in champagne. He slept 'like a log' last night, and is at present preparing for the balcony with the bath chair to follow. I can hear him whistling. If only it will go on now. Your visit and Audrey's helped gloriously thro' those difficult days. Our love.

Remember you are expected next week.

Californie Palace, Cannes 14 January '29

Thus far into the bowels of the earth and I assure you it seemed a long way in that Blue train, which shall have no blessings dropped on it by me. In a sleepless night, when I constantly opened my door to peer out upon pandemonium, another passenger kept opening his door in the same clandestine way to peer at me, and he so got on my nerves that I meditated pulling the cord to complain of him. The dawn was coming before I realised that the ill-favoured loon was the reflection of myself in a mirror. However though it is all a horror to me I have things to be grateful for. The hot sun is genuine and the blue of the sky and the Mediterranean, and I walked two hours today without an overcoat in scenery tropical and lovely, though all as if painted by scenic artists on some theatre stage. It is rather awful to think that I have been here only one night yet, but on the other hand I slept better last night than for many a day. Sir Douglas Shields is very kind. The only lady I have spoken to (the youngest sister of Edna May) tells me her mother never comes here nowadays because she found she always got bronchitis at Cannes! The changes of temperature are what one has to be wary of, and at night the central heat is going as strong as at Bury. D.S. however has taught me how to turn it on and off at will so all is well. I have a little table in the dining room to myself, and generally speaking the aspect is much like a Brighton hotel. None of the eccentricities one hears and reads about. One of the rugs in this hotel is said to be over 100 yards long which interests (and damps) me as an authority on rugs. Now I go slowly to dress and slowly to dine (and Oh me!) I have only done them once yet.

[1] Nicholas, who was recovering from a long illness.

Very glad to have your letter, but I can, alas, see well enough that it is you who are not up to the mark rather than I, and that you should be in this sunshine and I in the cold and fog of London. I am so depressed to think of you woebegone as I feel you are, you who are so courageous and splendid. Well, I trust to be back by Saturday night, as we have now got our tickets for Friday on that Blue Train, which will be fiercely overheated and is not, to my mind, equal to the London-Scotland trains. The weather has continued fine, and to-morrow we propose to make our one excursion, to Monte Carlo—Shields, Frank and myself. A strange trio for it, but could we face you if we did not adventure. The Laverys are the only people I have seen, but I have dodged a bit.

Stanway, Cheltenham Christmas Eve '33

I do hope all is going at any rate in the normal way with whooping cough and that you are both recovering a bit from a very trying time. This seems so far away from you that I feel cut off from all knowledge of your condition and the best Christmas gift I could have would be to hear that you are again equal to your many kind and brave deeds. It won't be long till I am back in London as my week at Mells is going by the board owing to the scarcity of water there which prevents their opening the house. There is lots of water here but the electric light goes out for hours at a time and we have to do our best with candles. It is mainly a family party and great romps have been going on downstairs, with Didy,[1] who is evidently adored, treated as the queen of the festivities. I am however having a nice quiet time and loaded with kindness, and Cynthia is the heart and soul of the gathering.

I am feeling well enough to be thankful and am writing in the bedroom where I was ill. It is not haunted by as many shadows as you might think, as I have little memory of what went on at that time—a sort of coma in my days.

My love to you, always. You have been one of the happinesses of my life for many years.

Adelphi Terrace House 1 February '34

Your news is so far good and brings some relief at any rate

[1]Diana Batty, soon afterwards Mrs Michael Asquith.

but obviously you are far from well yet and shaken. I am pretty well myself and a considerable change for the better has taken place in my nights. I had been having another bout of insomnia, but now I can seek my couch with considerable confidence. Last night I dined at Algernon Cecil's, the first time I have been there since Guendolen died. I forget if I told you that Peter Scott has been doing a little painting of my fireplace, which is good.

My greatest adventure is that I have actually been to a theatre. Went to see Elisabeth Bergner, who is remarkable.

With my love.

5 March '36

I am so troubled by the fears that you are very overstrained. So am I for that matter. I am always wanting to see you, as you don't need to be told, but I don't want to add to the strain. I have a very good nurse (new but a blessing) and in day time get out to the Clinic where Miss Bergner is. I am at least a help to her husband. She had so far got on well but the two critical days are tomorrow and Saturday. After that I can come to you if you can't come to me. I am amazingly well but it is rather unnatural and I suppose I may suffer for it. Cynthia is being splendid. If you can let me hear either way how you are I shall be glad.

Stephen[1] wrote me a letter that is the best I have had.

★

To G. K. CHESTERTON, writer

Adelphi Terrace House 1 July '14

My dear Chesterton

It is immensely good of you to help us in our adventure while you are so busy and I am very beholden to you. Care will be taken of your arm—indeed, as I understand, the slower things are done for cinematograph the better, and in any case you shall do nothing you would rather not do. I hope Mrs

[1]Gwynn.

Chesterton is to be at supper also, as the plays are meant to amuse her.[1]   Yours, J. M. Barrie

25 May '16

Many thanks for telegram and permission to use your cowboy experiences for the matinée. It is for the Star and Garter fund of the Red Cross . . .

19 July '16

I am so grieved to have given you much trouble—nobly borne—for nothing, as those cowboy pictures will not be used in my play now, if it ever is produced, and I have decided to destroy them, which seems the safe and wise thing to do in the circumstances. No one could more appreciate than I do the splendid way in which you sacrificed so much time to other people's affairs, and I shall always be most grateful.

To Mrs CHESTERTON

28 July '30

I am hoping ardently that you are both coming to Stanway. I know Lady Cynthia has written you with no doubt all directions, but as she had not heard when I saw her last I add my plea. It would be an immense pleasure to me. There are few people in this vale of tears that I admire as much as your husband.

[1] Barrie's 'Cinema Supper.' 'Invitations issued to about a hundred and fifty guests, to repair to the Savoy Theatre on Friday July 3rd. Here a banquet would be served—described as Act I on the programme—and an entertainment would follow. *Frank Tinney's Revue;* consisting of Frank himself ("Hello, Frank!" "Hello Ernest!") and a whole series of all-star sketches by J. M. B. Miss Marie Löhr and Dion Boncicault in *Why? A Conundrum.* Miss Lillah McCarthy and Henry Ainley in *One Night.* Miss Jean Aylwin, with Edmund Gwenn and Henry Vibart, in *When the Kye Came Hame.* Miss Irene Vanbrugh and Godfrey Tearle in *Taming a Tiger.* Interpolation at this point, in her own material, of the lovely and gifted Miss Ina Claire. Gerald du Maurier and Granville Barker in *The Bulldog Breed.* To conclude with "still another version of *The Adored One*," in which the players were Miss Marie Tempest, with O. P. Heggie and Graham Browne . . . And the extraordinary scheme of stationing men with movie-cameras to film the guests as they arrived or ate and drank. For it was Barrie's fantastic intention to employ shots from the Cinema Supper as introduction to a scene in his revue . . . The day after the party he was down in Hertfordshire, with his technicians, with Barker as joint-director, and with a cast consisting of Lord Howard de Walden, Bernard Shaw, G. K. Chesterton, and William Archer. Cowboy suits had been provided. The company put them on, and ran about and leapt as they were ordered. Chesterton was set to cross a stream in a boat, swamped it, and waded ashore.' From Denis Mackail's *The Story of J. M. B.*

To G. K. CHESTERTON

Instead of giving Frank Thurston[1] this truly fine gift would you mind giving him one of your books inscribed. I know he would rather have this from you. I forget if I told you he is a Catholic. A number of years ago he said to me, 'A man at the door wanting help said he had come straight to me from Mr Chesterton who had suggested his coming, but I knew Mr Chesterton was in Edinburgh to-day, so I sent him away.' It may not have been Edinburgh, but the story holds. Here is the latest—of a fortnight ago. The four of us left at Stanway after the last guests were gone were Asquith, Lady Cynthia, their elder boy and myself. Scene, the dinner table.

J.M.B.: The only lines in an Oxford prize poem that have lived are 'A rose red city half as old as time.'
Asquith: What city was it?
      (No one knew)
Thurston (passing round the meat): Was it not Petra, sir?
(Exeunt the hangdog company into the adjoining room).

I am at Brighton for a few days and so much better that I walk on the windy side of the pier while the 1,000 other visitors are on the sheltered side.

You gave us a glorious time at Stanway and I do wish I had been a more capable host. However, Mrs Chesterton promised that you would come and see me in London.

Returning to the Edinburgh tale, if I had had a letter from you next day dated Lands End I should still have known you were in Edinburgh. Though you were to wire me now that you had never been in Edinburgh (if it was E.) I should still know better. If you say it wasn't Petra I shall be sorry for you.

To Mrs CHESTERTON

I am hoping G.K.C. is all right now. I have just got back from Scotia where no writer is heard of this year except Sir Walter, so I have no knowledge of what is doing at Top Meadow. When you come to London, and the sooner the

[1]Man-servant.

better, I wish you would stay here if you don't need to go back same night. I fear you have other places you would prefer but please give Thurston and me a trial.

To G. K. CHESTERTON

6 January '36

I am glad at any rate to have a letter from you. But there is nothing I can do, as all parts connected with my play were assigned some time ago. Of course if I should hear of a play that held promise of a part to suit the stately lady, whom you describe very attractively, I will let you know, but truth to tell I have lost contact with the stage for so long that I don't know any longer of its people or its doings and had to let the management find most of the people for me. If I had had any sense I should also have asked them to write the play for me. I don't belong any more. With all warm regards to Mrs Chesterton and yourself.

★

To Miss NAN HERBERT (later Lady Lucas)

Adelphi Terrace House 14 December '12

Dear Miss Herbert

I hope that waiting for the steamer was the worst of it.[1] Something like the cricketer's feeling, I expect, when he goes in to bat. Certainly it is a venture that was bound to make you run cold at moments on the way, when you had so much time to think of it, but there is always a true satisfaction in trying to do a good thing however much one may blunder it, and you are probably too much occupied now to think of anything except just doing your daily job. From here it all seems strange, but on the spot I expect it is full of a blessed routine. I fancy one soon gets used to any change of conditions as long as there is the daily work to do. I remember Joseph Conrad telling me that running a boat in the wildest part of the South Seas became before long as matter of fact as driving a bus in London. Speaking of London, you probably are as acquainted in

[1]Miss Herbert had just left for Montenegro as 'bottlewasher' to the Red Cross unit there.

Montenegro with what is going on here as I am on the spot. Such papers as you see you will read as one doesn't at home. I remember long ago having a friend in India who kept so much more in touch with London than I was doing that I got most of my home information from him.

My most real news is that Michael went to his school party today in 'Etons'—first performance therein and was secretly much excited. His white shirt has filled the house (I am writing from there) since early morn, and in short nothing else is talked of in society. Our special correspondent recalls a similar todo up in Harris when a cow made havoc of a lady's wardrobe.

It is whispered in Downing Street that Nicholas has gained a prize and spells it prise. Is this the same Nicholas (says our stop-press news) who has just come home from the party top-heavy with his first meat-dinner.

I am feeling pretty well again, and would feel still better if you would let me know what your life now really is. It is so good to be doing something, and doing it with one's own hands. And such good as you can do you see the results of day by day, which is rather fine and prevents 'that tired feeling'. So far as the map tells me, you are on the sea with mountains behind you. I suppose you know Henley's Hospital poems, and I expect they will come home with some added force. I rather wonder how you will spend Christmas day. Also whether you can read my writing, tho' this is done more properly than my usual.

Yours always, J. M. Barrie

25 March '14

My dear Nan

The salmon is great and glorious, and I have been going through it with the sort of dogged enthusiasm with which, I hope, the boys attack a book of Homer.

Well is well, there's no good trying to write a letter, for in truth this bargain with these officers has turned it into a day of anguish.[1] I don't know what is to be said to-night, can't have much hope. I feel like pulling down my blinds. Home Rule or not becomes a very little thing, and so does what party is in power and whether troops were sent judiciously or not in

[1]After a mutiny at the Curragh.

Ulster; but officers allowed to bargain—we have suddenly ceased to live in a free land and are a shame to all who have struggled in the past to make it free. So far as I can see, that must be so if this bargain is not torn up and those men ordered unconditionally to obey orders and dismissed the army if they decline, yes, though every officer in the land followed suit. Without that, the people of this country have ceased to be its rulers. Alas and alas!

I hope the rank and file will shake the House to its foundations to-night.

J.M.B.

To Lord LUCAS (Auberon Herbert, 'Bron'), secretary to the Board of Agriculture, Nan Lucas's brother

Scotland 31 July '14

. . . Nicholas is riding about on an absurdly fat pony which necessitates his legs being at right angles to his body. The others are fishing. The waters are all a-crawl with salmon, but they will look at nothing till the rain comes. The really big event is that Johnny Mackay (Michael's gillie) has a new set of artificial teeth. He wears them and joins in the talk with a simple dignity, not boastful, but aware that he is the owner of a good thing—rather like the lady who passes round her necklace.

To NAN HERBERT

Auch Lodge 4 August '14

Your postscript is good news, and I was very relieved to get it. Now that Fripp is satisfied, Bron should soon be able to be up and doing again. As for you, I don't know where, when or how this may find you. We are so isolated from news here, that when I wrote last I was quite ignorant that Europe was in a blaze. We occasionally get the morning paper in the evening, and there may be big news to-day.

I don't see myself how we can keep out of it long in any case, and if so, probably the sooner the better. You will be terribly far from the centre if you go to Servia, and I should think you ought to wait, but you know best. It seems awful to be up here at such a time catching fish, or not catching them, for it has rained four days and nights and is still at it, and all the world is spate and bog.

Hotel Knickerbocker, New York[1] 22 September '14

We are somewhere near the top of above stamp. Weather tropical. We dine in a garden restaurant 20 floors up on a higher hotel, but it is not high enough. There are inviting targets here for the German siege guns.

This, I suppose, is private. Our 'mission' here has been bungled somehow. No intimation sent to Spring-Rice, who doesn't want us. I have therefore pretended to interviewers etc. that I came here to attend to my private affairs of books and plays—which degrades me in my own eyes and doubtless in those of other people, for it sounds a contemptible reason for coming to America at such a time. However, it suits those in authority.

I think I would have done some useful work if they had just left me alone, but it is not greatly needed, as I find America is quite splendidly on our side. I am sure that 90% of the population (practically all except Germans, *and many of them*) support us cordially. Further, Bron can assure Sir E. Grey that his action throughout is as much supported here as at home, and the White Papers have been issued as extras to the newspapers and are familiar to the masses. The only possible trouble is that (largely, no doubt, for commercial reasons and perhaps because of notions about their own importance) they may want to interfere on the peace question. But Wilson is first-rate and will control them, I feel. The justice of our cause is believed in everywhere. I suppose Germany's Ambassador has to make himself the servant of the Press out here. Only orders from home would make him do as he is doing. It is laughed at, and as good for us as if we paid him to do it.

News of the sinking of the three cruisers has just come in and saddened us.

I'll probably stay about three weeks to put a face on things, and then come back. I'm hoping, if you have time, to hear from 'our' hospital.[2] Thank heaven, that's one thing I can help with in a way.

Oh the heat!

[1]Barrie spent nearly four weeks in America, where he and Mason and Gilmour had gone on a 'mission', which the English Embassy at Washington, however, did not favour.

[2]Lord Lucas, with the help of his sister, had opened a hospital at Wrest Park, his Bedfordshire home; Barrie assisted them.

Adelphi Terrace House 9 December '14

I understand the prize report absolutely, and am also elated to know that you don't. I could have told you that you wouldn't and couldn't. It is a comparatively easy matter to run a hospital, but to work the billiard room thereof requires a strong man—as someone said it needed a strong man to find Ruth in the Bible. I think this was in one of my own works. I am rather excited about my works at present, because a man was telling me of an incident in a book lately, and I was impressed and said 'How splendid,' and he replied, 'You ass' (or words to that effect), 'it is in your own book.' I am quite seriously thinking of reading the book to see if it is full of such forgotten treasures.

I hope to get down soon. Generally a boy appears and blocks the way. I expect George to-morrow for a couple of days. As he has not had leave before, it may mean that he is going out soon.

I shall bring out some more billiard conundrums, but never, never, never will you understand them.

Tomdoun Hotel, Glengarry 8 August '15

Up here now with Michael and Nicholas. Have been far travelled since I saw you last. I went to France to see that little hospital[1] I told you of. It is in a desolate château consisting largely of under-ground passages where French officers wander, and is on the Marne. The guns are to be heard in the distance all day, and I was usually wakened in the morning by aeroplanes. In the stillness they fill the world with sound. The patients are children and women, either extremely wounded or destitute and ill. One little boy had his leg blown off by a shell at Rheims, and so on. The villages in that part are in a dreadful condition, some of them have about one house standing in fifty. They were destroyed by the Germans in their rush for Paris. There are thousands of Germans buried thereabout, and a grim notice has been issued on the Marne ordering all people to chain up their dogs at night. The dogs have taken to wandering and digging. The Germans stayed in the château but didn't damage it.

The Highlands are very lonely this year. Almost every able-

[1]Château de Bettancourt.

111

bodied man seems to have gone, and we are alone in a big hotel. I was loath to come but it seemed best for M. and N.

I am wondering whether Bron has gone yet. Give him my love, and do let me hear from you and how things are going at Wrest. I wish I could be walking up the steps at this moment and seeing you come down the stairs in your nurse's garments. This is a big job you have taken on and trying to keep at it so long, but at any rate there is no doubt that it was worth doing.

To Lord LUCAS

Adelphi Terrace House 29 September '15

My dear Bron

I am very pleased and not only pleased but proud that you have sufficient faith in me to make this proposal, and it will be an uncommon pleasure to me to undertake the thing and do it to the best of my small ability.[1] I have seen enough of the soldiers' life in city hospitals to know how fortunate those are who have a Wrest to go to, and tho' I think you have been almost wildly generous (my contribution was a small affair) I do believe that the results are fine.

However stupidly I may do it I feel I won't enrage Nan as a Committee would do. Conceive the two pictures—
(1) Nan with the Committee—oh, what a gracious woman!
(2) Nan when she has shut them out—oh what a . . .

I expect to see her on Friday. I wish you were coming up. I hear you are having a rather glorious time. I watched the Zeppelin from my window, and could not help thinking as the guns were plugging away at it that, exciting as life for the moment was down below, how wonderful it must be to those in the Zeppelin.

Yours always, J.M.B.

30 March '16

Hail! To report progress here. To begin with, Nan does look ever so much better now. For a long time she had a rather broken look—curiously and solely I think because she worked

[1]Lord Lucas, though he had lost a leg as *Times* correspondent in the Boer War, had joined the Royal Flying Corps, and more of the hospital management devolved on Barrie.

on and on and wouldn't give in when the strain was telling too much on her. She is so fearfully conscientious about Wrest that her heart gets no rest if everything is not absolutely perfect, and that with the sheer grind mentioned did pull her down. One great blessing is that the people at Wrest in this quiet time are all doing exceedingly well, which puts her mind at ease.

She told me of your project for Wrest, which I think quite splendid.

I think the feeling in the air here (that phrase has another meaning for you!) is one of more hopefulness about war-matters than it has been for a long time. I don't know with what justification. Verdun is big and the strain on Germany grows. Stirring things in the North Sea and on our coasts too are looked for very soon.

The Zeppelin brought down a month ago near Verdun by the Ravigny guns nearly fell on my children's hospital. They had an anxious time watching it, but it really fell a mile away. Next morning the children were skipping about gaily with a franc each, which they call 'the tears of William'.

Observe the ways of authors. A remark in one of your letters to Nan entertained me, I collared it and put it in my new play,[1] it is received nightly with a roar of rapture by cultured London audiences, and I calculate it will be worth half a crown a night to me for ages. By and by it will be brisking them up in U.S.A., the aborigines of Australasia will be dressing to get in to hear it, Fiji islanders will quote it to their papooses, Chinamen will run about telling it to the Japanese, but I disdain even to satisfy your curiosity by telling you what it is. But go on sending more.

It's a long play with du Maurier and Hilda Trevelyan in chief parts, and in one scene there are seven beauts so beautiful that we have almost to stop the piece to let the audience vote on them. And some frocks! I don't know what Gilmour and his Economy Reform would say. I went to Economy meeting at Guildhall. The pathetic waste of a big opportunity.

★

[1] *A Kiss for Cinderella.*

To Miss MITCHELL INNES[1] (*Mrs Josephine Maitland Edwards*)

Adelphi Terrace House 28 June '15

My dear Josephine

I send you on those other letters in a box.

It was very nice seeing you, and still nicer liking you as much as I wanted to do. But I was not afraid. I knew there was one matter on which George could make no mistake. I hope we shall always be friends, though it has begun in a way so much more sad than it was planned.

Yours affectionately, J. M. Barrie

★

To Lady JULIET TREVOR

25 July '16

My dear Juliet

. . . Peter[2] writes me that he has a beard now. They are not sure whether they have beards or whether it is only crusts of mud. I have a nephew 'missing' from the Somme and am afraid he is dead.

I met a man the other night with an impediment in his speech and I think he had set off to tell me he was your cousin but I had to catch a train.

Yours, J.M.B.

Glan Hafren, Near Newtown, Montgomeryshire 23 April '17

I hope you get away for a little from the eternal round of the hospital. I have been at Littlehampton and now we are here, Michael, Nicholas and myself, and grim contests go on between M. and me at golf-croquet, the last pastime at which I can stand up against him and I'm afraid that my supremacy even at that is shooting down the horizon. Near Littlehampton I looked into a shed (now occupied by a barrow) in which I wrote one of my books *Tommy and Grizel*—nearly seventeen years ago. The shed remains but all else that was there, or pretty nearly all, of a delightful village has given way to villas that I almost wish the enemy would fire some shells at. Revisiting the glimpses of the moon is not a cheerful pilgrimage.

We have had a burst of sunshine here for two days, and the daffodils and scyllas and the like have rushed into their holiday

[1]This letter was written after the death of George Llewelyn Davies in France.
[2]Llewelyn Davies, in France.

clothes and are dancing about the lawns. They will probably be enfiladed tomorrow or next day by a spell of snow.

It seems an age since I saw you and I am looking forward thereto as soon as we get back, about the first of May. It makes me sad when I don't see more of you.

Michael is waiting to 'pulverise' me at the hoops so off I go with sinking heart.

Trossachs Hotel, Loch Katrine 14 August '17

I don't know if you were ever here. It is pre-eminently the spot where you are supposed to stand on a rock and recite Sir Walter Scott from the guidebook. A very wet rock too at present. May is the best month for fishing if you come in August, and August is the best month if you come in May. You can, however, fall in all the year round. (I hope Knobloch is falling in at Vaynol).

We have had exciting visitors, to wit, our sailor boy, Jack, with the lady of his heart, our first sight of her. We were all outwardly calm, but internally white to the gills; Nicholas kept wetting his lips, Michael was a granite column, inscrutable, terrible; I kept bursting into inane laughter, and changing my waistcoats. So the time of waiting passed, the sun sank in the west and the stars came out with less assurance than usual. What is that? It is the rumble of wheels. Nico slips his hand into mine. I notice that it is damp. Michael's pose becomes more Napoleonic, but he is breathing hard. The chaise comes into view. I have a happy thought. They are probably more nervous than we are. But you have had enough of it, and you have so much to do in that garden and Knobloch has fallen into the lake again and Michael has caught him with a boat-hook and Veronica is giving first aid, and in short if there is any more of it you must decline to go on reading, and in any case you can't make out half the words.

I once won the writing prize at school! Heigh ho!

I hope you are having a happy time. In a way I am sure you are, for some form of happiness does come as the result of doing one's best and working hard, and you have been doing that for a long time now. Do write to me when you have the time—from the window overlooking the new garden.

We shall be wandering from here in a day or two to some other highland pastures.

Hotel Meurice, Rue de Rivoli, Paris 17 November '18

Have been motoring chiefly in the Argonne, two or three hundred miles a day on roads often two feet deep in mud. A night in the citadel at Verdun was good. Paris of course is very gay and *all lit up*. 'It's *finished, finished*' is the universal cry rather than glory. You would make a pleasant boudoir out of many of the German dug-outs. I saw German prisoners being brought in who didn't know of the Armistice, they had been dug out of the ground. Now everybody is converging on Paris, which is an American city.

I expect to be home end of week. I wish you were here. Come and dine tonight at Henry's!

Stanway 16 August '28

Alas, I cannot go to you because I am here till the beginning of September and there seem to be visitors all the time—your position repeated. I am glad to be able to imitate you even in so small a matter and there are all sorts of other ways in which I should rejoice to be like you. In appearance, for instance,—what a dash I should cut if I were like you. No more feeble books and plays—no, I'd be out in the open, making woman tremble. As it is, I pursue a humdrum life and am ticketed as harmless, one of those dear creatures of whom no one knows whether he is present or not. I sit with knitted teeth watching the play in which I am not permitted to take part. I am like the man whom pitying friends did invite to delightful Vaynol but who made no impression, while other guests were surrounded by the Juliets. He saw that the other guests were all attractive for some special quality and decided that he must be so too. But he knew he couldn't do anything difficult, so he made up his mind to take off his shoes. The next time he was at Vaynol, kindly treated but as usual making no stir, he sat down amid the company in the drawing-room and began taking off his boots. Soon the ladies were all around him, and the one cry was, 'Darling Juliet, do let me sit beside that delightful man who takes off his boots.'

★

To Lady NORTHCLIFFE (now Lady Hudson)
Red Cross Offices Books and MSS section, 20 King Street,
St James's, S.W. 11 January '18
Dear Lady Northcliffe
  (He then mutters to himself 'After all, it was she who got me
into this in spite of my better judgement, so why shouldn't I?').[1]
  I feel that almost fabulous sums would be paid for some
autograph documents connected with the war. They may be
inaccessible themselves, but replicas written by the same hand
would be nearly as valuable. For instance some order in a
historic moment issued by Sir Douglas Haig which he could
write out again for us in a minute or two. Who gave the order
for the first advance of the tanks—or something else about
tanks? Could we have it? Some historical political documents?
The declaration of war for instance. Messages that have passed
(probably by wire or telephone) to bigwigs in allied countries.
The same written out by Lloyd George etc would swell our
funds and only take a minute or so to do.
  In short the whole thing is who is to get at these things? I
reply your husband. Please get at him in the still night and help
a CHAIRMAN.
                                 Yours sincerely, J. M. Barrie
I don't suppose we could get the Kaiser to send us a message of
hate?
                        Adelphi Terrace House 21 February
  I had no luck this time, as I had been fixed for some time for
Saturday. It has struck me that you might ask me oftener if
you knew my telephone number. At any rate it is worth
trying. Gerrard 9674 (not in book). This ought to have been
put more cunningly. When you show no sign life becomes as
dreary as a telephone book (in which by the way my number is
Gerrard 9674). Sir R. Hudson and Mr Lucas have installed
telephonic apparatus in their dwelling-places. What their
numbers are I do not care a hang but mine (curiously enough)
is Gerrard 9674. The *Daily Mail* says 'There are now hundreds
of thousands of Londoners on the telephone. Singular to relate
the only person who has chosen Gerrard 9674 is Sir J. M.
Barrie.' I could keep this up. Will probably do so. There are
9674 varieties.

[1]At Lady Northcliffe's suggestion Barrie was Chairman of a Books and
Manuscript Collection to be sold for the Red Cross.

Alas, I had to ask them here this morning to ring you up and say I must put off my cinema-dinner as I'm down with influenza. Temperature so high I had to get an extra pillow to see over it. I am so sorry.

★

To A. A. MILNE, writer

Adelphi Terrace House 13 October '10

Dear Mr Milne

I see no one among the young people with so light and gay and happy a touch as you show in this book, *The Day's Play*, and as I read it last night I was putting on my guards once more and taking centre for the last time. You have given me one day more. It set me looking for a little booklet of my cricket club to send you but I seem to have no copy. We were all mad and glad. I elect you the last member.

The gaiety and irresponsibility of your work (I know it in *Punch*) are rarer gifts than you wot of now. When you know you won't be so gay. So don't know as long as you can. Something else will take their place by and bye—something very good I hope, but don't be in a hurry. Hide and seek with the angels is good enough for anyone.

I feel an affection for the man behind your book, and hope all will always be well with you—or thereabouts. Perhaps some day you will lunch with me. I wander about alone.

Yours sincerely, J. M. Barrie

1 October '12

That book[1] was fought for in the wilds of Harris by five boys, George got it first, stolen by Peter, recovered by George, handed on to Roger, again boned by Peter, recovered by Roger, handed on lawfully to Peter, boned by Michael, disappeared with Gerald while Peter and Michael were hot over it, finally fell to me and just read with much glee. It is delicious and I applaud heartily.

I hope you can read this. Discussion in *Times* about bad hand writing, which I take to be personal and am in hiding till it blows over.

[1] *The Holiday Round.*

Excuse pencil—am in Switzerland—no blotting paper.

I think it is a very good little play and sufficiently you to have its own particular quality. In my opinion it would act very well if it had good actors and not well at all with indifferent ones,—by which I mean that unless they could get that quality out of it they would get very little. It is about our old friend (damn him) the artistic temperament, and that is not easy to convey so that the public in general can understand. I am quite sure that with the right people it would 'carry' thoroughly and be a very good introduction to the stage for you.

As a 'curtain-raiser' it would almost certainly be flung away. They are nearly always put on merely to prevent the pit and gallery becoming restive because the long piece is beginning late; they are put on cheaply,—swell actors and managements hold that they don't affect 'business'. Occasionally some star person falls in love with a part in a one-act play but not often. Du Maurier would do your man as no one else would but I don't believe he would want to, and it is improbable you would get others who are less good but still good—I mean for a 'run'. What I believe you should aim at is to get it produced first on some special occasion such as does occur—a benefit—special matinée—with another piece by someone of repute, etc.,—your sole purpose being to have it tried in circumstances in which you *could* have hopes of its being well done. Then the thing would be to try to get Du Maurier first. You should let me write to him about it if you like this idea. Don't be silly about bothering me. It isn't any bother.

Another notion would be to let me show it to Barker to whom I think it would appeal and he might put it on in regular bill.

Don't have it done at all unless well. It makes me feel you have a natural instinct for play-writing—which you might not have despite the *Punch* things, and I wish you would tackle a three-act piece, not because I personally prefer them to one-act, but because it is easier to place them satisfactorily. If you do please let me see it.

I enclose the play—no, I'll keep it to see if I may do anything I have suggested with it.

20 September '20

All my heartiest congratulations to you both, or strictly
speaking to the three of you. May Billy be an everlasting joy to
you. From what you say I gather he is already a marvel but I
shall decide about this for myself when I see him which I hope
will be soon. I am also now settled down here and do hereby
challenge you to Slosh.[1] Your letter has been to Eilean Shona
and followed me to London, coming with a tanned complexion,
the result of a week among the mountains around Acharacle,
which, sir, is a fine-sounding word but a difficult place to get
away from, the first thirty miles taking seven hours.

★

To 'PETER',[2] of Glan Hafren, Newtown, Montgomery
                    Adelphi Terrace House 22 September '12
My dear Peter
    Your mother rote me a letter but she did not tell me her
name (which makes me like her better becaus I see thro' her),
but she sent me some fine ~~pietyours pikturs~~ (dash it all) u drew
about P. Pan, and they are just like the picters P.P. would draw
himself. i like u and i like your mother too, and i hope u will be
a great boy to her and a fine man. Peter's mother thinks Mr.
Barrie has a lot of people admiring him, but oh, Peter's mother,
u are mistaken and he is a lonely dreary person and is *very*
pleased to hear that some one thinks him nicer than he is
(which is what you and I, Peter, and all our sex are after).
                                    Your friend, J. M. Barrie

To Mrs HUGH LEWIS
                    23 Campden Hill Square, W. 27 December '13
Dear Mrs Lewis
    I am a great knut in my scarf. So the boys say. It will
probably change my mode of life. May as well go the whole
hog now and let out the lowest button of my waistcoat. May
take to a fur coat. May become one of the fat men with chins

[1] A cross between billiards and pool, a favourite game of Barrie's. When
Michael Llewelyn Davies died he dismantled the billiard-room and played
no more.
[2] Peter Lewis, aged four, whose mother had written (but without disclosing
their surname so that Barrie should not be troubled to reply) a letter that was
the beginning of a long friendship with all the family.

who spring up in a night when new restaurants are built. The boys go off with all my beautiful garments (as bought by Brown) but I shall stick to this one. Peter[1] was mauled in the 'Wall game' three weeks ago and in bed ever since (kicked on shin) but got up yesterday with the demon of unrest strong on him. A very happy new year to you all.

Yours, J.M.B.

Cuilfail Hotel, Kilmelfort 1 September '15

I wish there were a few more like you, but it is perhaps better that you should remain unique. I wish we could hurl ourselves straight upon Glan Hafren, but we shall be here till the 8th and that only gives us an exact week before Michael returns to school, and we need that time in London. It shows how we must have talked of you that he (the dark and dour and impenetrable) has announced to me that he wants to go to see you. I was never so staggered.

It has been rather grim in Scotland this year. The highlands in many glens are as bare of population owing to the war as if this were the month before Creation. I have just Michael and Nicholas with me and they feel it too, but they climb about, fishing mostly, and if you were to search the bogs you would find me in one of them loaded with waterproofs and ginger beer. We are just off in intense excitement to have our hair cut.

Adelphi Terrace House 31 December '15

I hope you will all have a very happy New Year, and I can picture you at it tomorrow about one o'clock in that nice dining room. The frame is a beauty and I wonder you weren't frightened to send me anything so nice. Here I am all alone as M. and N. are in bed and I've come back to the flat for to-night. Christmas evening was even gayer as I had to come in to town and Brown and his wife were away, so I had to make my own fire and dinner (eggs) and bed. The fire was worst, as there were no sticks, but I found a straw basket Mrs Brown goes to market with—or rather went, for it will accompany her no more. Otherwise I have been at Campden Hill and tomorrow am taking Michael and Nicholas for a week to the sea. Peter is probably on the Channel at this moment taking a draft to France. Jack in the country.

[1]Llewelyn Davies.

21 March '16

Dear J.M.B., I *could* write you a nice letter, but you would perhaps be bored by it and think you had to answer, so I'll just send three words (do you think three is too many, Hugh?)

As far as I can recollect that was your last letter to me and willful women must have their way, and literary characters will go on spelling wilful with too many l's in it, which now that I think of it is probably 'the Barrie touch'. You can see I write rather gleefully, the reason being that I have just enough of a chill to be abed, which is the pleasantest place after a bout of tiring rehearsals.[1] It's a very small chill indeed and unless matters improve in the night I shall have to get up tomorrow morning.

Peter is here for a special course on flag-signalling and it is great to have him.

There is much talk here of (and preparation for) a coming 'invasion' as the last throw.

30 July '16

It is very nice of you, and our firm intention is to swoop down on you early in September. Michael goes into camp till about August 10, and then I think we shall go to some seaside place till end of the month with Mrs Lucas and Audrey. I must be in London the first week of September, and I am wondering whether you could put M. and N. up then and I join you as soon as I can. It seems bold to think of movements at all just now, with such things happening. Peter has been in violent fighting for four weeks now, north of the Somme (I think, but secrecy is great) and has seen grim things. His colonel was killed the other day and there have been many casualties in the Battalion. I confess I never come into this flat without looking fearfully for a telegram. Mr Lucas's brother was killed on the Somme and a nephew of mine is either killed or a prisoner. So many people one knew have gone this last month.

I think Peter would like your parcel. I expect you have had a lovely time on the river today with all your armful. They shall get a talking-to if they don't all come running into my arms.

23 Campden Hill Square 20 September '16

All alarms and excursions since we left you. Obviously we should never leave you. A bone of a partridge stuck in my throat at Wrest hospital and no tubes etc. could force it down

[1] Of *A Kiss for Cinderella*.

Surgeon was to do a little operation and I set off for a nursing home (when Michael wrote you). Then another surgeon preferred to treat it medically for a few days first. Now there is so little pain that I probably have swallowed it, but I'm to be x-rayed to find out. Rather useful to be useless just now because Peter arrived in England last night invalided (not bad —a sort of eczema apparently that is very prevalent at the Front owing to general unhealthy conditions). He is in a hospital at Wandsworth but is to get round to us for an hour today and then I take Nicholas to Eton. About the film the only two I know of that are really good class are the *Birth of a Nation* and the Somme one. The former can't be got (and is 3 hours long in any case). I'll try if the other is possible but don't think it will be obtainable. Nico has been for days in the middle of a letter to you. We discuss what you are all doing at all hours of the day. 'There is Mr Lewis coming back', says M. 'I think it will be plum tart today', says N. We had indeed a glorious time.

[On receiving a war-time birthday-present of potatoes.]

Adelphi Terrace House 10 May '17

How truly splendid and magnanimous of you to send the potatoes. When they were revealed to my astonished eyes my hand (I am sure) went instinctively to my head to take off my hat. Brown looked as if he ought to be singing the national anthem. Cheers for Glan Hafren! How sorry we were to go. You will be interested to hear that Nico finished *Ivanhoe* several minutes before returning to school and came out head of his division in the exam. Michael is now captain of his house XI 'with power to tan'.[1] Nothing so triumphant to record about myself. My love to all and looking forward to seeing you before long in London.

16 July '17

I found your letter on my return. I managed to get Peter away with me for 48 hours which was beyond my hopes. I saw a rather remarkable sight from the Messines ridge. A German aeroplane darted out of a cloud and ran the gamut of our six balloons, burning four of them to ribbons. The sight however was the four balloonists descending safely in their parachutes. The only time of any danger was in seeking for George's grave, which I found.

[1] Inflict corporal punishment.

It is hugely good of you to speak of Glan Hafren again but (1) we haven't the face, (2) I can't decide anything about holidays, not till a matter about a play's production is decided. Enjoyed much seeing Hugh, Mary and Bittie. Flat still a muddle.

To Miss BITTIE LEWIS, Glan Hafren, Montgomeryshire

[Eiluned Lewis, now Mrs Graeme Hendrey. Bittie was her family nickname, and to Barrie she was often 'Jane'.]

27 January '18

My dear Bittie
  To think of that red head being laid low! Though pretending to be a literary hand, I am not really sure whether it should be laid or layed. To ordinary people I play for safety and write it so that it can be either. I often write my works differently to avoid ticklish spelling. The more you think of these difficulties the more perplexing they become. One conceives sympathy with the little old (Welsh) lady who felt convinced that two and two make four but never dared to say so because on reflection it seemed such a small number.
  Whatever am I talking about? It's obvious to me that I am dodging some difficult word. Yet the only word that springs natural to my pen when you are ill is dearest, or a combination like dearest Bittie and I find no difficulty in saying that. So dearest Bittie I am sad to think you have had this trying time and glad to hear you are now mending, and Oh dear, dearest May has also caught it and what a house of anxiety and also of love, and years hence you will look back on the days you had measles as very happy memories of that home which was so much your best thing in the world. Is Peter[1] to escape? I hope so. It reminds me of Michael in his extreme youth having to get a tooth extracted. As he left the dentist's he said 'Peter must come and have one out to-morrow.' Speaking of Michael he has had an -xtr-rd-nary -dv-nt-r-. By his orders I can say no more about it except that you are implicated in the str-ng-st w-y. The rest you must wheedle out of him.[2]
  My love to you all.

[1]Lewis
[2]Michael Llewelyn Davies had taken his uncle, Gerald du Maurier, to visit the boarding-school attended by Eiluned and her sister, with the result that Angela du Maurier was sent there for a time.

To Mrs LEWIS

22 November '18

Just got your letter as I have been a fortnight in France and got back only last night. I thought of your drawing-room fireplace—time about 11 p.m., and our talks there—on 'Armistice Night' which I spent in Paris. By far the most memorable thing there was the happy faces. Everyone seemed to have changed permanently in a night, and what the faces, as well as the cries said, was 'It is finished' rather than 'we have won'. I was at Verdun (spent a night in the citadel, 40 feet underground), Ypres and a lot of places, came back dazed from motoring 200 or more miles a day. I think the most interesting man I met was Colonel House.

So it actually is ended! It was dear of Peter[1] to say that about Michael. You can guess how thankful I am. I don't think he will be wanted for the army now, and I'm going to Eton on Sunday (Nico's birthday) to 'go into his future'. He writes 'I'll do anything you like. P.S. How about my going round the world?'

They marched at Eton with their bath-tubs as drums and the night ended with Michael getting 500 lines! (For standing on his head on a roof when he should have been in bed, or something of the kind.)

Thanks immensely about the butter idea, but I fancy it would lead to trouble with our ration books. The thing we shall suffer from most this winter is want of coal. It threatens to be rather grim up in this big room and I may have to give up using the kitchen and take all my meals out, which would be trying. Wherever I went in France was warm as toast—overheated; and as to meat, as much as you liked. But that was probably only on the surface. I had an amusing dinner here before I left—just Mr Asquith and Mr Birrell, but Lady Cynthia and Lady Dufferin dressed up as maids and waited on them and completely took them in.

I am heartily glad that Hugh is so much better and that you have all avoided the influenza as we have done. I forgot to tell you I saw a band of German prisoners brought in near Sedan, two days after the 11th who knew nothing about the Armistice. They had been dug out of holes.

[1]Lewis.

125

23 December '18

Mind you drink our healths on Christmas day (proposed I think by Peter,[1] in one of those neat speeches for which he is to be so famed in after life). We shall be drinking yours. I love to think of you all gathered together again under that happy roof. How we have all wished to live on to see 'what peace is like', but what is it like? Very silent I think, because of the dead men, as if we had difficulty in realising that they were not dead merely for the duration of the war. My love to all round and round. Michael is going to Oxford in January, to Christ Church. One boast! His report ended 'He is the most admirable boy I have ever had in my house'.

To Miss BITTIE LEWIS

16 February '19

My dear Jane

You have now put yourself into my hands. If they write me from Oxford (but I'm afraid they won't) I shall tell them *the truth* about you. So there.[2]

I hope you will be at Lady Margaret's Hall next autumn. Michael says there is 'something about you' that will suit Oxford. He didn't say what it is, so I am left guessing. There is a dean's daughter there so appallingly attractive that all Oxford is flung into a state of unrest when she walks abroad. Undergrads reel. She has to be accompanied by dogs and chuckers-out. Michael is to have tea there to-day. What times we live in.

My love to the coughers. I am giving a pretty good imitation of them.

[The Lewises' plan of a trip to Holland was shattered by the illness of one of the children.]

20 May '20

Dear Mrs Lewis, dear Hugh, dear Medina, dear Bittie, dear Mary, dear Peter, oh dear!

Such is life, but we must all go together some day to Holland and wear baggy trousers with our hands in the pockets and

[1]Lewis.
[2]Barrie's name had been given as a reference to the authorities at Lady Margaret Hall.

126

smoke large cigars and gaze contemplatively at the canals and afterwards go on the music-hall stage as 'the Tulip Family'. You, Bittie, will please now to drop that temperature and be nippy about it, or we shall call you the Black Tulip. You, Medina, will know how to water and weed us. At last we see for certain why you became a horticulturist.

I am going to Ireland to-morrow for a week to stay with friends (Dufferins) but not in a perilous part, else would I, dear Peter, take with me the revolver which I used to fire out of my pocket, in the days when I was a cowboy. I'll be back in time to see you in London town, temperatures permitting. Love to all.

[On the death of Hugh Lewis.]

To Mrs LEWIS

19 April '21

My heart goes out to all of you, and especially to yourself, at this sad time. Even to attempt to comfort you would be to hurt you, and I am only taking your hand in sympathy. When you are a little further away from it there are many things I should like to say to you. Of him it can certainly be said that he was one of the most lovable most honourable men I have encountered in my wanderings through the years; every one who met him whether intimately or casually must have been the better of it. He not only gave much happiness but received it. I think I can really call him about the happiest man I have ever known. He had his anxieties like the rest of us, and he had the one hard blow which you shared with him, but on the whole it was a life of fine serenity in a family circle blessed beyond what is given to many. He knew what was the best thing in life, and he had it in abundance. In a way your household often reminded me of that of the Vicar of Wakefield, as on Sunday evenings at the piano. He knew he had such a wife as are granted to few. I am sure you are not at all satisfied with yourself but never was there a wife who had more reason to be. I wish very much I could have come to you on Thursday but it just happens that I have a troublesome business matter that day which I must attend. I want to know what you are all to do in the near future and I need not say how much I am at your service. Our partings are all for such

127

a little time that we should smile even when we grieve. You have only to turn a corner to see him a little ahead. I am proud that Hugh was my friend. To all of you my warm love.

2 May '21

Yes indeed it is the one left who is struck dead. I am sure that even the sunshine is painful to you just now. I am even glad that a cold has driven you to bed for you can keep your eyes shut and physically you must be worn out. The plans you speak of seem to me wise ones. It is quite certainly right to keep on the business. The very last time I saw Hugh he talked of the pleasure it was to him to have the business for Peter to carry on if, when the time came, that was Peter's wish. The Eton expenses including the extras and so on come to about £300 a year. Would you like me to write to Mr Brinton now and go into matters with him? I should like to do it. Bittie will let me know when she and Mary get back. I trust to them looking upon this flat as the natural place for them to go to when passing through and as a sort of London home. I hope you will all do that and always walk in and out of it in that spirit. If I don't see the girls' hats lying about I shall get angry. I was very pleased with Lloyd George's letter, so warm and true.

I am alone again now except that I have Freyberg with me until he goes off to New Zealand, having got his six months leave for health and to see his mother. I could have given Hugh and you a pretty picture of how F. has been excitedly hunting the shops for furs and dresses as presents to her and of my solemnly sitting in judgment on them.

To Miss BITTIE LEWIS

12 July '34

Dear Jane

I have got much happiness out of your book.[1] There is a fragrance about it which takes me back to the well-loved home of all of you and loved by me as well as by you, and lo, you are all small again and there is a terrific contest proceeding on the croquet lawn and enter the yellow ball as bright as once he was thereon but not so bright now, and not all the figures once

[1] *Dew on the Grass.*

128

there can be there again. Judged by this book you have grown into the woman we wanted you to be and with the graces developed that had already begun, and much art of writing (that one always felt was round the corner) and with (in 1934!) an unsullied mind. I welcome you among the writers with pride and affection.

★

To a BEREAVED CORRESPONDENT

Adelphi Terrace House 13 March '19

Dear ——

It is a pleasure to hear from you again, but I am sorry indeed to hear of the sadness that has come into your life. The war has brought so many tragedies to our doors that those waiting to hear the fatal knock sometimes forget that the other partings are going on also. I send you my respectful sympathy, and can understand what a difference the little boy made. With kind regards,

Yours sincerely, J. M. Barrie

To Councillor JOHN WILSON M'LAREN, of Edinburgh

30 June '19

Dear Councillor Wilson M'Claren

Thank you heartily for your letter and enclosures. There can be no one, I should think, who would not be proud to have such an honour from Edinburgh,[1] but I must say no more of that till we hear that the Council agrees with the Lord Provost's Committee. In the meantime it is very pleasant to me to find such a good friend in yourself.

Yours sincerely, J. M. Barrie

8 March '21

Thank you heartily for sending me the cuttings about your *Weir of Hermiston*[2] play, which is evidently very good. I wonder

[1] The conferring of the Freedom of the City of Edinburgh.
[2] Produced at the Edinburgh Theatre Royal.

whether you know that R. L. S. himself wrote a long play on the subject called *The Hanging Judge* which was never published though I read it in MS long ago.

To Mrs GEOFFREY WHITWORTH[1]

13 November '19

Dear Mrs Whitworth

Don't think me a curmudgeon (please). But I suppose I am a bit of a hermit and can't help it (alas), and I shun social functions, so please excuse me. I hope it will all be a great success and applaud you from my fireside.

Yours sincerely, J. M. Barrie

27 October '27

Alas, that play would not do for your purpose at all. It was written for some eight children all cousins and was about them and their relationship and was full of local quips and was written to fit a particular room and in short it expired gently after a 3 days' run. Children of 7 and 4 played leading parts. So there! Otherwise you should have had it for so good a cause with pleasure.

★

To CHARLES WHIBLEY, *writer*

Adelphi Terrace House 25 November '19

My dear Charles

. . . You see I am still left-handed, and like to remain so. It isn't so difficult as you might fancy to write with the left hand but 'tis the dickens to think down the left side. It doesn't even know the names of my works. Also it seems to have a darker and more sinister outlook on life, and is trying at present to egg me on to making a woman knife her son.[2]

Always love, J. M. B.

[1]Mrs Whitworth arranged Christmas performances of two Barrie plays, *Quality Street* and *The Admirable Crichton*, by the children of famous actors and actresses.

[2]*Mary Rose.*

13 October '21

It is good to know that the pain has lessened so much,[1] and encourages one immensely for the final go. No doubt you are miserably uncomfortable, but all that, including the swollen face, is of the moment, and if the pain were once stamped out you would soon be yourself again. You know how devoutly I hope therefor. Cynthia and Beb are here now, and it is awe-inspiring the way she bangs straight from breakfast to letters, etc., instead of doing as I do—stagger to a couch with the *Times* and a pipe. It's like having a child in the house. It will be great to have you well again, to kill the fatted calf and see you able to eat it.

8 January '22

I am so much moved by your letter. No man ever read one from a friend that he could well value more. It is splendid to me the way you have come back into my life.

Freyberg is here, staying, and we are just going off to dine at some agreeable pothouse. How we both wish you could join us. We should be three brave if battered musketeers. I hope it will soon come about. We are anxious to know how you are, and indeed F. nearly went down to see to-day. If this other visit to the surgeon must be, we can at least hope for the big result, and after all another operation was always said to be a probability. Very keen to see you when you get up. I am feeble and futile but better.

14 March '22

You have either heard or will be hearing from St Andrew's that they want to give you the LL.D. in May when I go up for rectorial address. I trust you will be able to go and support me. Freyberg is also to get it, and we should have a good time once the loathly 'address' is over. They are offering it also to Housman, and it would be nice of you to encourage him to accept, as I don't know him personally.

19 December '26

I should have written to you ere this about your introduction to Peter's[2] *Voltaire*. It is to my mind a little masterpiece, and

[1] Whibley had much painful illness.
[2] Peter Davies, publisher.

131

I can never hope to see Peter so well served again till you write him another.

9 October '27

This is indeed great news, and I need not say I shall be proud as well as delighted to be your best man.[1] Cynthia instructs me that the club is to be your address to-morrow so I write there. It is splendid to me to know that you are to have a real home again, for you must have been very lonely for a long time. Take you all over, sir, I consider you to be one of the bravest and the best I have ever known, and I have known some good ones. I feel sure Philippa is fine, I remember being so struck by the something unusual in her the first time we met that I wrote to Walter about her—which was something unusual in me. I am not certain when it is to be, but command me, and if in London do please stay with me the nights before.

18 March '29

I am indeed sorry to hear from Philippa that you are having a rough time. The strained heart will get all right if you obey its desires very literally for the necessary time, really lie about a lot and avoid stairs—very irksome but it is the one way out as every one knows who has experienced it. I wish I could comfort you in any way, and I'll be down to see you soon if there is anything in that. I'd be over-joyed to have you both here any time my rooms are free as they mostly are, and the lift can't count as a stair. I am quite well myself and rather proud of having had the energy this fine day to go out and have my hair cut. Freyberg was in yesterday on a flying visit from Folkestone where among other duties he has the looking after of 80 married Tommies and their wives and children. Being on his own instead of carrying out instructions makes the real Freyberg of him. My warm love to you both.

2 April '29

I do trust all is going well with you, and that it has not been too wearisome. As for the Derby if you are equal by then to facing it I shall consider you in real form and will ask you to put something on it for me. I always want to be in the thing, but never knew how one betted except once in a nursing home

[1] At his marriage to the daughter of Sir Walter Raleigh.

132

when the nurse knew the ropes. Once I went to the Derby
(my only race) and though my horse didn't win I by skill won
a gold watch by throwing a ring round it. I have had a quiet
Easter as the only man in London, and now have the Principal
of St Andrew's with me for a couple of nights. We are going
to a revue—my first since Nicholas grew up.

7 April '29

You are evidently so far out of the wood, and I need not
say I rejoice thereat. But of course you must gang canny.
This weather ought to help you along, at any rate while the
sun is out. I don't know whether you have heard from Cynthia
that her father fell two days ago stepping out of a taxi which
had not drawn up properly at the curbstone and broke two
bones in the lower part of the leg. He seems however to be
getting on well, but won't be able to walk for a good bit. I
hear 'Pink Eye' is the latest epidemic among humans. I
thought only horses were subject thereto, but perhaps there are
no longer sufficient horses to go round. As for the coming
election I am one of the dodderers who trot along rather
regardless. I shall be seeing the P.M. this week, which may
fire me up. To-morrow the Literary Society meets but as no
Charles no me.

23 April '29

I hope 'The Old Ship' and the Brighton air will do you a
world of good. I can see you doggedly walking along that pier
which is associated in my mind with a fascinating game called
Skee-Ball. The highest scorer in six months carries off a motor
cycle as the prize, and I—I sir, your friend sir—was once
(under an assumed name—written up in chalk) champion for
one half hour of glorious strife. Think of the horror of it if
it had fallen to me to carry off the prize (with you and others
like you running along side cheering me—not that there are
any others like you.)

My speech is to-night.[1] Just as well you are not sitting there
to put me out of countenance.

22 May '29

I see you have been going through a bad time, and I am so
very sorry. You go to bits more completely than I do but on

[1] At the annual dinner of the Newspaper Press Fund.

133

the other hand you rise to a gaiety that is beyond me, like one more thankful to the gods for small pleasant mercies. Yours is the better nature, certainly the braver one, indeed I think the bravery of you, as I have often witnessed, is what has above all other qualities endeared you to me these many years. The dullness in which you have to live at present till you are vital again must be a much greater strain on you than it would be on me who am dull at all times, but I can see you battling with it and emerging victorious and gay again. That voyage should be a great help and the month before will soon pass. In the meantime I want to go down to see you next week, and Cynthia has written you I understand proposing various days when she can come also.

I am so thankful you have Philippa. She is truly splendid.

★

To Mrs F. S. OLIVER, of Edgerston, Jedburgh
                         Adelphi Terrace House 7 November '22
My dear Katie

All my best wishes to Beatrix, who indeed—but this is no way to behave, and I shall write them to herself. Edgerston must already be in a commotion over the coming event, and I perceive a strange new gleam in your eye. It will be very nice their being so near. It brings back to me Jack's[1] telegram down at the lake, and we are all getting ready again for Edinburgh, with the most important person[2] back again. I associate him with so much happiness at Edgerston that I go looking for him there still by the burns pretty well every day of my life, and your home there and you will ever be to me inexpressibly dear on that account. And so you may well believe that the happiness of the daughter of the house has indeed my fervent good wishes.

I have not indeed much to tell you of myself except that I jog along more listlessly than perhaps I ought and succeed more or less in presenting a wooden face to the world or that narrowing part of it I know. Nicholas is still a bright feature and soon the clock will strike his nineteen years. As you know

[1] Llewelyn Davies, announcing his engagement to Geraldine Gibb of Edinburgh.
[2] Michael.

134

he is now at New College, living out in Abingdon Road. He is very gay and also doing some work, and his letters would brighten any one. He had nearly all the Eton XI down for a week at Stanway, where we were this summer, and they played many cricket matches and danced many nights, and at the last dinner all made speeches and mostly took me aside to ask me which I thought did best. The worst ones were certainly the best.

I am not sure that you know Brown has gone—if not it shows how long a time since we foregathered, for he left in July. A sad parting for him and for me too, but the doctors insisted that to live in the country was necessary for Mrs Brown's continued existence, so there was nothing else for it. He is now a farmer in Lincolnshire, owner of his home, which he calls Mürren, after our visit there once upon a time, and I eat his apples. I feared a bad time, but am very fortunate in his successor who is not from the north yet is a better scholar than Eton (for instance) often turns out, being familiar with Latin, Greek, French and Spanish and also very good at his job. Odd, for he seems always to have been at this sort of job except when in the trenches. I tell visitors that if they go to bed with an Oppenheim work they must put it in the boards of Pliny. Not that I have had any visitors except Mrs Lucas and Audrey, who are about to run (for a firm) an old furniture place at Melton Mowbray. I see Charles Whibley on occasion and find much pleasure therein. He is ever so much better, but the eye is little use for seeing with. However, no pain, which is a blessing.

There is a general election on, and I find that I know neither who is standing for this division nor even what the division is called. Long ago a man used to boast not without justification that he had bribed me to vote with a glass of beer. I think I have voted once since then, but would not swear to it on the Book. And so goodbye just now with my love to you all.

Affectionately, J. M. B.

20 January '27

It was very nice for me to get your letter. That last night of the year I was in the midst of anxiety because a child at Stanway where I was staying was very ill and had just had the mastoid operation but all is going well there now. I saw Charles

Whibley yesterday on his way to Stanway, or rather I saw such of him as could peer forth from his bandages, and though he has had a bad time he is sanguine again. Of course he has a happy and indeed a gallant way of being sanguine at the first ray of sunshine, but it sounds as if those last operations had been very thorough. He gave me his news of you all, and I was so glad to have his good account of Fred. Jock must be cajoled ordered and begged to come to see me, whichever is the most efficacious. Peter has been over-working relentlessly but is getting off for a fortnight or so to-morrow. Nico flourishes like the green bay tree and Jack is getting encomiums from the high command. I have rather lost sight of myself but when last heard of there was nothing much the matter with me. I wish that any time you are in London you would come and have a meal with me. You would be received here with true joy.

To FRED S. OLIVER

Stanway, Cheltenham 11 August '28

I shall be proud to be a 'Freeman' of Jedburgh, and indeed the thought of it gives me much pleasure.[1] Charles Whibley and his wife arrived yesterday by their car and he is in good fettle, indeed last night I left him and Birrell to put out the lights, as they seemed to have settled down permanently on the sofa to thrash out the question of the day, which seems to be something secretive about Bunyan and Defoe.

The Manor House, Mells, Frome 29 September '28

Must answer such a nice letter. I am not thinking of the Jedburgh office I assure you as an ordeal. They have all been so pleasant about it that I quite look forward to it and, of course, far more to being back at Edgerston. Sad that you have had bad weather. I have never known the like of it in the south for persistent sunshine, and even now if it tries something autumnal it gives up by the middle of the day. Jock and his airplanes! How old it makes one feel.

(Queen Mary's veil—the white one of the butchery—is in this house.)

[1] The Olivers had presented to the town of Jedburgh the house where Mary Queen of Scots had stayed, and Barrie was to speak at a bazaar to raise funds for its upkeep. He was also to be given the Freedom of Jedburgh.

Californie Palace, Cannes 12 January '29

The above will show you that despite your views I have come here. Arrived this morning, and you will overlook it for several reasons: (1) For a fortnight at most. (2) All I seemed to need was to get out of doors, and this place is belching with sunshine so that I wander along without an overcoat and could be in shorts. (3) I look as drearily at it as you could wish, so nothing is given away. I hold therefore that I am forgiven.

The Manor House, Mells, Frome 18 May '29

Charles and Philippa were in London for the day a week ago and gave a little luncheon at the Café Royal. That sounds all right but I felt it was a rather forlorn attempt at old times and that he was not himself. I had to leave before the others, so had no real talk, but I'll go down to see him when I go back to London on Tuesday. They talked of going to Norway in a fortnight or so, and vaguely of New Zealand later—sea voyaging being advised but this may come to nothing. They also want a flat in London. Of course he does pick up wonderfully in quick time and I trust it will be so again. My idea at present is that he is in no pain but depressed mentally and physically. Probably his heart is the cause.[1]

I want to hear more of Jock and his lady. Such a short time ago since he was an infant asking questions about everything on earth and now taking the only way of solving them. Nothing happens now to the youth I have cared for without my seeing Michael in the same circumstances.

Peter has just published a translation of a short German novel, *Carl and Anna*[2], which seems to me the most remarkable and at times beautiful 'love story' that has come out of the war. Nico is in the midst of changing his house, going into 'more commodious premises' about a 100 yards away—in Bedford Gardens.

My love to Katie who when she has settled the politics of Edgerston might have a go at me.

[1] Charles Whibley died in March of the following year.
[2] By Leonhard Frank.

137

Adelphi Terrace House 19 September '31

I wish I was still among your rounded hills. You have a prospect as fair I think as any in Scotland, and though you all love it, it means most to Fred. One day as I watched him from a window stalking in the garden with the round hills for company I made a discovery about him that I have probably been on the verge of discovering for years and then missing—that he is really a figure in some unwritten tale by Walter Scott. The scene of it is certainly Edgerston, and the whole thing would begin to move if something very small could happen, such as the opening of a gate down by the burn. I could go on in this way for a long time, and for the moment at any rate it is my chief memory of that happy visit. I seem to know a little more of Scotland than I ever knew before.

I liked specially a little talk I had with him about Charles. I think he and I understood Charles and loved him more than any person, and feel him still as a presence in an unusual way. I continue to see him setting forth alone on a dark journey and to feel that it is wrong that our Charles should be alone with those poor eyes of his, climbing obstacles—dauntless nevertheless. For sheer clearness has there been anything much better than Philippa and he both knowing what was the thing to do.

I felt very much at home at Edgerston. I give you many thanks for that. You were the chief conspirator.

21 December '31

I was very glad to have your kind letter about Peter and your news of Edgerston also. I have been seeing a good deal of Peter's lady of course and like her very much and they are both very happy. The event is one I have long hoped for and when it is accomplished I suppose I shall feel that my task is over and, as Henley wrote, the long day done.

I have been seeing Lady Betsy and she is as delicious and dogged as if the scene were Edgerston. That photograph of us that you took at Fernhurst is me as I wished to be, and I have as yet hardly turned my eyes from myself to give a careless glance at Lady Betsy and Beatrix. It is the stature of me in which I so rejoice. Six feet three inches I should say. If I had really grown to this it would have made a great difference in my life. I would not have bothered turning out reels of printed matter. My one aim would have been to become a favourite of the ladies which between you and me has always been my sorrowful ambition. The things I could have said to them if my legs had been longer. Read that bitter cry to Fred and watch a complacent smile spread over his countenance.

That story of Robin liking to fight his friend Bobby best is a good intimation that all is well with him. His diversions in bed when prostrate remind me of a boy I know who spent a similar time learning to write with a pencil between his toes.

6 February '32

Here are the lines I spoke of by Jamieson of the Scottish dictionary:

> And Prosen proud with rippit loud,
> Comes ravin' frae his glen
> As gin he micht auld Esk affricht
> And drive him back again.

(Two rivers near Kirriemuir that swallow each other.)

9 October '32

It is not so good in London as at Edgerston though it is quieter. No swarms of people at tea for instance. In fact it is rather a desert island. I see there has been a 'cruise' to Robinson Crusoe's island and that it is alleged they went to the wrong island. I believe Defoe was thinking of London when he chose his island. I can't remember ever having a talk with Fred about Defoe, and would like to know if he does not think him one of the very greatest. However I don't see what Defoe is doing in this letter, which set out to thank you very warmly for having me for such a long stretch in the house that now means more to me than any other in Scotia. I shall never forget that first big breath of my native air when I alighted at your door. The express is the most beautifully fitted train I have ever seen, but it was taking me in the wrong direction. The only person in my carriage was a terrific swell about seed potatoes. He introduced himself by showing me his advertisement in the *Scotsman*, and we talked about seed potatoes for many hours. Next to him I am now the greatest living authority on seed potatoes. I don't mean that he tired me, he made it most interesting, and I see now that seed potatoes are more important than Ottawa.

The Jedburgh Abbey floodlit is fine and I am showing it round to the glory of Scotia. As for that play[1] I know the 15th Feb. was spoken of for its production, but such dates are often changed. All those children at Edgerston, they must be making the house ring and I wish I was there ringing it with them. I brought in the New Year staring solitary from my window. Thus it has often happened—too often.

★

To Lady GUENDOLEN GODOLPHIN-OSBORNE, on becoming Lady GUENDOLEN CECIL

Brighton 9 July '23

Dear Lady Guendolen

I have just sent a little masterpiece of a letter to your mother on the subject of your wedding. No one reading it will be able to see what lies between the lines, except yourself,—and catch you bothering to read it! So I will only say that every word is true. I hear them giving a little cry as they plunge into the waste-paper basket but you don't even hear the cry. Better doubtless that it should be so. The happiness of woman is built on the miseries of man, and now that I think of it I am at least proud to have added to your happiness! I don't suppose I shall have the courage to attend the ceremony, but I am coming up to see if I can get hold of a wedding-gift that cuts both ways.

Farewell in a sense. I think I shall go and live in the Ruhr.

Yours, J. M. Barrie

Californie Palace, Cannes 20 January '29

I expect that when you are in such parts as these you are unafraid, but I am unused to them and they frighten me. When a boy approaches with a telephone-message I hide in the bathroom and if he has a card in his hand I feel then my last hour has come. Otherwise I am ever so much better than when you so dearly came to brighten the invalid of the flat, and I go long walks in certainly broiling sun and study how villas are built till I could almost build them.

[1]*The Boy David.*

140

Adelphi Terrace House 6 November '29

I sighed indeed to have to send you that message, but it had to be, as I am for the time being under the weather with some ailment that only sheep seem to have had before. I have however for long been haunted by a feeling that I am a sheep. 'Know thyself,' as Descartes used to say.

12 November '29

I am hoping your cold is better, and am looking forward to the proof of it on Monday. I am not quite so sheepish as I was, but sufficiently so to make me at once recognisable when I enter your withdrawing-room. Looking forward modestly to making a sensation at last.

11 April '30

Yes, I am sad about Charles Whibley of whom I was very fond. He had a remarkable individuality, sometimes wildly extravagant in talk and again so modest and delightful, you would have thought at times that he wanted to reduce (by drastic means) the population of his country, though if you knew him closely you would know that he wouldn't kill a fly; he was really hopelessly lovable and kind. At his best he wrote about the best English of his day.

24 February '32

It makes me sad to know that you still have the doctors worriting you, but if on the other hand they are this time getting at the root of the trouble how overjoyed we shall be—especially this one. I think you have been very gallant through all this bad time, and you need no longer affect gaiety as you have so often done (tricking us) when you were having needle-thrusts that would have made any Mere Man, V.C., squeal. It is so good to know you have been a brave one. I need not say how I should love to come and see you any hour you feel equal to it. I am quite well myself and am leading a sort of dream-like existence, all owing to Biscuits. A few weeks ago I discovered Biscuits. They are little things which one crunches in bed when all the rest of the world is still. They are probably Victorian as they are called Alberts. You should see my smile when I open my bedroom-door o' nights and see them waiting for me. Suggested invitation-:

Lady Guendolen Cecil
At Home to J. M. B.

R.S.V.P.   *Alberts*

141

It is rather terrible to reflect that at this moment you are almost certainly telling lies to somebody. And so it will be (as Shakespeare says but with less point) 'to-morrow and to-morrow and to-morrow.' You cannot need any explanation of the indictment but it amounts to this,—that however over-long visitors remain (and you can't think how loth one is to leave you) you will pretend that you would love them to stay longer, and whatever pain is shooting through your head you will swear that you are much better to-day. It is angelic but devilish. I believe if you were left alone with a carrot you would be radiant to it so as not to hurt its feelings.

To ALGERNON CECIL, writer

Adelphi Terrace House 27 February '33

My dear Algernon

I am wondering whether it would not be good for you to be away from 43 for a bit and yet near enough to do things that must be done.[1] I have here a large bed-sitting-room which I should love you to make use of if you think such a proposal of any use. I am usually alone and would be very glad of your company. Also even if people came you need not see a soul unless you wanted to, and could have meals in your own room as much as you liked. I wish this would appeal to you as much as it does to me.

Affectionately, J. M. B.

Here is another thing which I wish to urge on you at present: I have a feeling that as an outsider I could give you some counsel on such matters as you cared to consult me about. It is the *practical* friend I want to be just now, for it is as much needed probably as the more intimate. I have a dread of your being one who may feel starved of affection when there are few for whom so much of it is waiting.

11 April '33

The flat seems very empty without you. Even the fire keeps going out. I have sometimes thought of following its example and seeking company in a restaurant but the desperate idea has come to nothing. A possible alternative is to have Mrs Stanley bring me in two teacups at 10.30 p.m.

[1]Lady Guendolen Cecil had died in this month.

Well, it can't be done as easily as that. You must come in frequently and help me not to miss you so much. I knew your visit would be good for me, but not quite how delightful you could make my evenings, though I had a comfortable guess about that. It was a great compliment to me that you could come at all, and I treasure the thought that in a way it came from you both, and that things were made easier by another presence in the room. That must have been why there was never any constraint over what we said or did. A pretty complete understanding. I am proud to have your letter and to feel as certain as you that our friendship is too well-founded ever to break.

★

To Mrs THOMAS HARDY, of Max Gate, Dorchester

Tandown Hotel, Glengarry, N.B. 15 August '15
Dear Mrs Hardy
    I am wandering about in the Highlands in such remote parts that it has taken your letter this long to reach me—partly because the highlands are as bare of man this year as if it were the day before Creation. I'd give some books with pleasure but don't know where to have them sent me, so please accept enclosed small cheque for the bazaar instead.
    I was on the Marne in France and I saw an old lady knitting placidly by the door of her new wooden house. On the same spot she had been ill-treated by two German soldiers in the dash for Paris, & they destroyed her home. Now they are buried beneath her potatoes & she is there knitting. It grips me like a poem by your husband. I hope you are both very well. I lift my hat to him. He is our great man.
                        Yours very sincerely, J. M. Barrie

Guilfoil Hotel, Kilmelfort 31 August. '15
    That is very delightful of you, and as there is no house in England where I would be prouder to hang up my hat than

at Max Gate I eagerly take you at your word, and when I get back to London I'll write and propose a time, and if that doesn't suit you I will propose another. No getting out of it for you!

Adelphi Terrace House, 2 January '16

It is a great pleasure to me to have your letter, and I wish you both as happy a New Year as any one can have in these sombre days. Certainly Hardy had a feeling of happiness when that poem of the oxen came off his pen. It is a thing of haunting beauty, and I think I for one will associate it with any Christmases that may remain to me. This sort of thing is indeed the pure flame.

29 December '16

I often think of my happy visit to you. It was a singularly happy one to me. Hardy's fireside is a very cheerful place. I have my boys home now for the holidays. Three of them at present, and the flat is for the nonce a noisy spot. Just listen for a moment and you will hear another plate go smash.

20 June '17

The time you speak of between the 25th and end of July sounds like a most excellent time for me, so I hope you will come then. I shall be very delighted if you do and very sorrowful if you don't.

About the going to France. I hear Hardy has been invited for the 8th July when I am going also, and I can't help hoping that he will make up his mind to come. As you may guess I would do my very best to look after him and mighty proud to be in his company, and I know from others how well this sort of thing is done. As I understand, the bigness of the things being done cannot be understood till one is there, and that brings comfort and pride rather than sadness. Long after the war is over (I don't doubt this) England will know that the biggest Englishman in it was Hardy, and I think it would be of some historic interest that he had been there. A car is put at our disposal and we go quite quietly where we choose. I should like to go to Ypres, as one of my boys is buried there. Of course he understands he is not expected to write of it or anything of that sort. I daresay the invitation has reached him by now, so do think it over. It would be a good plan if he goes for you to come here and wait for him.

I am delighted. Tuesday suits me admirably. I'll expect you between two and three. I'll tell you about what I saw at the front then. On the whole I am glad I went tho' it doesn't help one to sleep. I was able to get my boy away with me for two days, which was fine.

My love to Hardy. I'm so happy about your coming. Heather just arrived. Many thanks.

25 January '18

No doubt you have had an acknowledgement from the Red Cross about the MSS.[1] but I want to send my warm thanks also. I chuckled over the message you send from Hardy about the modesty of authors. As for the privately printed pamphlets I bless Mr Cockerell for having made that suggestion to you. They are the very things for our purpose, just what collectors jump at, so do please oblige again.

I should love to come down to see you again, you don't know how much. The Red Cross business will be over in April and I shall venture to propose myself.

My love to you both.

14 February '18

I have just discovered (and wonder if Hardy knows) that Turner when very young used to come to 8 Adelphi Terrace and paint panoramas of the river.

27 April '21

I wonder whether you would both be persuaded to come for a day or two to me in the end of May, to include the 27th, on the afternoon of which we are opening a new theatre for the Dramatic Academy students. It is to be rather a function, with the Prince of Wales, etc. and I have written a half-hour play[2] for it. It would be a great delight to me if you could do this, and the Academy would feel very honoured.

The Barkers and Galsworthys were in last night, and the B.s gave me nice messages from you, and also said how well T. H. was looking. Lady Cynthia and I are looking forward to coming down to you for a night some time this summer. Nicholas would send his love if he were in. I must tell you

[1] *Far from the Madding Crowd.*
[2] *Shall We Join the Ladies?*

about his last birthday. I had promised him a motor bicycle, tho' I shudder at the things and the danger of them, so conceive my delight when I got a letter from him saying 'I have changed my mind, and would rather have the complete works of Hardy.' You may conceive how I rushed out and got them. His brother tells me privately that Nicholas has since written to his old nurse saying 'Nobody knows about life until they have read the works of Hardy.'

Stanway, Winchcombe 1 Aug. '21

I wonder if it would be possible for you and Mr Hardy to come here for a few days—say next Friday or Saturday till Tuesday. I should be so delighted if you could, and so would Lady Cynthia who would be here with her husband and children. This is her birthplace and is let to me for a few weeks. Nicholas will be here and possibly Charles Whibley—no one else. I should love it if you could come. Your best way evidently would be train to Cheltenham, where we should meet you with car.

[Note in Hardy's hand on back of envelope for Mrs Hardy's instruction: 'Many thanks etc. etc.
'My husband says it is impossible for him personally. He has discovered this year that he cannot go visiting any more—a person over 81 must stay at home. But I could etc.']

Adelphi Terrace House 12 January '22

I am damped to hear that T.H. is down with a temperature and trust it is not influenza. I daresay only a slight chill and hope he is much better already. A line about how he progresses would be very welcome, tho' it may be a shame to bother you. I want you to be very sure of one thing, that if ever you felt lonely and suddenly wanted a friend you have but to write or wire and I would be down by the first train. I shall come soon in any case, and, as a proof of how well I now am, take this—I have a lotion I should have been using, and before the doctor came today I poured some of it away to make him think I had been behaving well. Then in the evening I found that what I had destroyed was my precious sleeping draught! I wish I was by Hardy's side as he lies cosily abed, telling him of some of my adventures when I was prone. I had a nurse and Freyberg, the V.C., you remember, staying o' nights and they were in terrible rivalry. Each had strings from my room to

146

theirs which I could pull to rouse them, and constantly in the night I fell over the strings with the result that they came rushing in, each glaring at the other. I am practically right now, and Lady Cynthia who was a jewel all thro' has gone away for a week.

That was a splendid message of T.H.'s about coming up, and I look forward to it enormously. Tell him I saw a good deal of Michael Collins when he was in London and was greatly impressed by him. Obviously a leader of men and with a boyishness at times almost as gay as your favourite Sassoon's (I am jealous of that youth!)

19 January '22

Thank you so much for letting me hear the good news of T.H. For the moment I am so relieved that I don't worry about the folly of the doctors, but by midnight I shall be furious with them. That they should unnecessarily have given you such anxiety is very hard to forgive. I am much amused by your scoring so neatly over the nurse, more amused than surprised. I love Hardy's message about coming back to the Adelphi. Tell me, if you have time, did he manage to avoid going to Buckingham Palace in knee-breeches for the O.M.? If he did manage, how did he manage?

I can, however, see him cutting more of a figure in the said than I should do.

Lady Cynthia is looking forward to my having to do it, but if so this flat will be denied to her that day. I don't know that I shan't even post Thurston to the door.

For the moment even this does not really lower the spirits into which the good news has put me. I am indeed happy of it. My warm love to you both.

22 February '22

Hereby to assure you with my hand on my heart that I am so recovered as to be genuinely in 'rude health'. What a nuisance on the other hand that you should have had influenza, from which may your recovery be rapid. I feel I should like a breath of the country and to see you both at the same time, and am wondering whether you would put the dog on me if I came down on Saturday afternoon, arriving at 3.48. It is good to hear that T.H. has been so vigorous lately with the loathly pen.

147

I look forward to making him chuckle over my misadventures at Buckingham Palace. To put it cautiously, I have no skill at stockings.

Let me know, please.

5 January '23

You know how sincerely I hope for the best kind of happiness for Max Gate in 1923. I cannot think of that home without affection for you who have been such a godsend to it and to the illustrious name it covers.

T.H. would have chuckled if he had seen me at Cambridge the other day. I went to meet Housman but it was alas one of those dire dinners of dons and wines, and I knew I should be appallingly silent and dull, and I went and I was. The awful feeling that you will never be able to speak or think again! If you have never experienced it go to a college dinner. And yet, such nice people too.

20 May '23

I have been reading a number of the novels again and found that *The Woodlanders* is the most complete, so to speak, of all. I have seldom known any book that makes the reader so much one of the company, that leaves him with the feeling that he was there. It really is an epitome of life with its joys and sorrows, and it is also a very consoling book. I get a lot of comfort out of Hardy's books, despite the wind that shakes them.

23 December '23

I am very glad that all is well and happy at Max Gate, which tendeth to make all well and happy here. Not absolutely well for the moment, as this is written with two hands and one eye. Good subject for a painter—and the whole remark reminds me of the kindly criticism 'Mr. So and so is a d—d scoundrel, but it is his only fault.' All which merely means that I have had a neuralgic needle in me, but am nearly all right.

What you say of Lawrence[1] at the play[2] is very interesting. He was evidently moved to the quick, and it seems to me to explain a good deal of his own wonderful life. 'The quick.' What a bond of comradeship it is—jumps all gulfs, takes him to poesie, T.H. to the East. (Also makes me mix my metaphors.) I expect though that he was wrong about the giggling behind him,

[1]Colonel T. E. Lawrence.
[2]Hardy's *The Queen of Cornwall*, at Dorchester.

148

which was very likely merely strain. I have often heard such sounds in a theatre from people who were the most moved—often in Shakespeare—it is a form of boiling over. Or of course it may just be loutishness. I look forward to the performance for the London Dorsetshires.

I have two of the 'boys' with me for Christmas, Peter and Nicholas, and we shall spend it alone, but in good feather. Most of my Christmases of the past few years I have been by myself, and cooked my dinner (as you and I did), not liking to show in a restaurant or a club. For New Year, though, I am going to Stanway, where Lady Cynthia and her people are.

5 November '24

It is good to hear from you. I shall be more than common delighted to go down and see *Tess*, and if it is the same to you I propose myself for the dress rehearsal of Monday 24th. I like dress rehearsals and all the odd thrills and flutter of them, and of course it would be great to be with Hardy. If Col. Lawrence can get away for that night so much the better. I like the account you give me of the enthusiasm of members of the company, and also there is not a bit of doubt that those journeyings will help them in their playing.

Don't be surprised if you see my pipe again. I did not abandon it for good but just to watch myself squirming for a time without it, with the hope of being temperate presently (though I was never good at being temperate in anything).

I am quite well, but like T. H. don't sleep easily. Oh, the blessedness of books in the night! I am sending you a novel by a woman said to be about 24 years old, which seems to me to be rather astounding—*The Constant Nymph*. If it strikes you try to get Hardy to look at it.

1 February '25

I am always uncommon glad to see your handwriting and I like that postmark Dorchester, but sorry to hear Mrs Bugler has decided against coming to London to play Tess. It would have been such an opportunity for showing what she could do, but on the other hand the disturbance in home life would necessarily have been considerable and it may be a wise conclusion to come to. As for myself I am not writing any play just now and don't know whether the wish to do so may come

149

back, but if I do and there is a part that seems to fit her I should be delighted to have her help, and certainly will keep her in mind. I hope you are both well—you ought to be well in Dorchester if one can keep alive in London through these fogs. The last one was the worst for a good many years, or at least so I thought. I forget if I ever told you how much I like you. No, too shy, but I do like you very much.

19 January '27

Alas, poor Wessex. It is a very pleasant part of Max Gate gone. You can't think how often I have talked to people about that dog and his ways. He had got into the Wessex tales so to speak, one could see him running about in them and telling certain famous characters (all incredulous) about the wireless that was coming. One of the best advertisements for wireless,— 'Wessex liked it.'

I would have written long ago, but on the very day you wrote, Stanway, where I was, was in great distress over the sudden illness of Lady Cynthia's youngest child who had to have the mastoid operation and was dangerously ill for some time. All is now well, however, and he is happy and gay sitting up in bed writing books from morn till night. One is a dictionary with his own meanings to the words and another is entitled 'The Holy Bible, by God'. I had written a play for the children to act, but of course that had to go whistling down the wind, for this season at any rate.

11 January '28

I left Max Gate yesterday feeling more buoyant about T.H. than when I went down, for among other things there is obviously a good deal of strength in him still, and it is certainly encouraging that there is no fever. For his sake (and I know you think of nothing else) you must husband some little strength so as to be equal to the days ahead when he will need you quite as much as now. It is true he cannot easily bear you to be out of his sight, for you are the one person in the world to him (as well you deserve to be), but that will go on, and if you break down it might mean your being unable to be with him. So, please, you will in the long run help best our great man to whom you are indeed a great wife.

Your letter is so kind and dear that there is no reply to it except just to say that the little I did was only what every one at that ceremony would have been proud to have a chance to do.[1] I should like you to know too that it was not merely the greatness of the man that made him wonderful to me. Suppose he had been just an everyday person—I should still have thought him one of the most lovable human beings I had ever known. It is this part of him that lies at Stinsford and the other in the Abbey. Each place has got its rights.

The tributes to him, apparently without a dissentient voice, have been extraordinary. I wonder whether it has ever had a parallel. Of course they will be arguing about him and taking sides for hundreds of years, but at his death I question whether any man of letters was ever so acclaimed. A proud woman you, but such a lonely one; I dare not intrude on that, I suppose you have to pay for your unique position. The last thing I shall forget about Hardy is the change you made in his face. I had known him long, and I think the heart that is now at Stinsford had been calling long and bleakly for what you were at last to do for him. I honour you very much. I need only repeat that I want to go to you at any moment that you think I might be of the slightest service—it would be a privilege to me, as also if you would come here where you would be absolutely secluded except to any one you wished to see. There may be matters you would care to discuss with me and I would give you the best counsel I could give. Of course the book of him is what I want to see more than anything. I should like to have two or three weeks to think it all out.

I have written them at the Abbey to add the 'O.M.' and I now agree that it is better so. Nice of the Dean to suggest it.

I am reading the *Life*[2] with huge satisfaction. I couldn't help reading the London days first, but am gone back now and reading it straight through. If it is all as good as the first sixty pages it is to be a book indeed, and unlike any other Life ever written. So far it seems to me quite ready for publication.

[1]Hardy had died on January 11th. Barrie was much concerned with his burial.

[2]Typescript of Mrs Hardy's *Life of Hardy*.

3 February '28

The book is a remarkable achievement, and if I thought of you mighty well before I think even more of you now. I could go on expatiating on its beauties, but for the moment let me mention the two things that I think are wrong. (1) The intrusion of so many names of people in society he met in London. To my mind they are an excrescence on the book and get an importance in it, and so in his life, that is in false proportion. I believe it was a very fortunate thing for him that he had these holidays away from himself so to speak, they probably freshened his brain and spirits as nothing else could have done. But given so elaborately they don't belong, they would be misunderstood. Enough to my thinking to mention Lady Jeune and Mrs Henniker and that he visited in many houses. Of course I don't mean taking out any of the many fine jottings of his own or summing up that you record and that are probably as thick here as elsewhere. The man could not look out at a window without seeing something that had never been seen before.

(2) The book leaves too much an impression that any silly unimportant reviewer could disturb and make him angry. He was subject to as much rot about *Jude* and the poems as ever writer was, and sometimes it came from people of distinction, but though he was naturally wounded I don't think they should be given this opportunity of finding him replying to them or meditating replies. I like best the statement several times repeated that his sense of humour was too strong for them. This by no means would cut out the expressions of his views or his aims, and what he considered art of any kind to be, which occur frequently and are among the best things in the book.

By the way *the* most striking thing in the book is that all his life he was preparing, getting ready, for his *Dynasts*, chopping his way through time to the great event.

15 February '28

I have a receipt for the lettering of stone from the Abbey and a promise to send the design back when they are finished with it. I had also a good talk today with Mr Cockerell, in which a volume of letters was mentioned as a possibility you had been thinking of, and I agree that Sir Edmund Gosse would be an ideal man to undertake it.

Here are the words proposed to be put on the panel in 8
Adelphi Terrace, and if there is anything you prefer altered you
have of course only to say so. There can be no doubt that poems
were written in that room and the mention of them seems to
give a halo to it. I am looking forward much to being with you
on Tuesday and should like to see the monument at Blackdown
on Wednesday.

I can see what feelings must overcome you when you open the
Biography and attempt to work on pages every one of which
must have poignant memories to you of the actual moments
when you and he discussed them. I think you have now entered
on the hardest time of all, when the immediate necessary
things are done and the blankness comes with an added force.
There is something painful even in seeing the sun shine and
flowers spring up as if it was all nothing to them. I feel very
close to you about it all, and so helpless.

I am so sorry that our jaunt to Blackdown has laid you low
and feel I am rather heartless in having to say that it evidently
had the opposite effect on me, for I have been tingling with
health and spirits ever since. As we went round the monument
I was reminded of the snell air of my native place, quite as if I
had foregathered with an old part of myself, and there was a
happiness as well as a vitality about it all. But on top of all you
have gone through it was doubtless too cold an excursion for
you, and instead of revelling in it as I did I ought to have been
your stern mentor and made you sit in the car.

At any rate my last visit to Max Gate makes me only the
more desirous for the next one. It is almost strange to note that
at such a time I find the house the reverse of gloomy;—I mean
that it, or our talk, has a brightening effect on me, perhaps
because everything there is so real, and I feel I go on false
pretences, for though certainly my intention was to attempt to
comfort you I am the one who is getting the comfort. I have
read the letters to Mrs Henniker, and want to keep them a few
days longer if I may so that I may re-read them and see if I
agree with myself (I am wondering how many more there are).
As provender for the Biography I am a bit disappointed in them
as they give on the whole little of himself. They do of course

show that here was a lady of great charm to him, for whom he had more regard than for any other person in an important time of his life, and it is valuable to the reader to know of her as such. We see him seeing her often and wanting to see her oftener, and it is pleasant to read of how much kindness he gave her in the matter of her literary work, helping in so many ways. But the letters deal mainly with arrangements about seeing each other, advice to her, comment on what she is writing, and, alas, so little about what T.H. is writing. Nor much about what he is thinking, his views on life, etc. I rather grudge her being a writer at all, and indeed I believe he did also. Of course the pieces about *Jude* and the *Well-Beloved* and the poems are the kind of thing one is searching for, but would that there had been more of them. She was delightful and cultured and could take him on holiday from himself (for which I bless her), but she did not in these letters draw blood, so to speak; there is no indication to me that she influenced his work in any way. She was a pleasure to him, and to have been that is something she had a right to be proud of. I suppose no one ever influenced his work. He was a masterful man. Egdon Heath influenced him. That name and his own became one.

1 May '28

Have just re-read *Pair of Blue Eyes* for the nth time and started on *Under the Greenwood Tree* (ditto). When I read him I can't turn to anyone else.

17 May '28

Of course the letter about the Palmerston ceremony must go in. It is in itself a delightful letter and comment on a memorable occasion, and readers will naturally think of the similar ceremony in the Abbey that was to come so long afterwards. I think in the Life there is a reference to the incident, and that would be the place for it. It should go in complete I think without a word omitted (with of course the sketch of the place). Palmerston born 1784 takes one back a long way. Making use of T.H. being at the funeral one could go back to Shakespeare with about five people, all great, each of whom could have known the previous one. It could work out with them all literary men.

Of the other two letters certainly we should get the bit about

his going to St Mary's Kilburn and Roman Catholic churches.
His liking for going to churches, sacred music, etc, is a very
interesting part of him, not generally understood.

24 June '28
I have no doubt at all that these are 64 pages of superlative
merit. I don't know what pieces to give the palm to. Perhaps
on reflection the way his knowledge of and interest in religion is
shown, so remarkable at that early age. Yes, I think so—the
growth of his mind toward what it was to be later should get
first place. There is no heavy labouring to show this—it just
comes of itself, a natural growth, and a growth in the
courageously honest straight line that was to be his whole life.
If this is not fine biography I am a Dutchman and will also eat
my hat.

31 August '28
Here I am again back at the old place in the old rain, but
with one attraction added to the view. It is your flat, which
already assumes the appearance of a friend. The boards have
been trundled off somewhere else, and even your garden is
getting ready for you, the window boxes now presenting a neat
look, evidently having been combed out by a master hand with
a small rake or perhaps ten fingers. I almost see you at those
windows already and exchange greetings. I only got back to-
day and it is very fine to me to think of you as a neighbour.

2 September '28
Many thanks indeed for the rug, which is delicious. I am so
glad you are coming up on Tuesday to see about your flat which
of course I am avid to see also. Tea time will be ideal for your
coming in here. Thurston off for his holiday but Mrs Stanley
(housekeeper) is here and will be proud to give you any
information about tradespeople, etc. Till Tuesday then.

9 September '28
That is tremendously kind of you, and it is just the sort of
thing I have in the back of my head to ask of you on occasion
when you are in the Terrace. Just now I am all right or will be
at any rate by Tuesday when Thurston comes back, and Lady
Cynthia who has been abroad comes in end of week. I am

feeling well but in the desire to be still weller have a man who comes to pour electricity into me though I am not certain it does not pass down immediately into your mat.

And I am so glad you are sleeping well at last. We might have a string between the two flats, so that when you tugged I could send the sleeping draught bottle down it.

16 September '28

I have taken a good deal to writing at my bedroom window as it gives me much more daylight. Frank is back now and Lady C. returns tomorrow with an appalling dyke of letters awaiting her. It was time Frank was back, and Mrs Stanley has been telling him tales about me, as that I went out to dinner one night blissfully unconscious that I had a 'dress' shoe on one foot and a country affair on the other. Wish I could compare notes with T.H. about that sort of thing. It becomes exciting as the publication of the Life and the poems draws nigh.

18 September '28

A collected volume of my plays is coming out, and I wonder whether you would mind their printing at the foot of a frontispiece portrait of me those eight lines of T.H.[1] with of course his name. They hit me off in a way that I like, and of course I love the connection, but if you think better not, all right. I have them framed now. Be sure to say just what you feel.

[The letters from now on begin: 'My dear Florence'.]

7 May '29

That there pain is not so bad now. I think it has been frightened away by my fierce fight with the bandage that affects to hold the thermogene in place. Also I have returned to my own sleeping draught with grand results. Yesterday if you had been in Robert Street you might have suffered from

[1]Hardy's lines, after attending a rehearsal of *Mary Rose:*

> *If any day a promised play*
> *Should be in preparation,*
> *You never see friend J. M. B.*
> *Depressed or in elation.*
>
> *But with a stick, rough, crooked and thick,*
> *You may sometimes discern him,*
> *Standing as though a mummery show*
> *Did not at all concern him.*

one of the windows in this room, which was blown clean away by a gale, but cleared the people in the streets, like a low flying aeroplane.

I am now going off to a rehearsal of *M. Rose*, not such an interesting rehearsal as one you wot of. Are you remembering to consult Augustus John about a sculptor?

Your door and windows in the Terrace now present a melancholy appearance—at least they do to me.

23 June '29

I am surprised that things have gone as far about Epstein, not knowing (as I am sure you did not know either) that anything of the kind was being done at all. Nevertheless I feel sure that Augustus John has only acted out of great kindness, and that all he has really done is to interest Epstein in the subject—which is valuable. Out of what I must admit is my small knowledge, I believe Epstein to be the big sculptor of his day but he often does strange things that are at any rate beyond the understanding of plain men and women, and even actively repugnant to them. He would probably do either the best or the worst statue of T.H., while various others would do something pretty sure to be satisfactory, though not notable. With them 'safety first' would be the words again, while with him there is a real risk but a possibility of something fine beyond any others' attainments. It is a pity Mr Hornby is away, but of course nothing could be settled till the small committee meets and makes a recommendation to the larger one. That is the situation from the business point of view, and Augustus John will understand it. In interesting Epstein he has probably done what none of the rest of us could do, and therefore we may say so far, good. That would still remain the business situation after they went down to Dorchester and see you and talk about site or anything else. You can have ease of mind because it is not you who decides but the committee.

Stanway, by Cheltenham 8 August '29

I trust all is going pretty well with you, and that you are keeping at arm's length the self distrust that so often floods you and is so uncalled for and yet is, I admit, an endearing part of you. You are always doing your best and it is a very good best. Though you had your life with T.H. to live over again I cannot

157

see that you could have done much better, though you will go on ransacking the past for little things left undone. You are really his Vol. 2, and he lived through it brightly because of you. Triumph enough for any woman. Things here go on sedately, always with some visitors. Birrell who leaves today has been a great stand-by to me—also one Stephen Gwynn, once an Irish M.P., whom you may not know but is good to know.

5 September '29

I have thought a better plan than Mr Kennington bringing photographs of his work here would be for me to go to his studio and see the actual work. I have arranged with him to go there tomorrow afternoon and will let you know what I think. I hope you agree that this should tell one more. I ventured to consult Evan Charteris about sculptors as he is an expert, and he said there were several very good men among whom he placed Kennington and Dobson as about the best. He thought any of them would endeavour to do the kind of statue that was asked for. I question whether there should be any panels even tho' they were good.

30 October '29

It seems to me very satisfactory that Mr Kennington is desirous you should give him suggestions, and my first thoughts are that of course you should do so, but that it will be more difficult now than when he has something however rough to show you. Nevertheless even now you could help to some extent—as to the manner of his sitting in the open, the turn of his head, familiar ways with his hands, and so on. All this you know of course as no one else does.

1. As for any suggestions from me, among the first would be that he had the figure of a young man—the sculptor can hardly grasp how much this was so without its being impressed upon him, it was so unusual and so marked.

2. As for any eccentricity of dress (a real help of course for Mr K.) it should be emphasized that there never was anything of the kind, that he was essentially a man to whom calling attention to himself by dress or indeed by any sort of mannerism would have been detestable and that he just wanted to look like other people. If he could have made his face like other people's he would have done it.

3. In most statues the figure whatever its position is triumphant. If you think this out I believe you will find it is often the proper course, but surely it would be quite wrong in the case of T.H. Triumphs abundant came to him but they were not responsible for one line in his face. He liked people of understanding to see what he was trying to do, but he asked hardly anything else of them. I think the triumphant effect in statuary must come largely from the poise of the head, its erectness, the eyes so satisfied. I don't myself see T.H.'s head erect, I see him looking down or even away from us. Not assuredly self-consciously, but leaving the impression so to speak that here is a portrait that he would not have sat for but that has been snapped by a Kodak.

4. If Wessex is to be in it, as I should like, I see him alert, calling attention to himself, in fact the triumph should be left to *his* face. I conceive T.H. *not* looking at him.

5. I have sometimes wondered why statues are always of a man as he was in his last years. I can conceive of a man who lived to an old age being sculptured as he was in youth. But I am not suggesting it in this case.

These are just some thoughts, too vaguely set down, and others will come to me. Mr Kennington has a very difficult task but one likes the spirit in which he approaches it.

I have been in bed for a day or two rummaging in an ancient medicine work to try to find what was the matter. I fixed on Vertigo—or is it Vertigris? My doubt shows how much better I am.

7 March '30

I have taken on a heavyish job that necessitates the writing of heaps of letters which heigho are expected to be in my own hand. However that won't last long and I am so well as a whole that I'm quite taken aback when people say 'What a cough you have.' I suppose it's like Big Ben, not quite as loud, but so frequent that I have ceased to notice it. I trust foreign parts have not given you a scorn of England.

21 May '30

I don't believe you have seriously contemplated that American lecturing tour. I never did anything of the kind myself, so can only speak from hearsay, but I understand that few experiences can be more grimly tiring. Rushed on long journeys from one place to another. On the other hand to make a trip to U.S.A. and Canada for a short time and get to know on the spot what T.H. means to them would I think be a capital thing to do, and in that case you would add to the worth of the whole thing by preparing a lecture or two to deliver just once or twice, not arranged for beforehand but as you found fitting. I think everyone who can should go over there and get more in touch with the people who are our chief concern outside ourselves, and they are splendid hosts and would be specially so to you. A dreary dribbling day here, and I have just remembered that it is the opening of the flower show.

15 September '30

Here I am again, and Mrs Stanley has the flat looking rather dapper with various walls touched up and fabrics cleaned, but has not dared to do what she would like to do most of all, namely to get at the ceiling of my study. The canary looks as if it should have had a coating of something also, as it is once more in the moulting stage. Your plan of taking a flat such as those in St James's Court (which I think I have never been in) while you look about seems to me a good one. Your mind gets so troubled and uneasy when you think of taking a house in London that I believe now your best plan is to do as before and just take a furnished set of rooms somewhere for a period—I use the word set of rooms rather than flat because it sounds more cosy and also less decisive. At any rate I hope you will come up soon, and of course I am all in agreement about here or Westminster being a pleasanter part than away out in Kensington. I must say things strike people differently though, and I always remember that old Mrs Drummond, whose husband owned the district, when she once came up to see me said that how anyone who could live anywhere else would reside in my flat fairly beat her. She herself lived in Eaton Place or Square which has always seemed to me one of the dreariest of regions. So there you are.

The new hamper was delicious, and first among its contents I put the carrots. I never knew carrots could be so splendiferous.

4 September '31

Just in case you care in the least to have the MS. of my remarks at the unveiling here it is. I am so sorry I did not do better, but it was not from want of trying. The occasion was certainly a very moving one, and when others felt it so how much more must you have felt it. I avoided, as I daresay you know, talking of the matters that I knew were lying nearest your heart lest you should break down, mentally as well as physically, for you were near both. But there is now a satisfaction in the knowledge that the right thing was done that day and that the statue is a worthy one. I feel sure T.H. was pleased with you on the 2nd September.

[Enclosed in previous letter.]

Unveiling of the Hardy Statue

For a very few minutes only shall I venture to stand between you and what we have all come here to see, the figure that is behind these sheets. He was a great man. That was his hard fate. In this matter, you and I are the lucky ones. Our lot to be soon forgotten, not to be messed about by the spade-men of the future; but Hardy has to miss it. I believe he would have preferred to share our right to the shorter span, once his 'task was accomplished and the long day done.' I believe indeed that in one way this statue must be a failure. If it is the living image of him whom it portrays you will find when the sheet is removed that there is no statue there. It will have done as Mr Hardy would have done, if he had heard that there was a great concourse of people to do him honour,—slipped quietly away. I hope I have made our sculptor a little uneasy. It will be a warning to him not to do so well in future.

What is it precisely that we are expecting to see? Our ideas must be very varied. When the child Hardy was born the doctor thought him dead and dropped him into a basket. That was an anxious moment for this country. But a woman stepped forward to make sure, and found he was alive. A statue to this woman—Mr Kennington could have done worse than give us that. Knowing what we know of him now, we may think that at his first sight of life he liked it so little that he lay very still. There was never any more faltering. The undaunted mind. That was Hardy.

That is a statue I see. Let me admit to you a certain

longing I have. I know some things about Hardy that I feel sure cannot be in Mr Kennington's work, and I should like to come here some night soon—maybe to-night—when all of you are in bed—especially Mr Kennington—I should like to steal here in a white coat, with a hammer and chisel and chip those little bits in. Perhaps I shall find the statue surrounded with critics, all in white coats, all chipping; each one of us so zealous to get in some favourite bit of his own that he forgets it can only be done by chipping some better bit off. The darkness of his spirit, for instance, which some people, long forgiven, took for pessimism. There were years certainly when I thought him the most unhappy man I had ever known; but if he had escaped his weird we could not have had our Hardy. And, after all, can one be altogether unhappy, even when ridden by the Furies, if he is producing masterpieces? May we not suspect that he has moments of exultation which are denied to other mortals. I daresay the shades of the departed great gathered in that room at Max Gate to watch their brother write the last page of *The Dynasts*. Happily after that he was to pass into a long evening of serenity. The President of the Immortals had ended his sport with Hardy.

I will not further delay your seeing the statue. Our sculptor has chosen, I think very wisely, to show Mr. Hardy as you knew him best in Dorchester, as you may often have met that quietest figure in literature on your country walks and his, as you and he went home-along. I am as anxious as you, for I saw the statue only long ago in the making. I hope it has grown so true to him that I shall know even what is in his pockets; probably a piece of string and an old knife.

September 1931   J.M.B.

16 October '31

It is a long time since I heard from you, and I am wondering if you are at Max Gate, and hoping in any case that all is well with you.

I am all right and no doubt wasting a good deal of time in reading about elections. It seems obvious that the Nationals must be given the best sort of opportunity to get us on to dry land again. Ramsay MacDonald is doing valiantly and my only fear for him is that he may not be able to stand such a strain o work. I went to the House several times and heard Snowden on the Gold question. He was very impressive, and I felt he belonged to the really big political figures, most of whom are gone. I have been rather disturbed by hearing that people have been writing their names on the T.H. statue. Perhaps they can be stopped from doing this without putting up a railing but otherwise it should certainly go up. The Committee's decision to wait a little seems to be sound. What a strange passion this is, writing names on works of art—it seems to be common to the whole world.

28 October '32

It is long since I heard from you, and I should be glad to hear that all is well with you. I am pretty right myself again after my visit to Scotland. Began to pick up as soon as I swallowed the first mouthful of my native air. If you open your mouth in the dark in Scotia you can make a good guess at what country you are in.

All well in the flat except that the canary has a corn between its toes which keeps us all busy.

24 May '35

I have been away on the Continent for nearly a fortnight (Frank with me) and only got your letter on my return an hour ago. I followed the condition of Lawrence[1] in the papers there in tortured suspense, and when it was evident how dreadfully he was wounded I felt, as you may have felt, afraid of his recovering as a wreck. The thought of him, above all other men, in such a state seemed almost more than could be borne. You of course know much more than I, who only saw newspaper accounts of how it was with him, but better it seemed to me that this glorious and gallant English figure should be suddenly knocked out of the world than linger maimed. I see that his brother is there but I can't intrude on what is such a catastrophe not only to him and his but to the nation. Sometime nevertheless I should like you to tell him that I knew his brother and thought him a pillar of a man, a figure in English history.

---

[1] After the motor-cycle accident from which T. E. Lawrence died.

9 February '36

There is alas no good news to tell about Margaret[1] except that she suffers no pain. It was about six weeks ago that she became rapidly frail of body owing to bad blood circulation and a weak heart. As the doctors say, it is as if old age came upon her suddenly, and though for a week or two they succeeded in restoring her to an extent and even to playing to us on a bed-piano we got for her, the weakness is now much greater and her heart feeble and irregular. She sleeps practically all the time and the opinion is that she cannot be long for this world. She has always been serene but does not know one now. I can't write more about it but you will understand what it means to me and William.

10 May '36

It was dear of you to remember my birthday which I spent amidst the fall of stone and dust which again is now my out-look. The poor terrace has now most of its inside torn out and there are more gashes in its walls. None save familiars can do it reverence nowadays, and one ought to look the other way instead of gazing at its shame as I find myself constantly doing from my eyry. Perhaps I too should have stolen away, indeed perhaps I'll have to as the noise and dust may prove un-endurable. So rapid is demolition of this kind that in a week many landmarks go. I am going away tomorrow for only two or three days and I daresay there will be big changes when I return. We become like the birds' nests one finds in hedges, half torn away and pieces of egg shell scattered beneath. As for health it is pretty fair at present—as they say in the north. Nothing to boast of and nothing to complain of. What I have lost in Margaret is unspeakable and the worst times are when night falls when we used to have so much to say to each other. So many things to say of an intimate kind that would have no meaning to others. But you know all about that, having gone through it yourself to the nth degree.

1 January '37

My christmas and New Year might have been as quiet as yours as my rheumatics still have me in their hold tho' I am really a bit better. Last night my nurse and the canary and I

[1]Barrie's sister Maggie.

celebrated alone at the window, and today the nurse who has been with me many weeks succumbed to this influenza and has had to go, so now there are only self and canary when night falls, and the canary is the merriest.

I can picture you at the birthplace almost as if I had been looking on.

★

To Miss ENID BAGNOLD (Lady Jones), author
2 Robert Street, Adelphi 29 June '20
Dear Miss Bagnold

I am so sorry I cannot be in London on July 8 to attend the wedding. This ought to be a formal note to your parents, but you must forgive my writing to you instead, because I have a gleeful hope that you wrote that book about the hospital[1] which I liked immensely—my glee by the way is because Sir Roderick is marrying into my calling, which I take to be a feather in the cap of all literary characters. As for yourself you have had some very good ideas, and I think that to marry Sir Roderick is quite one of the happiest. I am sending you a little wedding gift which please accept with my warm wishes for the best kind of happiness.

Yours sincerely, J. M. Barrie

Eilean Shona, Argyllshire 26 August '20
Dear Lady Jones

Here in this distant isle have I been reading your *Happy Foreigner*, with the result that I applaud Roderick more than ever. It is a delicious companion on an island and gets better and better unto its last page. No, I won't quite say that, as the gem of it is that adventure of 'the River', which is indeed in the true spirit of romance. Yes, Roderick, you have done well.

★

To Mrs PEARSE, of Lanarkshire
Adelphi Terrace House 1 February '21
Dear Mrs Pearse

I am very proud of the kind thought that made you write me

[1] *A Diary Without Dates.*

165

so dear a letter. When an author is at work on something he often gets lost in it, thinking a good deal of it, and then is sadly disillusioned when it is finished and he reads it over in 'cold blood'. You have found in this play[1] things I tried to put into it but so feebly that to many they are not there at all. I have no doubt that there is something of your boy in your letter, and that you are a little kinder, so to speak, to me because of what the three of you were to each other.

Yours sincerely, J. M. Barrie

★

To A. B. WALKLEY, *dramatic critic*

Adelphi Terrace House 3 February '20

My dear Walkley

I expect you are right about alterations. I must admit I was very annoyed with the revisions of Meredith and James, especially James because he was so much better a writer in the earlier times. Meredith I think did make some improvements. However I am apparently so constituted that I couldn't sit out a month's rehearsals if I didn't meddle with the MS. What does touch me a good deal is that you cared enough about *Crichton* to say 'hands off'. Your original writing about it gave me more pleasure than I have got from anything else I can remember said about my plays. And I think this 'admonition' after all these years not less pleasing.

Yours very sincerely, J. M. Barrie

2 July '26

It makes me uncommon sad to hear you are giving up the dramatic criticism which has been for so long one of the happiest features of the *Times* and, as I suppose everyone will admit, incomparably the best work of the kind. In my own little corner as a playwright you were my great encouragement; it was certainly mainly because of you and Archer that I went on with it,—and him, though I cared for him much, I could very seldom please, while I have the gratification—and it is the best the theatre has given me—that quite often I pleased you and you were most generous in what you wrote. At any rate I look forward to reading many another paper by you in the *Times*.

[1] *Mary Rose.* ★

166

To Miss MARY CAROLINE WATT

Adelphi Terrace House 19 September '21

Dear Miss Watt

I have been trying to find out whether I could put you in the way of such work as you speak of. I haven't succeeded as yet but I have now written to Sir Walter Raleigh at Oxford and told him to communicate with you and tell you if there is any chance of work on the Oxford Press.

I was interested to hear from you and of course I remember your father[1] well and much esteemed him and also admired his scholarship, and also I like your letter which has a courageous 'tang' to it if I may say so.

Yours sincerely, J. M. Barrie

12 May '27

Congratulations to you on having finished your job[2]. It is a very pleasant experience with often a touch of sadness and at times a sinking because of the 'What next' feeling. But these pass and I wish you heartily much success with the book.

The Convent sounds a very restful place. I did not know you were a Catholic but it by no means lessens my interest. If you find that paper of mine[3] in which your father appears it would be nice of you to let me see it again. My best good wishes to you and the other daughters of John Watt.

30 July '27

I am interested to hear of this new book[4] and wish it much good fortune. I expect that Saints *are* difficult!

I am glad you love seeing your name in print, though I may whisper that this is a pleasure which does not last a lifetime.

★

To W. H. LESLIE ADCOCK, *then literary editor of the* Evening News

[Mr Adcock wrote to Barrie: 'I suppose you hold the record as the author of the greatest number of polite notes declining to write articles, and I will not presume to be the inspirer of still another. But I cannot resist the opportunity

[1]The Reverend John Watt, D.D., of Aberdeen.
[2]Translation of de Ségné's *Marie Antoinette*.
[3]'A Spring Fishing Party' had appeared in the *St James's Gazette* in March 1885.
[4]*St Martin of Tours*.

for a flank attack which this morning's *Morning Post* presents. In its column of gossip the *Post* quotes you as the author of a short story, which, as a subtle hair-raiser "far exceeds any of . . . Ambrose Bierce, and certainly stands alongside Scott's 'Wandering Wullie' story in *Red-gauntlet* and Stevenson's 'Thrawn Janet'. Sir James's tale remains buried in the oblivion of the already nigh-forgotten *Scots' Observer*, which only the name of W. E. Henley, its editor, keeps in recollection. Written round, undoubtedly, the age-old mystery of the house of Strathmore, Glamis Castle, the reason why this, one of the best stories of the supernatural, has never been reprinted is in itself a mystery." Now I venture to ask: Could we have your permission to reprint this story in *The Evening News*? I appreciate, of course, that an author might reasonably be reluctant to permit such an exhumation, but in this case, if we may believe the writer in the *Morning Post*, there seems no reason to suppose that the skeleton would be a very grisly one, if, indeed, it were a skeleton at all.']

Adelphi Terrace House 2 July '22

Dear Mr Leslie Adcock

Best let sleeping dogs lie I think. I have not seen that old story of mine since I wrote it so long ago, but I know I thought it a failure at the time. Do you have access to a copy? I should rather like to pass the time of day to it again, though I don't expect I should change my mind. There was another whose title sticks to me agreeably, 'The Body in the Black Box,' but where that appeared I know not.

Another thing against re-digging is that it might set others thereto, and as I used for years to write two a day there must be as many of them as would break the axle of a luggage van. I sometimes come on old copies when I dive into dusty drawers. I can no more burn them than you can destroy your love-letters. Henceforth I shall associate them with your love-letters. At this moment there is nothing I see so vividly as the little faded ribbon in which your love-letters are enclosed. As time rolls on I shall probably get mixed up and think you wrote the articles but that the love-letters were intended for me.

They had their day and ceased to be
But, oh, the meals they meant to me.

(This refers to the articles).

Yours sincerely, J. M. Barrie

[Mr Leslie Adcock wrote: 'Although your Red Herring was attached to the pink ribbon from my love-letters, I scented it. I have also nosed out the story from the British Museum. It appeared in the *National Observer* (which was then being printed in London and Edinburgh) on May 9, 1891, and even in those days you were keeping the best company, for we found R. L. S., Kipling (*Barrack Room Ballads*), Henley, Andrew Lang, Alice Meynell, Oscar Wilde, and A. B. Walkley crowding the same columns. "The Family Honour," which I send herewith, has been dressed in print simply in deference to the rules of decency, as one dresses up a child about to be re-united to its parents.

'Something tells me (I suspect the Voice in *Mary Rose*) that you will never let it go; that my mission in life is to go on writing to you for the article you will never write, and for permission to reprint stories that you will never allow to be reprinted.']

Adelphi Terrace House 9 July '22

Dear Mr Leslie Adcock

My hearty thanks to you for the copy of that old sketch and the trouble you have taken in printing it for my—edification? No, alas, I should not like to have it republished. I don't think well of it. I feel your letter should have been pitched thus— 'Dear Sir J.B., I have read the article 'Family Honour' you submitted to us and now return it as not suitable for the *Evening News*. You seem to me to have a good story to tell, but tell it crudely and in an affected style, which I advise you to get out of if you can. Yours sincerely, W. H. Leslie Adcock.'

Yours sincerely, J. M. Barrie

★

To Mrs ANNE ELIZABETH WHITE, of Holywood, Co. Down

[Mrs White, who was unknown to Barrie, was the widow of a newspaper-owner and journalist in Co. Armagh.]

Stanway, Winchcombe 2 August '22

Dear Mrs. White

A little bird has told me of your contemplated visit to your son in New York, and I hope you will let me have the pleasure of contributing the enclosed cheque towards the journey. I have some right, you see, as your husband was of my profession and we writing people stick together. I hope you will have a very happy time in America.

Yours sincerely, J. M. Barrie

To Miss KATHLEEN WHITE

[Mrs White died two years later and her daughter Kathleen sent Barrie a copy of her mother's passport photograph.]

Adelphi Terrace House 18 July '24

Dear Miss White

You did a kinder thing than you knew when you had the (for me) happy impulse to write me about your mother. I wish I had known her and had the right to leave some flowers on her table as a greeting the day she returned from visiting her sons in America. I can see all right that she was one of my ladies, the ones I crib things from though I may never have set eyes on them. The bits she liked best [in *Margaret Ogilvy*] were probably just her own bits, and if I had met her I should have said so, and shaken a finger at her. I like her photograph much, for though to you it may be a poor thing I see a delicious face, benign and with such humour in it that one can almost hear her laugh— rather a child's laugh I should guess. Of course I know how poor and trivial my things are but nevertheless I am glad that shrewd face did not find me out.

Believe me, much your debtor, yours sincerely, J. M. Barrie

★

To Lady *CYNTHIA ASQUITH*

Adelphi Terrace House 7 May '19
Thomas Hardy has gone. We went to the Academy dinner. Winston spoke grandly in a voice which he managed to charge with emotion. I cheered him most. I like them like that. He is the man who won the war. I thought the Prince of Wales looked very attractive and nicely shy; and when he said that the subject deep in his heart was how the war would affect the art of this country no one grinned except his brother. But Haig was the hero of the evening and the way the gathering let him see this was rather heartening.

[To Thorpness] 20 June '19
I don't suppose I shall be able to get down. I want to come but I should have done it before Michael got back. They shrink, these boys, from going anywhere; the death of their parents is really at the root of it and down in my soul I know myself to be so poor a substitute that I try to make some sort of amends by hanging on here when there is any chance of my being a little use to them. Even in admitting this I am saying more to you than I do to most.

6 July '19
Letters have been thick as leaves in Vallambrosa;—indeed you could eat a meal off the floor of V. more tidily than here.

I have answered a lot and mostly said the wrong thing. (I am down for several dinners.) Will hand you on some tomorrow.[1]

Michael got his two-seater, took nearly an hour's lesson, and then went off in it through the streets alone. I then sat with him in it for two days so that we should end together, as I think we nearly did.

I went to the Thanksgiving Service at St Paul's today. I think this is the only public function I was ever at. Beautiful and memorable of course and full of colours—and what a glorious organ—it nearly made me musical. Few things could make one's mind travel so far back into history. But the blinded men! No, no they don't look cheerful as we are told. They are the saddest thing I have ever seen. They seem so far away. If you want to punish the Kaiser you could do it by leaving him alone with his thoughts among these men.

I hear Charles Whibley is depressed. Probably nothing in it, but just in case now is the time for you to write him a nice letter.

Now for the grand meal of my week—I dine alone at a restaurant, lucky dog! 'Sir Jas was the envied of all observers as he took his seat.'

20 July '19

I had a very nice time with you and am glad I went to Thorpness.

Recd. with thanks much enjoyment. J. M. Barrie, 20/7/1919. (I hear you say 'You sign your name here').

My luck pursued me all the way, which may be briefly translated: There was a dining car in my train.

Grand offer from Mary Pickford. Replied with an honest kersey 'no'. I have sometimes regretted saying Yes but don't remember ever regretting saying No. That is an aphorism, or pretty nearly, and should be inscribed on the seats in my Walk.[2] I was a bit hurt at not seeing extracts from my works neatly painted all over the place.

[To Stanton, Broadway, Worcestershire]   19 November '19

I have no doubt something of the kind could be done and of course I would be delighted to do my very best therein. I think it all very plucky of you and don't doubt you would find some

---

[1]In August of 1918 Lady Cynthia had become Barrie's secretary.
[2]At Thorpness many places were found to have been named after Barrie's works, and a road called Barrie Walk.

entertainment in it also if you were physically fit for strenuous work. You are not at present, and not a finger would I raise in the matter till you are, that's flat. I mean you could not do the actual work yet, but of course we could go on with the preliminaries.

The Admirable Crichton would have been the very thing for you—Lady Mary—and I presume I could have arranged this, but it is already done though the film is not yet 'released'. However, it would have necessitated your being in U.S.A. and indeed for a month on an island in the Pacific where they lived the wild life of the play and had (Ian Hay who went with them told me) an extraordinarily good time. However, there are others of mine as well as of other people's, which will be done here. I know the head people on both sides (it was they who gave me that cinema machine) and the chief ones are in America. I'd write them or wire them of course with pleasure. I'd better know first what precisely you mean by saying you think you would get an offer from them here. At any rate don't get it yet. Probably best not to do anything till I can have a talk with you about it all. What you ought to do for the present moment is to stay on where you are as long as you possibly can (and a few days longer) if it is suiting you. You have got to get fat and we shall weigh you daily in the scales that Simon[1] has doubtless already made the acquaintance of. I have a feeling that you worry about lots of things unnecessarily. You have got to take life as a comedy though it is often a pretty bloody one. Fond and foolish mothers tend mistakenly to think they should be wealthy for the sake of their children who will otherwise miss this, that and the other. On the contrary, blessed are they who are poor (which does not mean that we mustn't get all we can out of the cinema!) It begins to look as if the pulpit were my proper sphere, so I desist. In finding those cheques you have presented me with at least £1,700.[2] If you were a boy (as you would have had to be in *Crichton*) you would cry 'Halves' before opening your hand on these occasions. A long letter for a left hander. There seems nothing worth sending on at present. P.S. You are the most abject object before a glass of wine that I have ever known.

[1]Son of Herbert and Cynthia Asquith, born in 1919.
[2]In the clearing out of drawers forgotten cheques to the value of £1,700 had been found by his secretary.

You are evidently having a more hilarious time than I, as the
boys went off with their old nurse to the seaside on the 23rd,
and I have been sitting in my room practically ever since,
sometimes without Brown or anyone, and sneaking in the dark
to restaurants where they don't have any interest in me, as a
person not in demand. (It would be rather a neat ending to
hang oneself on a Christmas tree.) This all looks like an appeal
for pity, but I have been able to work and so am contented. I
have also got gout (hurray!)

Enclosed is a note about your filming. They are cautious
coves, you see, but from a covering letter I know they are very
interested. This Mr Ford is to see me soon as he arrives. In
the meantime I warn you you make a great mistake if you don't
get those photographs done I spoke about. Of that when you
return.

You will be uplifted to hear that all those cheques you raked
out are good, except about £30 perhaps. Rehearsing *Crichton*
now. I sometimes see you walking on and whirling Miss Julia
James out of the way. I'll get a box sometime for Michael for
P.P. It will give you some awful hours in after evenings
probably.

3 January '20

I shall be so joyful to see you on Friday, and won't you just
find a pillowcase-ful of letters on your desk. I hope you all at
Pixton Park said 'Rabbits' as soon as the clock struck twelve on
New Year's eve. According to Nico it makes you secure for the
year, and he yelled it out triumphantly on Big Ben's heels. We
then retired to bed with an unwonted feeling of security.

Freyberg was in last night—the first I had heard of him for a
week. The fury of writing, for which he has a great natural gift,
is the cause. I have seldom seen anyone so struck down by this
malady, he already looks the pale student of the midnight oil.
He may talk vaguely of mundane affairs but all the time words
like 'no adjectives', or 'the art of writing' or 'by style I mean'
keep falling off his lips where they gather unbeknown; and
every hour of the day, so to speak, he is going over the top,
waving manuscripts, and reading them to enemy prisoners.

I got a lot of New York press-cuttings about *Mary Rose*
today, contradictions of each other, etc. The only good thing I

found was that what my work failed in was robustness. I haven't seen it put exactly thus before, but I fancy it is exactly right. The Peter Pan Co here are in great feather, as they have beaten all the box-office records of the St James's Theatre.

Why can't I be more robust? You see how it rankles. Also, I am very distressed at the way our cricketers are doing in Australia. I almost weep over them, tho' not robustly.

[To Sussex Place]   Royal Albion Hotel, Brighton 17 Mar. '20
We have had a gorgeously sunny day here for our first, and who knows but I may soon be challenging Carpentier and wearing him down by my superior agility on my pins. We have had some bouts in the bowling alley on the pier, and if I was beaten it was a pretty near thing. The only person I know here is Miss Marie Löhr. She sent her child, Jane, up to play with me, but Jane after a brief scrutiny of us elected for Michael. However, I was allowed to be a dog and a chair and a telephone receiver and things like that. Harry Preston[1] still shakes hands after what I conceive to be semaphore signalling. He gets more out of life than most of us. Hotel is quiet just now but the stars will no doubt come in a rush for the week-end. Your letter has just come in and I was very glad to have it. It is a nice sort of a letter. Now to dress for our fashionable meal. When I mention that I wear a made-up tie I have probably told you the most damning thing about me. No, I don't know about that.

[To Margate]   Adelphi Terrace House 10 May '20
Such a birthday I had, and all owing to you. I wonder how many years you knocked off me at that little table. I think I must have seemed to be getting young again to everybody at the other tables, and I was revealed to their startled eyes as a stripling—I expect I looked handsome (I felt it), and I talked (this is the impression I carried away) like a Greek God. Here I sit, thinking of myself as a remarkable person—I could rush out and be photographed—I beg to state that I am a wonder. Of course it is you who are those things, you who are the wonder. You are an artist, and I am your chief work, and to think that you made this grand thing out of me in an hour or so, with the Ritz for your atelier! You see it is over myself that I am elated. I give you all the credit but I am drunk over the result. I don't

[1]Sir Harry Preston, Brighton hotel-proprietor.

know that I do give you all the credit. I give you most of it, but I hang on to a feeling that there must have been lying dormant in me qualities—absolute qualities, so that you did not create them but only fanned them into life. Wasn't I witty? Those sparkling things in your frock were not there when we went in to dinner, they were just bits of my conversation that stuck to you. All this letter is about myself—can't be helped. I am hoping though that you are having a 'lovely' time at Margate with Michael and Simon, and that Michael is telling you wonderful tales suitable to your years, and Simon pulling your hair, and smiling. Tell him he can have all mine on condition that he smiles as he tears it out. May they have as good a birthday as mine when they are my age. And so, goodnight.

4 June '20

. . . I had a visit at tea-time from General Maitland, the man who crossed the Atlantic twice in air-ship, and has the simple far-seeing eyes of those who have done the big things. All soldiers have it nowadays to some extent. Nansen has it more than anyone I have seen, as if the eyes—holes in his case rather than eyes—were fixed for ever on scenes dark to me. I want Maitland to meet you. He is bringing in the surrendered Zeppelin tomorrow and feels rather sorrowful for its officers, who have to hand it over on English soil. They are to be chivalrously treated. (There is also the possibility of their leaving an infernal machine in it.)

6 June '20

I got some paper from the Hardys[1] to write you a letter in the train, but I am not clever enough, the words got jumbled like a broken film and I fear this is too late for the last post. A man sat opposite me writing with the greatest ease—nothing else dashing about him except that he carried his handkerchief in his sleeve, which also is beyond me. It was lovely to get your letter this morning, and I had a very good time altogether at Margate. Hardy took me yesterday to the place where he is to be buried, and to-day he took me to see the place where he would like next best to be buried. There is something about him more attractive than I find in almost any other man—a simplicity that really merits the adjective *divine*—I could conceive some of the

[1] Thomas Hardy and his wife at Max Gate, Dorset.

disciples having been thus. We went to see the rectory and church that was Barnes's (the Dorsetshire poet). I should like you to read to me that beautiful thing of his in the Oxford Book of Verse. I want you to read much more to me. The Hardys both want you down there, and said you were a lovely person which of course I pooh-poohed. You delight and alarm me by thinking I still have it in me to write a good book, not to speak of a play. There was a time when I rather thought I could do something good if I could find some person who thought so too. Vanitas vanitatum.

Tremendous long journey back. We stopped an hour or so at a place called Westbury junction, apparently just to give us all a rest. Several times we left it, but we always hurried back. I seem to remember an old lady travelling from this country to Australia who said that the worst part of the journey was over when you got past Westbury junction.

I went to bed last night at 11 o'clock. What do you think of that. And I fell asleep too, but woke up about 1. This makes your going to a ball on Tuesday seem like turning night into day. Your only dance of the week—regular hours and Bengers all other evenings. It was sad the car's behaving badly—my own experience though is that they are always hours later than they think they'll be. I read the play —— gave me. Dreadful rot. It is now somewhere about midnight, and I have not been up so late for a round of the clock.

18 June '20

Ichabod! The glory has departed from this flat. You have taken it away in one of those boxes, I suppose.

I have been busy with poor Freyberg most of the day, got him to 17 Park Lane[1] about 3 and have lately got back from a second visit. It was very necessary he should be there, as his leg has all gone discoloured, and at the best this will spread before he gets better. They have had many such cases with soldiers as the result of wounds, and the best that can be said at present is that though troublesome it is not considered dangerous. If it is an average case he should be pretty right in a week—it might be quicker or a good deal longer. They hope to get the headache and temperature under control soon. You should write him tomorrow. I told him of your threat to read to him, and I saw

[1]Sir Douglas Shields's nursing-home, much used by Barrie and his friends.

176

him giving you another point. Though not crushed by your writing another letter to your godmother I keep wondering what she could have spotted as un-Cynthiaish in mine. If it was the spelling I beg to say that I left that in all confidence to you. Besides you can really spell better than I do. This is so at any rate in that book about your children, which by the way is a lovelier book than I could ever write. In your poetry book there is a poem with no words to it called 'Cynthia' which is your contribution. You have often read it to me without knowing, but I am rather good at reading it myself.

I am so glad I like all your friends. On the whole the one I should most like to like me is Mary Herbert.

Now for the post.

10 July '20

You wouldn't recognise the flat now. Three youths in it for the moment—Michael and Nicholas and Michael's friend Buxton. M. in Spanish garb, N. magnificent in Eton rosettes, cane, tall hat—B. sublime in mauve waistcoat—a Harrow lad but otherwise commendable. No Bengers at night in kitchen—sardines instead. Hallo, are you still there? Buxton went to a dance last night and took the key of my desk instead of key of the door. M. sat in lift at foot of stairs from 12 to 3 awaiting his return—with claret and a loaf.

I went with N. to the Lords match. 15,000 tall hats—one cad hat (mine); 15,000 stiff collars, canes, shiny faces—one soft collar, cudgel, dreary face (mine). The ladies comparatively drab fearing rain but the gents superb, colossal, sleek, lovely. All with such a pleased smile. Why? Because they know they had the Eton something or the Harrow something. They bestowed the something on each other, exchanged with each other as the likes of me exchange the time of day. I felt I was nearer to grasping what the something is than ever before. It is a sleek happiness that comes of a shininess which only Eton (or Harrow) can impart. This makes you 'play the game' as the damned can't do it; it gives you manners because you know in your heart that nothing really matters so long as you shine with that sleek happiness. The nearest thing to it must be boot polish. Does this bore you? Am I at it again? Observe I say nothing about Winchester, nor the little cane with tassel that Simon will carry some day.

I shall be so glad to see you again on Monday. It's sad your being so far away though I know you are being an enchanting mother all the time.

[To Amiens]   20 July '20

I don't expect you will get this for years and years. You won't go to Amiens, or it won't go, or they will give you someone else's missive, or the French president will fall out of the train with it or on it, or some such mishap, and then some day when you are quite an old lady, Simon 'now grown to man's estate', will be aeroplaning you over France and will drop down at Amiens for petrol and the tin will be tied up in my letter, and you and he will read it at some auberge over a bottle of wine and compare notes about the writer. Simon will be jocular, but you perhaps will be pensive.

You will see a good deal in the next few days to make you pensive, and though there may be sightseers about who seem blatant and noisy they will nearly all be people who have lost some of their best on those battlefields. Sad enough hearts among them, though their faces may belie it. I think it good for you to go, must be good for everyone to get means to a knowledge of what 'glorious war' really is. All the troubles that are in the world now are probably good for us for that same reason. I was never in Amiens, but I was in Cassel in 1916, and there got the help that led me to finding George's[1] grave. I remember Cassel as standing high on a level plain, and headquarters higher than the rest of it. Freyberg had a lot of association with it. He went with me last night to *Mary Rose*. Nesbitt was very good indeed as Simon but did not seem to last out for the final scenes. There is a chance of getting Leon Quartermaine, who I thought long ago would be very right in the part. You have probably seen him—perhaps as Mercutio when Ellen Terry was the nurse. I had Mr Hayman in yesterday, and Colonel House comes today and the U.S.A. Ambassador and his wife tomorrow, so you see I am for the nonce surrounded by America, north, south, east and west. I would so much rather have you reading Comus to me, and letting me know by your face when the special bits were coming. You do read beautifully.

Here am I forgetting that you are an old lady sitting at an

[1]Llewelyn Davies.

auberge with a gigantic Simon who has actually persuaded you to split a bottle with him. Funny that this letter should turn up after all these years. What a delicious old lady you look, sitting there in the shade, a trifle frail. Up comes Simon to take care of you just as you used to take care of him.

[To Stanway]   Eilean Shona 13 August '20

We have now been on the island a whole night, a wild rocky romantic island it is too, and if I had Michael of yours with me, as I do wish I had, we should have made great play of putting this in a bottle and letting it be picked up a la Crichton castaways. It might have reached you almost as soon, for the first five miles of its journey takes the better part of a day apparently as it lies at Acharacle a night before it sets out on the longer but easier part of its journey. You won't get it, I can see, before Sunday. Mothersil! I scorn your implication. All our sea-faring was on an inland loch as calm as the Serpentine and not much wider though there were a score or so of miles, and we had to stop now and again to get a bottle of milk from a rowing boat or give a sack of flour to another. All through the 'Pretender's' country—we lunched where he raised his standard and round about here he hid in caves when his sun went so quickly down. The sun has gone down for all who used to be great hereabouts—we look out on an aged keep where the last of the clan Ronald said farewell to his last acre.

This is a very lovely spot, almost painfully so. 'I am never merry' when I see sweet Scotia, or never merry any more, and have chosen a room where I can hide from the scenery. I should like to emerge with Simon in my arms, thus we could defy it together, laugh at it and still keep our feet. But for want of him I am better placidly peeping out on the rose garden to which I am still equal. It almost taketh the breath away to find so perfectly appointed a retreat on these wild shores. The Ritz could not do us better. Such bathrooms! Such a tennis court (the loveliest I should think in Britain—how could anyone with eyes let them rest for a moment on a ball!) Such boats. There is a tame lamb that would trot with Michael everywhere and lean against his legs when he stood still. Appliances to answer every thought. It is certainly a mighty fine present the Howard de Waldens have made us, or rather that you have passed on to us. Superb as is the scene from the door, Michael, who has already been to the top of things, says it's nought to what is revealed there—all the western isles of Scotland lying at our feet. A good spying-ground for discovering what really became of Mary Rose. Speaking of her, it was all fixed up before I left London that Nesbitt should play Harry and Simon in U.S.A. He is in great feather, as his salary jumps from £8 or so a week to £50, but he doesn't know that this was done mainly to please you, as indeed it was. So please be rather elated.

Picturesque outlooks do not an Eden make, and I daresay I shall be thinking with Dr Johnson that the best road in Scotland is the road out of it. However this month will pass like all the others and a good deal of loneliness won't blot out a single memory of your visit. As for going long walks, the island nips the project rather, though it is some eight miles round. I shall sally to the mainland at times in a boat, and set off alone for Ardnamurchan and other toothbreakers. The publishers clamour for more plays and I have brought *Kiss for Cinderella* with me with the pious hope of preparing it for them. It seems trumpery work. I like your wanting me to get started on a book but I don't have any book inside me to transcribe. Don't think I haven't gone a-fishing for it. I am not naturally an idler, it was always a glory to me to be at work, but I can get hooked on to nothing that seems worth playing.

It will probably be, as often before, that I shall kick up a pebble someday, and make more of it than ever a man made before. I am almost a genius at the occasional pebble. Funnily built man—especially to come from Scotland. Oh, how I grin at myself at times, but with the wrong side of the face. Did I ever tell you of the philippic I once wrote (anonymously) against J. M. B.? It appeared in Henley's paper, and some of my admirers were so indignant with him that they withdrew their subscriptions.

Lots of books here (finely bound) but last night I read in your Shakespeare book which travelled north without a ticket. It was the next best thing to listening to you in the chimney corner.

Don't you try to be funny about writing once a fortnight.

I dined with Freyberg and Mason before I left, and B.F. was at his best, talked in a way that made me proud of him far into the small hours. He didn't think there was much chance of his getting here, for which I'm sorry.

17 August '20

I had hoped to have a letter ere now, but the post has gone again. I do hope all is well with you. You get more delicate at a distance. This island has changed from sun to rain, and we have now had about 60 hours of it so wet that you get soaked if you dart across the lawn. It's dry for a moment and anon I will be observed—or rather I won't be, for there is no one to observe me—playing clock golf by my lonely self. I am mostly by my lonely self, and a little island is not the best place for strenuous exercise in wet weather, the roads—or rather the road—ending as soon as it sets off and the heather so wet and slippery that as you ascend you suddenly disappear from view. The others are out sea-fishing with Jock Oliver and Audrey Lucas who have arrived, and the party is merrier without me.

I have got started on the *Kiss for Cinderella*, rather like digging up the dead and holding an autopsy, but you are requested not to shout at the performer as he seems to be doing his best. You shall have your way about those spectacles but as for the sculpting of me, woman forbear. Michael has been drawing more sketches of me, and they are more than enough. He has a diabolic aptitude for finding my worst attributes, so bad that I indignantly deny them, then I furtively examine myself in the privacy of my chamber, and lo, there they are.

I enclose two letters to answer. The one about *Mary Rose* —refer him to the manager, Haymarket; the other to the committee of the Society of Playactors. Some other dull things I have answered or destroyed. One from a Californian lady says she had such a nice letter from you that she is encouraged to write more fully (and she does too). You should read Enid Bagnold's *Happy Foreigner*, very good, and with one chapter called 'The River' which seems to me to be rather fine romance. There are some pretty things about love in it, very delicately and freshly done as if they had come flying out of a nice mind. I am writing to Beb[1] about his poems, which have been forwarded. Simon comes handsomely out of them, but I think the 'Village Sermon' is easily the best, and a very fine thing, 'thoughts that voluntarily move harmonious numbers.'

[1]Herbert Asquith's nick-name.

Benger-time is the quietest hour of the day here, everyone else long in bed, and I can't even fly to the bottle as water is our only drink—water and an occasional two tablespoonfuls of my sleeping draught, as I have not got the hang of sleeping well yet on islands. However I am very well. I do hope I shall have a letter to-morrow.

22 August '20

I flatter myself I have my own way of spelling Cyncie, and that the others don't rise to the *y*. But my way gives it a rather cynical look, which is not in your character as I know it. Cynics become bores after 23 or so, up to which it is their solemn right. I don't know that I ever exercised the right much, though it may be that college mags would belie me. My first contribution to a magazine was perhaps a little cynical as it described my runaway marriage at Gretna Green some 60 years before and was written as by an old man recalling his salad days. Did I ever tell you of my two first tales, which were contributed to some newspaper that advertised therefor? My chief memory of them is that they had to be 20,000 words long and that the honorarium (as it was always called) was £3 a tale. (A three act play is about 14,000 words). The first was accepted because it was considered to improve as it went on but the lack of excitement in the first word was deplored. So I began the next with a wedding, and just when the words 'Do you take this man?' were spoken there was an eclipse, and when it cleared the bride was gone. (Highly commended.)

We have an addition to our party here of Mrs Lucas, who followed Audrey yesterday. I went to Acharacle to meet her, and had a sense of elation in being once more on the mainland. It was also pleasant to have a whole hour in which I did not see the sea. You credit me with more energy than I possess in thinking I look upon a 10-mile island as not giving me sufficient scope for walking. What we really are is a mountain stuck in the sea, with no roads round it except paths that give in after two miles. Of course I ought to bound up the hills like Robinson Crusoe after goats, but though I do climb a bit it isn't a daily joy.

To think of Simon having set forth on his second year! The caterpillar was a mannish way of celebrating it, but he doesn't really know what life is till he comes to wasps.

I am interested to hear that you have cut off your hair. I may say that I have cut off my head. It was rather an expense, and the general opinion here is that I look better without it.

I have now got to go out and play in the clock-golf tournament for the championship of Eilean Shona. How I wish you were here and that, instead, I was setting off with you along the shore, past the saw mill to the forest where the shy deer are.

26 August

Have just come in from a prodigious walk over mountains whose very names call for stout climbers—was cheered all the way by thoughts of modest boasting about it over the tea-cups; but all is vain—it is flouted by Michael as a thing of nought and a mere beginning of his excursions. I am chastened and reminded of a Swiss mount I left with the same pleasant sensation, to be told at the hotel that it was the local cleric's favourite morning stroll and that he had done it 250 times. That tennis court as to which you seem to have doubts is I assure you a good deal played on and I myself have not only performed on it but have been reading the Badminton book on how to become a dab at it. I am now a dab, except for (a) my service, (b) my difficulty in taking other people's services, (c) the net bars my finest efforts. If Michael is not playing (he is extraordinarily energetic up here) he is drawing such oil-portraits of me that if I believed they did me justice I would throw myself from our highest peak. I have an uncomfortable feeling that his portraits of other persons are rather like them.

I am hacking away at 'Cinderella', scarcely worth while perhaps but it makes me look less idle than the rest of the party, which has now been added to by a friend of Nico, a perfect Etonian and about seven feet high.

It does seem a pity that Michael and Simon are losing their Margate colouring, but I don't know that they would retain it over here. It is not very bracing unless you are on the heights, though very wholesome. The Scotch place for them would be Braemar or the like, where the air stings you as with pebbles. I am very glad you are happy in your old home, I don't think I could be happy in mine any more, too many ghosts though I can be very happy thinking of it.

You don't seem over-cheerful at being away from your children, but consider the coming reunion. Michael taking you as a fixture and entirely reliable has doubtless been exploring the uncertainties, and you will come on him again as something fresh, like a new game. Simon will deceive you with his smile, which is not really caused so much by pleasure at seeing you as pride in remembering you. I suppose there is very little about children that could not be learned from a puppy that a friend of Michael's has brought here. It too is full of fears about life and has an eye ready for the policeman, though one has never struck these shores. We are a very Etonian household and there is endless shop talked, during which I am expected to be merely the ladler out of food. If I speak to the owner of the puppy he shudders but answers politely and then edges away. Our longest conversation will be when he goes:

He (with dry lips but facing the situation in the bull-dog way): Thank you very much for having me. Awfully good of you.

I: Nice to have you here. (Exeunt in opposite directions).

Do my letters seem aged? I certainly feel so here. I have a conviction that they secretly think it indecent of me to play tennis, which however I am only suffered to do as a rare treat. They run about and gather the balls for me and in their politeness almost offer to hold me up when it is my turn to serve. By the way, what an extraordinarily polite game tennis is. The chief word in it seems to be 'sorry' and admiration of each other's play crosses the net as frequently as the ball. I fancy this is all part of the 'something' you get at public schools and can't get anywhere else. I feel sure that when any English public school boy shot a Boche he called out 'Sorry'. If he was hit himself he cried, 'Oh, well shot'.

It is a heathenish business getting away from these isles, which once they open to you are reluctant to let you go. At early morn you get across, then drive, then 3 hours on boat, then 3 hours' wait at Glenfinnan, then on to Fort William, where you start your journey. I expect to get back on Saturday morning, and it will be a joy to see you on Monday.

[To Grasmere]   2, Robert Street, Adelphi 17 September '20
You seem to have got into the hands of the right kind of landlady. She reminds me from your description of a real

angel who looked after me in my last year at Edinburgh University, and was loved beyond all words by every student who came under her spell. In after years I used to visit her, and she would say to me, 'There's one of your stage plays was at the theatre here and oh, I wanted to go and see it, but oh, I couldna dare.'

I am deeply moved by your giving me an address to go to for my hair restorer. I see myself setting forth, and choosing a wet day when I can dodge in under the concealment of an umbrella. You don't seem to be aware that I am rather proud of that bald spot. Also I can't find it in this flat. I remember a man in a club who had so little hair at the back, and that in isolated dabs, that at a distance you could not tell whether he was presenting a front or a back view. Bets used to be made about it, and then we crept towards him to find out. So much for hair.

Nicholas goes back to school today in all the excitement of a new house, as his old tutor is now vice-provost. He has a room in the new house which was the meeting place of 'Pop' in its 100-years-ago days, but little will the eminent ghosts disturb him.

I had a man in to-day to talk of *Peter Pan* cast. If you know of two engaging creatures for Peter and Wendy let me have them.

The pile of letters to answer grows.

Interrupted.

[To Stanway]   Adelphi Terrace House 9 December '20
If you knew how much you are missed here you—no, you wouldn't, you would be pleased. The lift even has got sulky, and taken to creaking and your desk is a most forlorn object. It will be lovely to see you on Tuesday. It does sound sad about Gosford but these enormous houses seem to have ceased to be natural homes for single families, and I suppose your mother is really 'gladder than she is sorry'.

There is a terrific number of the *Bookman* out with about 30 articles on me. Even Freyberg gave up trying to read them. There's a good one by Chesterton who says I am 'the most diffident of men and the most impudent of artists'. What do you say to that? There is an awful full-page picture of me, which is more like a tallow candle in distressed circumstances, or Michael says it's like a leper. On the other hand there is a perfectly superb one with flashing eyes and the noblest moustache in the Army. I think it is the finest thing I have ever seen, and in the dead of night I sit alone gazing at it with an exultation that even drink cannot give.

I went to the County Council's discussion about whether acting is a Fine Art. (Left sitting.)

Discussions at Dramatic Academy about a special performance—that single acts of classic plays by three different authors then in the room should be given. I proposed that my part should be to run the three acts together into a consecutive play. (No seconder.)

Hope you don't have to stay away longer than Monday.

[To Pixton]   23 December '20

My calendar says it is the 23rd of October, but I know better. How little I have done in these two months. On reflection perhaps it is the 23rd of October. Your note only arrived late last night, when Michael was sitting up with me, and conducting himself almost suspiciously delightfully to me. Then in the watches of the night came to the door our guardsman,[1] and he also was suspiciously delightful. When people are delightful to me I tend to wonder what you have been up to. When I use the word suspicious in this connection my eyes journey in your direction, I can't think of any one who is so eager as you to give pleasure to other people. Your first instinct is always to telegraph to Jones the nice thing Brown said about him to Robinson. You have sown a lot of happiness in that way. I see it growing like yellow corn here and there in desolate places.

I trust you will all have a very good Christmas at Dulverton. The nearest I ever was was when we were on Exmoor, and had the rectory where Blackmore wrote *Lorna Doone*. The great man who owned all the fishing was Nicholas Snowe, and the boys used to make Nicholas, aged six, intercede with him for fishing facilities on the grounds that they were of the same name—successfully too. Michael and Nicholas went off by the 8.20 today, very gay and confident, and I began my festivities by having a gorgeous long lie in bed. I then arose, and put on your desk letters that seem to me to have Christmas cards in

[1]Freyberg.

186

them. Two little boxes I opened—from people I had forgotten—and I at once hurled handkerchiefs at them. —— brought the cigars and I don't know whether they are a gift, but I have risked despatching them to Gilmour. One thing I shall never despatch farther than my pocket is my little knife, which is a gem of all the virtues, and I didn't know that there had ever been any one clever enough to invent it.

I am to dine with the Guards on Christmas Eve at St James's Palace, and expect it will be interesting or at least 'massive and concrete'. Tonight I am engaged to have a little dinner with myself and hope I shall get on well together.

27 December '20

Christmas on Friday, Christmas on Saturday, Christmas on Sunday, Succumbed on Monday. However, this is the last day of it. Don't give in. Pull hard, my hearties. See, little Katie, a glimpse of sunshine breaking into the dark wood as we break out of it. In a few hours Christmas will once more lie behind us. Eyes front, march . . .

Cables from New York about the *Mary Rose* production make me doubtful of its course there. They say the audience was enthralled but the press can't make out what it means. I wish you would tell me what it means, so that we can settle this matter once and for all.

I am entertaining myself successfully by going over the *P. Pan* film scenario again and putting in new things. One could go on doing this till doom cracks, and then put in the crack.

I have had some more Christmas offerings, nearly always from people I didn't send to, but as to handkerchiefs I have now struck. This office is closed.

I must now arise and have my silent lunch at the R.U.E. side of fireplace, as we say in the drama. Please pull in your chair.

31 December. '20

I can see that you are being very over-driven with this influenza ravaging the house and yourself so unfit, as unfit you must be with such a low temperature. It makes one, in my experience, more 'down' than a high temperature, and I feel so sorry for you. I trust Beb is getting right now, and that Michael and Simon have escaped. I am sure you are being very brave and good through it all. I expect you would all be better back in London.

You are right about the two friends of yours I met. The poor one sounds the more interesting. I like poor people best. They are so much more human if they don't get bitter, and they can also be human in their bitterness. The poor are at their best (and easiest) when they are all poor together, and not flung among the other kind. I have been meditating making the subject of my awful St Andrew's address 'On the Advantage of being born Poor'. You may say what you like (and I hear you) but I think I could make out a good case for it. But it is all much easier in Scotland than south of the Tweed.

I haven't, by the way, any hesitation in saying that you can without misgivings spend the money for the children on their garments. If the donors had meant necessarily toys they would have sent them. Besides, children have pleasure in their clothes though they may also look on them as their lawful right. I once told the boys, ages ago, that my only kilt was made out of an old pair of curtains, and for years they cast it up at me. I can't now remember whether the actual incident took place. At my school we used to play another school at cricket, and they worried us by playing the same boy in flannels for the 1st XI and in knickerbockers for the 2nd and in a kilt for the 3rd. We could never quite prove it but he was a great thorn in our side.

I haven't got Max's book yet, and I look forward to your reading his clergyman to me. I know the essay on 'Servants' which is vastly good. How I do wish you were back reading to me, but humorous matter is sacrilege from your lips which were made to read of 'magic casements'. The *Lost Girl* I haven't ventured into yet, except the first chapter, which is rather hard to the teeth.

[To Stanway]   1 April '21

I have just remembered that the masseur is at this moment on his way to me. When that April with his showeres swoote hath run his course, I swear no more massage. Nicholas has arrived with his young friend, and they have at once purchased gramophone records that roar and hiss louder than they ever roared and hissed before. I don't see how I can help becoming musical in the end.

I think the next time you go away I will take my revenge by stealing Simon. One leap over the rails when Nannie has turned her head in the garden. I seize him in my arms and tear off with him, shrieking- gee-gee, gee-gee. At the door I have waiting, not a taxi but a horse. We mount the horse and away. In case he gets tired of the same horse I have horses stationed along the line of route. We leap from one to another. We arrive at this address. We have a horse in the lift to brighten the journey upwards. Brown receives us wearing a horse's head. Horses are stabled where there used to be my desk and yours. A cot is provided shaped like a horse. Instead of rocking it neighs. Mrs Stanley gallops round outside the windows. I think in some such way I could keep him going for a few hours.

I'm uncommon sorry not to be at Stanway while Michael is there. It would have been my chance to wheedle my way into his good graces by the recounting of tales. Perhaps not. Perhaps all my capacity in that line has finally dried up.

[To Cromer]   27 April '21
    . . . Did I ever tell you of how the girls at the mixed school I was at in Scotland had a plebiscite about which boy had the nicest smile, and the brother of one divulged to me that I had won. I expect I was very elated, but it made me self-conscious with the result that I have seldom smiled since.

I shouldn't wonder though I nearly smiled during lunch to-day, when the great magnate of the movies was here, and our talk was devoted to the things that matter. An attractive little man—all his Ws' are Vs—with a wistful face that longed to be a hero. I think this is one of the best characteristics of the Americans, they long for the great and good and passionately resent the second best, though those who aspire to it only may rise higher than they. They can only be approached from the emotional side. He liked the pictures of Miss Sturt, and she is being asked to be tested in P. Pan clothes at the studio on Tuesday. This of course is far from meaning that she will necessarily be chosen to play it. He says there are 200 applicants of note in the movie world.

Friday morning I am going with Nicholas to see a private view of *Sentimental Tommy*. I dread this. And yet I remember very little about it, and have not read a page of it since I passed the proof-sheets. Did I ever tell you that I told R.L.S. in a letter that he was to be the hero, and that he came to a bad end. He wrote back 'Am I hangit?' which gave me the idea for the actual end. On the 'screen' I expect to see a very different end, though I don't know how it is accomplished.

Freyberg was in to-day, and I wrote in one of the books to his mother something about her 'splendid son'. He is to stay here from Saturday till he goes off, which is on the following Wednesday evening. On Friday I am going to the Academy dinner, but it isn't a late affair, as it begins at 7, and even Academy oratory runs dry in time so I hope you'll ring me up. I do miss you from this flat to which the dear nature of you has brought so much sunshine.

[To Margate]   17 June '21
I hope you are having a happy quiet time with the children and I wish I was on the sands watching Michael achieve his grand success of the day in handing the baby back to the Punch man or teaching languages and deportment to Simon whom I do assure you I love very much. Yesterday being Michael's[1] birthday seemed specially sad to me as it wore on but it passed as everything passes and I had quite a good night. I won't ever attempt to thank you for the loveliness of mind and heart with which you have helped and encouraged me at this time. Any courage I have got seems to come from your example.

[To Pixton]   7 September '21
Stanway[2] was, and the great glory of Stanway, or at least the happiness, or at least I was much happier there than I could have been anywhere else. It was even deliciously cool in the sun, though I didn't think so at the time—I know it now, for London is a mist of the accumulated heat of months—old dead air. My only news is that Bernard Freyberg is here, arrived this afternoon out of the blue and will be staying at the flat for a little. He got your letter about Michael only the day before he left New Zealand, and knew nothing till then. He felt a slight recurrence of his ailment soon after he left N.Z. but otherwise has had none for three months.

[1]Michael Llewelyn Davies; he had been drowned on May 19th.
[2]Barrie had leased Stanway for the summer from Lord Wemyss, and did this for many years to come.

I wrote your mother today. As to you, Stanway is just another name for you. Instead of going over the barn[1] with the Australians I could just have described *you*—not as being in Doomsday Book as a fact but as a prediction. I could elaborate that idea as a story for Michael. One of the best things that happened to me at Stanway was that he and I became such friends, and I think it will always last. Even Simon would cry 'No more' to deaf ears. I had a splendid letter from Bridgeman, and Nico wrote him at once of its successful reception. I'll keep it to show to you if my pockets don't bulge to bursting point before you come back. Remember how much I am longing to have you staying here again. I still feel, indeed it grows on me in absence, that you had a great deal too much to do looking after so many people and ever-lastingly so sweet and gracious to them while you were often not really well. I suppose those and other qualities had sunk into Nicholas when he delivered his eulogy. How many things I might have done to help you that I didn't do and how often I was irritable and depressed and selfish—it is as if I was trying to see whether I could break down the patience and sweetness and loveliness of mind that go to the making up of Cynthia. I never succeeded, and I hope I'll never try any more.

12 September '21

I hoped to hear from you to-day and am not at all sure that with the cares of Stanway off your shoulders you haven't collapsed and been put to bed. It might also be the best thing for you. It is all very well to say you enjoyed 'reigning' (as your mother puts it to me) at Stanway and of course it was a joy to me that you did, but at the same time there was little relaxation for you and I don't see that it can be accounted a holiday. My feeling, looking back, is that we were all people of to-day, really intruders, being entertained by a lady of the olden times who glided about in a long red gown (she never wore anything else) and was wondrous gracious and melting but composed of elements rarer than we could ever achieve. I think there is some room in Stanway unknown to the rest of us that she came from and returned to, and that if ever we could discover it (as by putting lighted candles in all the windows and then finding which window remained dark) we should see on

[1]Stanway's tithe-barn, mentioned in Domesday Book.

191

the door in the faded writing of an ancestress very like your mother, a card with the words 'Will Shakespeare's Room'. Then when all the other windows were dark that one would light up, and we might peep in and see Will and the lady in gay converse, or she reading Hamlet to him while he wonders whether it is necessary that Ophelia should be gowned in white. So gracious you were to us, but were we really of your epoch and did we ever really touch the gown? The Secret of Stanway. That is my new name for you. I have an idea that if anyone there is of your time it is Prew[1] and that he sometimes hovers round in Elizabethan garments.

To return to the mundane, life creeps on here its petty pace. Many letters, some of which I have consigned to the basket whence no traveller returns, and others answered, and others still I'll send or keep for you. Nicholas had good cricket at Talbots and made 84 not out in one match. Bernard is still with me, and I like having him. He is not quite the Bernard of old—as lovable as ever but as it were with a mystery attached. I am not certain that he is really well though he says he is—his eyes don't look well to me. Or it may only be that he has planned out a new mode of life—almost doggedly he eats little and drinks not at all. He has got a present for you—a frock, which may be professionally described as white with myriads of little holes in it. It is specially adapted he says for playing lawn tennis in. It is only partly made up I think, as there is a difference of opinion between us as to which is the skirt and which the bodice. He has given me a table cloth in so exactly the same style that perhaps it is the bodice.

We were flung into a pleasurable state of elation yesterday evening by the announcement that Charlie Chaplin had called. The manner of it was somewhat attractive. He asked the housekeeper below if I was alone, and being told that Colonel Freyberg was with me he shuffled and muttered that he had just come to have a look round and stole away. What a triumph if I could have ushered him into the Stanway nursery to teach Simon a new way of walking, also how to fire a custard pudding at his dear Nannie's face when she mentioned bed. Nicholas's grand ambition now is to escort him through Eton.

[1]Coachman.

[To Stanway]   15 September '21

Stanway revisited! It will seem rather strange, and now for
the first time I begin to realise that in a sense it was once mine.
My idea, if it suits your mother, would be to come down as
soon as Nicholas returns to school. He goes back on Wednesday
evening so I propose coming on Thursday, reaching Todding-
ton at 7.30. I like that quite as well as getting out at Kingham.

When you confess that you don't feel well you are certainly
feeling in a very poor way and much more in need of doctors
than I am. My opinion is still that you had a great deal too
much to do at Stanway, not if you had been all right perhaps,
but in your state of health—especially in getting up so soon
after that flu got you. That came of having so many visitors
and your determination not to give in. I don't know if you
know it but you are really a very determined character. I
thought Winter[1] looked so much better of his holiday when he
was up the other day. I was saddened to hear of Michael's
'stumps all pitched and no one to play'. I must have a special
game with him to make up. I went yesterday with Bernard
to the Oval to see the last match of the season, and saw
Tennyson much cheered for a good innings. I have had
Michael's landlady up from Oxford with some of his things.
She was extraordinarily kind to him in a mothering way and is
a very sad woman about him. I have been going through his
letters that were lying there. You are the only person I have
to speak to about him and for ever and ever I am thinking
about him. Nicholas was overcome the other day with what it
means to him, and it was only by real courage that he went off
to stay with his friend. Letter gets dull at the end but as I say
I can tell only you of those things.

                                                18 September '21

You are rather hazardous on the subject of Simon. As for
his passionate desire that the puffer should disgorge me, we
shall see. I expect to hear him being lured, cajoled, wished
toward my door on Friday morning, seeing the door opened
as if by him, seeing him enter as if not propelled by a hidden
hand—immediately after which——

'Do you want to go back to Nannie?'
'Ess.' (Curtain).

[1] William Winter, married to Barrie's sister Maggie.

193

This all seems to suggest artfulness on your part, but Nicholas confided to me yesterday 'I compare all ladies now with Lady Cynthia, and they can't stand the test.' As if that were not enough he tells me he has had a letter from Bridgeman asking him to find out quietly whether you read his Collins and what you thought of it.

I had a somewhat cold experience yesterday, going with Jack, Peter, Nico and Gerrie[1] to the storage place to have a last look at the old furniture[2] before it is sold and disposed. Hundreds of familiar articles once very pretty and much cared for, now dusty, disregarded and clammy cold. Even occasional garments of the days when they were babes. Many things they once exulted in. No sentiment about the visit. Only a bored look at the dead. Nothing to complain of in this, it is how the young must take tomorrow on their shoulders. But I felt as if I were one of the articles lying there much more than one of the onlookers. Lots of them I could write a chapter about. I could make a book of them that would give them another day's life. Such things as they wanted to keep were put apart for them.

Nicholas had a great time with Charlie Chaplin who came and stayed till two in the morning. Immaculately dressed in evening garb, and carried all off with ease and skill and grace. He has a rather charming speaking voice, and a brain withal. A very forceful creature and likable. The police who are put on to guard him all produce their own autograph books for him to sign. The ordinary stage drama he called the 'Speakies'. I like Prew's letter and feel more at home with him than ever. And I am glad Michael has managed to range those cricketers under his banner. You had better get a dozen in all of the Australian cricket group, as they seem to be in demand. I decided not to get a cricket ball for M. as the tennis one is safer. Thus careful am I of your progeny, or as Simon would say 'prodigies'.

7 October '21

You rather alarm me by saying you have planned out to 'live by rule' but far more do you alarm me by the dark suggestion that you are to make me live by rule. Freyberg is living by rule as far as I can make out, but how I could be

---

[1] Jack's wife.
[2] From the Llewelyn Davies' house in Campden Hill Square.

made to do it passes me. As for massage, avaunt. Poor Charles Whibley is having very much to live by rule. He returned to the nursing home today to have a second operation—not looking to me any better from the first, and his face much swollen, but he is fairly sanguine and so in rather better spirits. He expects to get down to his own home by Monday. I have just come in late from visiting Jack and Gerrie, Jack in bed after a struggle with the dentists, he pulling the one way and they the other. Michael is touching about the bulging foreheads. You can reassure him from me that if I have one they are of little good. By the way if it suits Beb better his room will be ready for him on Monday, though you don't come till Tuesday. I should certainly like to hear you reading my Scotch. It is always an effort of memory to me to think of you as in any way Scotch. I like to think it, though the symptoms are not apparent, you are so essentially English—Shakespeare's English, like Stanway. In W.S.'s lost work I am sure there is a stage direction, 'Enter Cynthia'.

And now to catch the last post.

[To Sussex Place]   28 February '22

It is just a cloud hanging over you because you have lost the physical power for the moment to blow it away. Matter and spirit are not only allied but may be practically the same thing, and I think this is especially so with you. When rundownness makes you despondent you fall into the way of accusing yourself of all the faults that you are so peculiarly without. Just because you are naturally the most brave person I know, if you falter one instant you turn on yourself for a poltroon. To my mind you are so brave that I should think it a vice in you to have an iota more of that quality. It is strange and almost terrible to me that I go on getting any happiness out of life since Michael's death, but I owe it all to you. You are the sunshine of this flat as much as of your own home and you never come into it that you are not a blessing to me. The good fairy indeed. If you were only a little stronger in health.

[To Pixton]   21 March '22

It must have been icy travelling. I have had both fires going—going up the chimneys mostly for there is no heat in the room. I expect to have to break the ice at the pump anon

when I prepare for that —— affair at which I boggle. Last
night I wandered into the House of Commons, lured by
Donald McLean. They were so soporific that as soon as one of
them woke up and saw that there were not 40 present they
promptly turned out the lights. The fairest sight to me was
Lord Windsor. He lolled, taking up three seats in the toler-
antly bored manner in which they always loll there according
to the pictures I know the House by. None of the others was
doing this, and you could see by his manner that he had been
a member for years and years.

There is quite a pile of correspondence on your desk already
and it is not the only thing in the room that already feels you
have been away for a long time. How I miss you! I feel very
un-gay at thought of the —— treat. I shall shake hands,
scowl shrinkingly in a corner, and so to bed.

St Andrews continues to loom. I write a sentence,[1] and then
walk round and round before I can write another, by which
time I am quite used up. I calculate that at my present rate
of inspiration I could write a three act play in twenty years.
Donald McLean has offered to find a hall for me where I could
practice delivery with no auditor save himself. Too solemn.
I could write a picture of that incident and sit down to it at
once. Anything except an address. My only hope is that
my gawkiness may prove an asset. When I stick, it may turn
out to be a 'Barrieism'.

It isn't that I worry over it. I don't worry enough, Ladies
and Gentlemen.

21 November '22

I have finished the *Three Musketeers* and feel I have now
bidden them a final farewell—*adieu* not *au revoir*. Glorious
rhodomontade or sublime balderdash, it is on the whole the
finest work of fiction in the world; even re-reading when you
are old and scared you can see your old self going strong with it.
Never was anything else quite so gay, unless the summer you
read it first. No 'character-drawing' worth speaking of. Any
dull dog of today could go so much deeper into Milady—but
hey nonny nonny.

For what a long time now I have been only half awake—
except sometimes in the night!

[1] Of his Rectorial address.

I feel I have scored over you by finding the shop where Simon's chocolate letters are sold. It took some finding too. Not for everybody would I go into shop after shop asking for chocolate letters. Speaking of letters, the pile that has faced me here staggereth, but I have been going through them. It was sad to me to leave that happy party in the car and plunge into the lonely train. I found on arrival at Paddington that I had taken a return ticket, as if to give myself an excuse for an early return. I enclose it in case Simon would like to travel up alone in a smoker with Nannie twisted round the window of the next compartment.

12 January '23
I can't settle down to write. I have to hang on to the memory that there were years when I revelled in being up and at it; and that long before I had written any books I was a sort of legend in 'Fleet Street' for the unrelenting doggedness of my turn-out. It begins to look as if you had got at my tap. All the same you really are doing too much, for though I slogged away I did not have in addition a house and children to look after, and a desk-load of another's letters to answer. That desk now with its correspondence presents the appearance of a cart-load of coal just deposited. Nicholas has returned looking as if he had not been much in bed, and completes that effect by a late dance last night and a throat this morning. With a yawn he resumes his belated enquiry into Roman law.

My newest imbecility seems to be that I keep dropping tobacco sparks on my clothes which leave 'round O's' that will engage the educational attention of Simon. I never used to do so, and take it to be the mark of the dodderer, though it may only mean a dampness in the tobacco. Frank puts it thus: 'You are becoming inimical to your clothes, sir.'

[To Stanway]   2 February '23
I got the book of Raleigh fragments, the best thing in it being the Will. That should go down. It would be nice to have an anthology of Wills—not perhaps real ones, but such as his—a lot of people persuaded to do fancy ones. I could probably do not a bad one. I have an idea I once made the Will of Nana in *P. Pan*.

8, Susseks Plaice 13 March '23

My dear James

i am very unhappy and neglected and sow is Michael. U.R the only one we have to look to now. Mother is writing a book about children and she takes notes of all the things we say. Father is writing a book too and he is putting us into it too, and he squeezes us to make us say litrary things. Mother crawls about the nursery stairs listening with the same objec. They have fights which is to get the study to write in. For a test case Michael ran down and called out 'I have flung Simon out of the nursery window same as Punch does the baby,' and all Mother said was 'I'll see to it at one o'clock,' and all Father said was 'All right,—I say, I'll put that in.'

Later. Michael has begun to write a book about children aged three.

Later. Nannie has begun to write a book about children.

What am I to do? Dear James, I appeal to you as the only person I know who is not writing anything. Simon.

P.S. I am writing a book about the kitten.

To Lady CYNTHIA ASQUITH

[To Margate]   Adelphi Terrace House 28 June '23

I am supposing you had not found Michael well enough for 'Dreamland' and are probably now sitting by his bedside instead, both seeing better fireworks. About the happiest times of my life were when I sat similarly with another Michael.

1 July '23

I have had a fear these last two days that you found Michael rather bad when you got down, and now Beb has just been in to say Michael is fairly right again but that you are down. I am so very sorry. I can't fathom this mysterious ailment that seems to haunt the bungalow, and I begin to think it is time you were all out of it, nice a place as it looks. Beb says you have no temperature, and that seems to make it odder.

I had a curious experience on Friday night when I was here alone—woke up on Saturday morning at seven o'clock to find myself lying on the couch in the study fireplace, fully dressed and all the lights on. All I can remember is that I sat or

reclined thereon reading the *Manchester Guardian*. After that a
blank for six or seven hours. I was quite well. All my life I
have had a belief that I could not fall asleep anywhere without
a rug or the like over me. I am rather shy of getting on to that
couch since then.

On our return from Eton Nicholas lapsed into depression—
all due, I think, to the pain of not being any longer an Eton
schoolboy. Eton is written on his heart as deeply as ever
Calais was on that queen's.

[To Lago di Garda]   17 September '23
   To think of your being already basking in Italy if basking be
the right word, for I fear you are not well enough to bask anywhere. It will be very sad to me if you have not enough ease
of mind and body to enjoy this Italian visit. The flat is most
dreary without you and I wander its deserted corridors. Nico
is by way of working at the Acts of the Apostles, and I know he
is doing so when the sounds of slumber reach me from his
arm-chair.

I have been to a rehearsal of *Hassan* and will probably go
to another two. It will be a fine production with a great deal
of poetry and has a striking ballet. The thing I felt to be wrong
was that Ainley as Hassan was superb in speaking the poetry
but was not sufficiently the confectioner—was too much the
romantic hero. A more homely confectioner, quite plebeian, is
my idea though his words often make it difficult. I have not
seen much of the scenery yet, but I think there will be much
beauty in it, especially in the last scene. I have written to your
mother and am now writing to Simon. I hope at any rate that
the film gives some real glimpses of him. The witches (from
my Macbeth thing) come to curse the interlopers at Stanway
but Simon smiles in his sleep and that turns them into beautiful
creatures who remain to bless. But unfortunately we can't
show his smile. It is a great joy to me that he beams on
me as much as ever.

[To Stanway]   11 January '24
  All alone in the flat, as even Nicholas is off for the week-end.
I like much having Maggie and William, but at the same time
it seems a law of my nature that I must be a good deal by
myself. Or with my cough for company, for I have seldom
heard it going so strong. Stout walls these, else would they fall

outwards. Yet it is nothing more than a tickle in the throat. I'd have written yesterday if my fireplace hadn't been full. I've been having a fierce altercation with Mrs Stanley about my pillows—to the effect that if she cannot get me harder pillows I shall have to buy or construct a board. How horrible are pillows so soft that they meet round your face.

Alice is not to be produced till about the 23rd. It is being quite adequately done, but is really to my thinking old-fashioned and little more than a charade. This week's plays in general have had a bit of a slump, all owing to the political situation, they say,—not *P. Pan* which draws its £750 a day regularly.

I am reading *Kangaroo* by D. H. Lawrence. In chunks I don't follow him, but it is very vivid, and the coarsenesses— as if those of an ugly youth creeping out of him like ghosts— are really a very small affair. There are power and poetry in him as in few. He quite misrepresents the feeling of this country in wartime, but perhaps no wonder. A very happy man, with such a passionate interest in himself, roaming the world in search of that self and finding it everywhere. But he is big, and I should think in some ways lovable.

[To Mullion, Cornwall]   18 September '24

It is the nicest of nice letters you send me and turns the soft paper into the finest thing produced by the royal stationer. Of course the Trossachs had their sad memories to me, though they were all memories of very happy times—that long sitting room was as full as any place. On the Loch Katrine boat too! Those hills on the left going from our hotel—I had once such a rush over them shouting his[1] name in terror that something had befallen him. And the joyous return together. But there are infinitely more memories here, and I did enjoy being there with you and yours, and in some ways that enjoyment was added to because of my having been there with him.

This is a lovely day for your first in Cornwall and I hope you will both have a very good time. I wrote to Turley Smith, and if he is back, as I think he is, he will be useful at all events about golf for Beb and perhaps about lodgings.

[To Stanway]   26 October '24

You are so often engaged on errands of kindness. This you

[1]Michael Llewelyn Davies.

will promptly deny, but you are, and I am glad of it and hope this one brings its own reward. Every time you come to me is also an errand of kindness. It has rained I think all the time since you went away—perhaps because you are away—perhaps because there is an election on. I have been smoking a little more, but have dropped the draught though my fits of sleeplessness came back. Fortunately I had a really remarkable novel to beguile the hours, *The Constant Nymph* by a writer unknown to me, a lady (of 23 I'm told) who must be a rather extraordinary person. Also it made me feel old and out of date beyond words. I am looking forward to seeing you on Tuesday and have got a table for five for our election dinner on Wednesday. Now Peter and I steal to the kitchen to cook a meal and how I wish you could be here to help, or to be put in the chair of royalty to watch your servants attending to your wants.

14 November '24

I am so sorry that Simon is unwell again. It may easily be that sitting about in the open air is not the right school for him —they can't always be on the move, and what may be right for one boy may be all wrong for another. I expect it is some very little thing but you will worry, being away. The moment he is ill one realises what a joy he is and most other times besides. I am so glad you can come to dinner on Tuesday and will promise there shall be no speech. Looking back on that effusion[1] it makes me rather ill, and I am very far from having any pleasure in it. No surer sign of mediocrity I think than being accepted as a successful afterdinner speaker. It is really a clout in the face. I saw the *P. Pan* piece of film today with all the cuts I had made in it carried out, and I thought decidedly more favourably of it, but so far it is only repeating what is done on the stage, and the only reason for a film should be that it does the things the stage can't do. I have a letter from 'Mr Owen' saying that life is very cold and harsh on the island where they are doing the pirate ship, etc., and he is sorry for himself sleeping in a wind-lashed tent. Think if you had gone with Simon! Yet he says that the part of Slightly is being played by a five-year-old—probably an experienced pro. Give my love to your mother. I trust that she is much better of the German

[1]At an anniversary dinner of the Printers' Pension Corporation, when the toast was proposed by Winston Churchill and Barrie made a speech.

treatment and hope she is pencil in hand, planning the cricket pavilion. One good thing of the Printers dinner was that I did manage to get my hat-trick in to several people—to some of them twice. Looking forward so to Tuesday.

[To the Hague]   11 April '25

Oh that I had the pencil of the artist that I could send you sketches of my present conception of you all instead of a feeble epistle. I see you wandering four in hand and mostly in the wide Dutch breeches and still looking rather pale. Michael is smoking a heavy cigar, as the natives begin before they are his age, and Simon is carrying a basin, no longer as the one thing needful but as a trophy. Or someone has taken both of them for tulips and is scattering the petals in a canal. So far as the vigilant eye I kept on the weather could tell, all was smooth for you, but one cannot judge from an eyrie, and it may be that you were thrown against each other like dancers in the cinema. Awkward if Simon refuses to return till the channel tunnel is built. However I think all must have been well, for with so much water inside me I must be a sort of barometer for the sea, and if it was rough I should probably have been all billows also.

Here I pause to drink some more water. Strange to think that all the time you are adventuring in a foreign land I am merely drinking water. Last night I couldn't sleep for a long time for no worthier reason than because in my mind's eye I conceived oatcake with butter on it and marmalade on the butter. One ought to have these little fasts often so as to revel in the good things when they come instead of partaking mechanically. No more efforts to talk at dinner parties. Everyone listening to the delights of the marmalade as it calls at the palate in passing.

I am longing to hear how the adventure really is progressing. Is Michael worried about Beb's safety when the Dutch constable clogs by, and is Simon in a dream thinking out a tale of the bursting of the Dykes?

(Pause here while I drink more water.)

So far very few letters, but as a matter of fact there has been only one post. Unfortunately my name has been put in an advertisement about the Henley funeral with the result that enquirers have already found the lift and I have a presentiment that the affair may become a newspaper stunt. Even Peter has gone, and Nicholas went off in the car yesterday for ten days or so with the Jameses. His leg still needs prudence, and he forgets in the twinkling of an eye though he has made all sorts of promises.

There came to me this morning a nice idea for that speech at the Academy dinner which I have already declined to make. I'm really glad it didn't come in time though.

(More water.)

I am feeling very well and not incommoded by Dr Laing's treatment. Also, lest you grow nervous, I am not drinking so much water as this letter seems to indicate. Nevertheless half measures as you know were never much in my way. It will be grand to see you again and you already seem to have been away for a long time. A fine view from my windows, but a better one of you at your desk.

[To Stanway]   B—— June '25

There have already been sixteen hours of morning and still an age till lunch. I don't have the spirit to say that I must go to-night (indeed I am in hiding) nor the nerve to cut and run. Occasionally I listen at my door to make sure that all is quiet in the well of the house and then I steal out for a walk. I walk miles and the clock says I have been gone ten minutes when I steal back. I have nothing to read but an Oppenheim I bought at Waterloo and find I read a week ago.

1.0. Thought I heard the lunch gong and by a mighty effort went down to face the function. Find lunch not till 1.30 and stole back to room less able to face function next time. Everyone is very kind and there are evidently lots of nice people about but I don't know any of them even by name except —— and he is no refuge in a storm. The new American ambassador is attractive and I cling to him till he bolts.

Reflection at 1.20. It isn't as bad as that dinner of dreadful memory, but it is longer. It is so long that I sit here thinking of my past. Do you remember when I had a flat in the Adelphi? 'Years pass' as we say in the beginning of the new chapter, and I am still here though less clear of eye and beginning to dodder at the legs. I recall (hazily) how long ago you and Beb and Michael parted from me at the door. You were young things then.

I went a walk for a long long time with a lady who talked about the New Rich. I am not going a walk with her again.

1.30. Now is the time when I would accept a challenge to play golf. How delightful to be sitting for my portrait. I would receive with rapture an announcement from Frank that a deputation is at the door wanting to chat with me about my opening a branch of the Ladies' Debating Society at Upper Tooting.

1.40. They are all so much alike and yet they can sort themselves out. This gives me the loneliest feeling.

1.45. Lunch looms. I have made one plucky resolution, not in any circumstances to sit beside the New Rich lady. But how to know which she is?

1.50. I descend. Several more arrivals. Long wait in hall in which I am imprisoned. I find a pretty lady and sit beside her far from New Rich.

3 *p.m.* Cigarettes. I decide New Rich is best one.

3.15. I steal off alone and go to look at the shrubbery, which I have been going to see repeatedly since arrival last summer.

5.0. Tea. Sat beside New Rich. Have decided never to leave her.

5.30–8. Locked self in bedroom.

I could continue, though that is the hour I have reached. Dinner shouldn't be so bad, and later I can have several looks at shrubbery. To-morrow early! But at last I miss the car, as many of them will be in my train on the journey! It is very cold and I have garments quite unfitted to cope therewith. This all sounds churlish as I have host and hostess who are both kind and attentive. Just means serve me right for venturing out of my natural ways of life. It might be a little easier if I had any idea of who the great throng of people are among whom I am living.

Stanway assumes a more than ever attractive air. Homely! (Think of it.) Yesterday I expect you had a grand tea with candles in Michael's honour and I dare be sworn Simon acquired illegal possession of some of the birthday gifts. I would love anyone who would burst into my room with a warm pair of socks. Oh for a sweater, or a dog to converse with. I shall never go anywhere again without my dog. And yet they are all quite nice. But who are they? And why am I?

Monday morning. Arrived London safely. Sunday evening

better than expected and evidently I was the one at fault. American and wife are jewels.

[To Stanway]　　　　Adelphi Terrace House 18 January '26
We got to London quite comfortably. The train was late at Honeybourne the better part of an hour, but with a wisdom for which I should hardly have given credit to either of us we sat on warm in the car till it came in. My cold is not bad, just stuffy and I haven't gone out yet as the rehearsal is not till seven when it will no doubt last many hours. At this moment I am presuming the thunder and wind and cocoa-nuts have just started at Stanway (5.10). Good fortune!

I do hope the play did help you all to get through this sad New Year time a little less painfully than otherwise.[1] If so it was so well worth doing after all the kindness I have had at your mother's hands. Very depressing to go with her laid low. She is certainly one of the most gallant and lovable figures I have ever known, and sets such an example by it that she does good to all who know her, every day of her life. You are pretty good at that also.

There is a woman ('a terrible woman', Frank says) who has been sitting on my stair for the last hour refusing to go till she interviews me and so 'becomes famous'. You may conceive me anon stealing down by the other stair.

I forgot to tell you that a week ago Mrs Stanley said to me she was wearying for you to come back.

　　　　　　　　　　　　　　　　　　　　　1 April '26
I am alone in London. Is zat so? Well, we shall see when I go out to-morrow for my stroll, the streets deserted, the taxi-drivers all gone to Paris. I remember ages ago being alone at this festive season, alone strictly speaking with half a crown, and as I looked at it and fingered it, it turned into a two shilling piece. That was the biggest fright I ever had in Oxford Street. I do hope you have all had a good journey of it and are now feeling very Wordsworthian in Grasmere, which I also seem to associate with wrestling. Perhaps Michael and Simon will associate it with that also by the time they get back. I'm afraid I have not done any work though it is so quiet. I sit in a blaze of light owing to my centre lamp having had the dust blown off

[1]Mrs Guy Charteris had lately died.

205

it. If only someone would blow the dust off me. In an hour I shall be in bed reading *The Virginians*. Extract from the *Times:* 'Sir J. Barrie having started on *The Virginians* has now completed all arrangements for the Spring of 1926.' Is Jasper with you on the English lakes, barking Wordsworthianly? I too bark Wordsworthianly——

> My heart leaps up when I behold
> A Cynthia in the lift.

'Going down', she immediately says, but she knows I mean coming up. Now I go down the lift with this.

21 April '26

Rushed all day to-day and now Principal Irvine has just left and we are having early dinner and going to a music hall at Nico's expense.

The usual result of a speech[1] already begins to show in people asking me to open things for them. Otherwise I have quite recovered.

Tell your mother I thought she was very very nice to me when she came up to my room to say good-bye. She has also been very very nice to me at other times. How is 'Sir James's beautiful place in the country?', as you may have read Collins called Stanway in his speech. I must keep my head or I shall begin to think it really is mine. I do hope you are feeling quite right again. If there is anything the matter with me I make a fuss and announce it, but you are the other way, just showing how much nicer and *manlier* you are, as indeed is the case.

[To Thanet]   6 June '26

Two good days for you to be wandering the shore with Simon and Co., and I do hope you have been feeling fit for it, for I know you will be doing it whether you are fit or not. In reality, though you never seem to be aware of it, you are constantly sacrificing yourself in the interests of others and are a heroine not merely in appearance. 'Enter heroine' is what the door says when it opens for you. I hope it was a good drive down with no mishaps. We had such a one to-day to Shields's cottage which is really a farm of the most up to date kind, ingenious beyond words and ideal for the athletic. You pass

[1]His cricket-speech at a Luncheon to the Australian team.

through the billiard room into ping-pong room across the dancing room to the tennis courts adjoining the swimming bath which leads to the fishing ponds near the squash-court. Wonderful dairy and cows and pigs and chickens all round and kept in fettle under the surgical eye, with hospitals, and temperature cards on the walls and I rather think thermometers twice daily in the mouths of the animals. I hadn't seen it since it was building but I'm sure it's a model and we had the heartiest of receptions. Last night Maggie had quite a musical conversazione, as the cricketer-writer, Cardus, is also a musical critic, so we roped him in.

[To Cannes]   10 September '26
I suppose you are about this time waking up in the train to find it is slowing down for Cannes. Or as this is noon Evan may be already reading you choice morsels from his Sargent[1]. I do hope it is all going to be a glorious revel of sunshine and sea for you, and indeed you can't be much sunnier than London is to-day. I have all the curtains drawn, yet sit sweltering at a desk not unknown to you. I have a grand letter from your mother in answer to one I wrote her about Stanway, but not a word about her health as to which I wanted some reassurement. In many ways she is about the best of all letter writers, for what she sends is a moving picture of herself, with the 'captions' written upside down on the edge and any number of speaking erasures. Woman thy name is Mary Wemyss, by which I mean she is an epitome of all that has been said or sung of them by flabbergasted and adoring man since the year One. Even the lads of penetration of to-day will need to leave her out in their understanding of the sex and accept her as the exception to all rules and join in the general thanksgiving for her. I question whether I know anyone alive of whom more people have reason to be glad than M.W. This sounds I think like a letter sent to the wrong person. However you are the best of all her works. My love to Beb and Evan.

                                           14 September '26
You will also be becoming that colour if Evan in so short a time has got to the lobster stage. We are having it fairly broiling here without any sea to bask in. Yesterday I had

[1]Sir Evan Charteris was writing the Life of John Sargent.

the idiotic idea that it was chilly and lit a fire that became a bonfire and nearly melted me away. I had a good time at Mells just pottering about and arguing terrifically with Almroth Wright though I expect he would put it that I showed skill in avoiding argument. I hope you can persuade Lord Hugh Cecil to move his quarters in his most querulous manner as he will add to your gaiety and there always seems to be an extra sparkle in your eye when he is in the offing. That railway journey from which you got (but perhaps chiefly on reflection) entertainment would I fear have maddened me and turned me into a Jasper[1] whom on all other occasions (I am thankful to say) I so little resemble.

In the photograph of your hotel there is a figure so like you (in the centre) walking with the Stanway cook that I see you have taken precautions against there being any falling away in the quality of the food. More to the side I see Beb in uniform apologising to a bright young thing for keeping her waiting, and Evan is seen to the best advantage gazing complacently at the statue of Sargent quickly erected under his auspices. The flat and its occupant await your return, one of them (I won't say which) looking rather spick and span and also somewhat empty since Nico's last visit when he carried off his bedroom. His house looks very nice, I think, and he is like two householders rolled into one. Jack is already off to his ship and I am wondering whether those troubles in China may affect the Home Fleet. It is delightful to me to know you are enjoying yourself so much and makes me, also, happy.

[To Freiburg]   21 October '26
I want so much to hear what that doctor says about you and your next letter ought to tell me. As to your having an indolent time that is certainly the time you need and will probably do you more good than the doctor. It will be rather fine if your June weather lasts for it is very cold here, my wood scarcely warms the recess and the dining room table is now at the other end of the room crouched close to the gas fire. The ideal garment here would be the fur bag, with Frank plopping about in another one. If you have been reading Sergeant Burgoyne on the retreat from Moscow it is but a grimmer account of life

[1] A barking dog.

in an Adelphi garret.[1] Fancy if he had had that bag. But never would he have been allowed to keep it. Napoleon would have slept in it nightly. The sergeant's account of his first hot bath when he got out of Russia might be modestly paralleled by my present feelings because news has come from the kitchen that there is to be a pan of hot water in the bath in half an hour. To increase the resemblance between the Sergeant and me I now for the first time in ages begin to think about food and wonder passionately whether there is any chance of my dinner being of a meaty kind, with red blood in it. But it is pretty sure to be six cold oysters and a bird. If one could choose one's dreams (delightful thought) I think I should see myself back at Stanway rolling from one bath to another—if indeed I could resist remaining all the time in your father's one.

Beb is coming in to lunch tomorrow so I shall have a bite Funny incident—I was standing today at the entrance to a London musical theatre gazing at the pictures of the beauts in some new piece when another observer got in my way. Turned out to be Beb. Note of exclamation here if it were not against my principles. He told me Simon seemed to be liking the school better. I enclose a nice little notice from *Punch* about the *Treasure Ship*. Simon must bring it back to me unless you want me to buy it. I don't suppose you understand a tenth part how interested I am in it, and in anything that has touches of you;—and anything you write or say or do certainly has that. I went to the Caves[2] to lunch and found they had not exaggerated their passion for Shuffle-board[3] as I was shown the room which is to be devoted to it, and the table and the disks are ordered though on a comparatively small scale. They seem to think somehow that the Stanway table was the favourite resort of Henry VIII, so I did not undeceive them, and we should all come to think so,—and that there was a disk for each wife. I go to dine at Denis Mackail's next week, my only engagement. The letters are pouring in but are mostly from would-be Peter P's. One very haughty because no reply had been sent by return, beginning 'It is not for me to say you are no gentleman,' etc. Laing is coming in tomorrow to disturb my throat.

[1] The coal-miners' strike, at the beginning of the general strike, was in progress.
[2] Lord Cave, Lord Chancellor.
[3] A mediæval game for which there was a long table at Stanway.

The rain it raineth every day. It stopped today for a few
minutes to let the Lord Mayor's Show get under way and then
went for them. I got caught in the show in my walk—I do every
year. I fancy Simon would have liked it better than the one
he saw, as they had all London conveyances, from sedan chairs
onwards and fire engines that began by being as small as per-
ambulators. I think of you as eating white grapes all day when
you are not under medical torture, and perhaps the grapes
are becoming by this time part of the torture. I knew some
people who were wrecked for several weeks with nothing to eat
but a barrel of Scotch shortbread, and oh, how they hated it
ever after!

The auction[1] of *Old Lady Shows Her Medals* was so successful
that I see you soon having to answer pressing requests for MS.
It was the seediest, most mildewed looking thing but was
knocked down to a second hand bookseller for 325 guineas. I
mustn't burn any more of them.

Tomorrow is the day when I go to Buckingham Palace, and
I am as perturbed as if it were to the Tower. Easier to write
the life of the Duke of York[2] than to go there. I used to walk the
three miles to Glamis to watch cricket matches, little thinking
that it was bringing me three miles nearer to you.

That blistering by the sunshine treatment shouldn't have
taken place. As for the injections they must I suppose make
one feel queer but at any rate I do hope they will achieve
their object.

Coal seems hopeless for a long time even after the strike ends
and I have ordered a gas fire for your special benefit instead
of the little stove. Ugly but sound. Am also having my geyser
bath put in order, and looking wistfully for a load of peat.

Dinner for Friday—Self, Oxford, Birrell, D. Maclean,
Galsworthy, Grey.

[To Baden]   13 November '26
I got on all right at B. Palace and indeed they gave me a
handsome reception—King, Queen, and Duchess of York. Last
night was my dinner here, and Oxford, Grey, Birrell, were all
at their best. I can't recall such a good literary dinner of the

---

[1] For the benefit of the Newsvendors' Benevolent and Provident Institution.
[2] Lady Cynthia was writing a biography of the Queen, then Duchess of York.

kind—for they talked only literature for several hours; it was like going back to another century.

The letters can wait all right as I have weeded out the ones that called for immediate answers.

[To Pixton]   26 February '27

I was so glad to have your letter, and as for the Emperor and Empress[1] of course I don't really mind at all—indeed I see that we are well out of making the attempt, and that I would, when the time came, have been the most depressed. Furthermore it would have thrown far too much strain on your mother who should have been my first thought. Otherwise the great thing is to get Simon well and keep him well and for the house and company to combine in an attempt to prevent my slipping things into his part to make him cock of the walk, a situation for which he has an aptitude to look after himself. I hope you got safely to Pixton and were not eaten up by the dogs. There is a part of Exmoor not very far from you which I once knew so well that I daresay I could go about it still, blindfold, without striking against many trees. Where Blackmore lived when he wrote *Lorna Doone*. Michael was ten then and I remember we had a grand scheme of reaching Dulverton and fishing some water there. Brown and his wife came in yesterday and you can't think how excited Mrs Stanley was. Her face agleam with the rapture of the occasion. I expect that with the vitality that lies behind her ordinary quietude she sometimes misses that merrier kitchen where he convulsed them with imitations of me and my visitors. I feel that Trollope and I are living here together, for I seem to spend so much of my time with him, especially in the long hours after midnight. We then wander about Barsetshire in a heavyish carriage drawn by two slow horses with long tails and the motors whiz by us, but with Anthony on the box we do reach our destination which they perhaps don't.

[To Montreux]   25 April '27

This is only Monday evening, so you can be not more than half way on your journey and perhaps not even left Paris, a pretty cold Paris, I fear, judging from the cold snap here. The

[1]Referring to a proposed addition to a Barrie play the children at Stanway were to act.

adventure of the night will be rather epoch-making for Simon and brings back clear to me our journey of years ago when the other boys were very jealous of George for getting sick. We tobogganed often down to Glion from Caux and even all the way down to Montreux, and I remember how frozen with ice was the mountain train on our arrival. You must go up to Caux and have a meal in my hotel whose name I forget, but there were two big ones and ours was a little higher than the other. I had learned on the train from a sporting-work how to ski by crossing my right leg along the line A.B. and my left along C.D. (as in diagrams) and when I fell, there I lay till I remembered how to rise by doing things with E, F and G. I hope you have wild flowers and sunshine but there may be snow near at hand as I suppose Glion is higher than any spot in the British Isles.

Had quite a luncheon party today. Jack, Gerrie, Peter and Gilmour—and Jack and Gerrie come to stay a day or two tomorrow. Elizabeth has been in arranging the spare room where the new things make all the old ones look very faded and wan, but I hope it will be a bright room for you when you return. I am looking forward to that with all the gaiety that is left to me. I have a depressed feeling that I did not play up well to the company at Stanway—I don't mean the actors —but was glum and silent and didn't half let your mother know how splendid I thought she was, but that was largely aspirin I suppose. I think I'm a bit better now. Went out this after- noon to my foot-man and encountered Cheveral[1] laden with Macbeth's headgear, donkey's ears, etc. *Sic transit.* I do hope you get some sun and warmth and I'll be so glad to see you back again as a resident. My birthday approaches!

[To Cadogan Square]   26 June '27
I hope it has not been as cold at Kingsgate as I had it at the ancient home of Ann Boleyn from which I have this moment returned—or rather first of all I have lit a fire. It wasn't cold inside indeed, but clammy out of doors. There were about 30 people there, I should say, who seemed all very nice, but I came away not knowing who most of them were, and the young ladies of whom there were many I put all down as John Buchan's daughters because he was there with one. He talked

[1]Parlourmaid.

212

a lot about Bibs[1] whom he seemed to have taken to greatly. Rather an ordeal to me to be one of so large a party, and how I should have loved to have Simon bring up my breakfast. Tomorrow morning at 11 I start off in quest of the Eclipse, which in this weather I suppose will not show at all or so little up to expectation that the sightseers may behave like the English tourists who reluctantly climbed a Scotch mountain to see the sun rise, and not thinking when it did rise that it was anything so special, hissed.

[To Aberlady, Scotland]   25 October '27
I hope your journey in the train proved to be all your fancy painted it. I remember a story of Mrs Carlyle, that she got into the train here for Scotland, feeling depressed as Carlyle hadn't been able to see her off. Looking up she saw that the only other occupant of the carriage was a man she had last seen 40 years ago when he proposed to her. He was just returned from Australia, and though he was not meaning to go to Scotland he went all the way with her and she was 'clated' as she says in the unpublished letter recording the incident.

I'll come to tea with Simon on Friday and perhaps sit to him for my portrait. It would be interesting if he were the one to solve the problem of how to make my face presentable for the papers.

                                                    25 November '27
I'll ring you up before I go out so just a line to say it's nice to think of you lying there basking as I trust you are still doing. Last night I was late at A. P. Herbert's, who is certainly a very lovable man with four children, all attractive. They have the nicest club out there (Hammersmith) I have seen in London. It is a skittles club in a delightful Shakespearian pub, and it would be almost worth while to go and live there in order to be eligible. I think Beb must come out with me one night and order a 'port and splash'. I'm thinking of popping in on Simon tomorrow. I wish to heaven you could pop in here, not that popping is any name for your elegant moves. 'She swam toward him' is better (Meredith isn't it?)

[1]Lady Cynthia's sister, Countess of Plymouth.

[To Thanet]   24 June '28

Simon's last days as he was! Heigh ho, at any rate the sun
is giving him of its best and will tinge his memories of all that
has been. He has had a lovely time of it, and though I talk
as if it were over the first sight of him will disabuse me. He is
an entrancing child and has given a good deal of radiance to
some days in my life. He is rather the boy 'who wouldn't grow
up'. Curiously in the forthcoming life of Hardy there is a
glimpse of Hardy when six or less telling his mother that this
is his wish. One hadn't thought of Hardy as a P. Pan. Re-
reading in pages the first sixty-four of the Life I think them
superb, but of course this is only the beginning.

Nico became a father at 8 o'clock last night of a girl, and all
well. Meantime I have acquired a canary.

Robb[1] went off almost drunk with joy, and the whole thing
is a great satisfaction to me. I feel I shall be driven to a cinema
tonight, the solitary's friend.

[To Cannes]   3 September '28

I suppose your train is now gliding or thereabouts into
Cannes in time for lunch. Yesterday looked like a perfect day
for the Channel, and I saw you and Michael pacing the deck
without a qualm, which is always a proud moment. I hope Beb
did not get lost in Paris in the throes of composition.

I had Rossdale in and he decides I have a slight attack of
sciatica. I am at present in a plaster and an electric rubber
comes tomorrow, but all I feel is just the slightest discomfort,
and Elizabeth is dining out with me tonight. The one thing
that maddens me is that Dr Rossdale insists on my sitting on
soft seats, and you know what that means to me. My black
velvet chair is now in the study with a cushion on it, and I
am squatted thereon indignantly. I have not looked for '6, 7
or 8 Women' or 'Half an Hour' yet, but you may conceive
me among my cupboards tomorrow (on a cushion). Gilmour
has been in and is busy over my 'speaking movies'. You will
have to give up disapproving that invention if it means they
are to be another source of income for me. This is rather a
lark. There is something in science after all. Your duchess
book is advertised in swaggering style in the Sunday papers—

[1] A Kirriemuir friend of Barrie's boyhood came to stay, and gave him the
canary.

also Lord Oxford's *Memories and Reflections*—both imminent. You can now go off and bathe while I address a few words to the canary. You were lovely in all ways at Stanway.

8 September '28

I expect you should be living at Cannes in the more correctly clothed manner that appeals to Michael (whose efforts I applaud), for your duchess book is evidently to make you a distinguished literary character, and there is no room in the water for two at once (Shaw being the other one). I have seen various reviews of the long important kind that is only given to nobs, and not only is it much acclaimed but you are in all cases applauded. I think that whatever may be the fate of such books in general this one is sure of much favour.

I cannot believe that it could be much hotter anywhere than it is here at present and we cannot, like you, take to the water. If we lived as sensibly as you are all doing the postman would be going his rounds in a towel and Gilmour would be dropping in on me in pyjamas. I have gone back to my coolest garments (at this point I pause to get rid of some of them). It is the most dreary job having to go over those little plays. I have searched the flat in vain for *Half an Hour*. I have knocked off a good many letters, and there is as yet no great pile on your desk.

[To Brighton] 26 October '28

What a day for your travels. I have shaken my fist at it through the window for being so heartless, and can only hope that the last of rain is left behind before you reach Brighton and that you wake tomorrow to sunshine. You are neither of you fit for beginning thus and I feel you are probably the more exhausted of the two. That complete rest seems to me to be calling to you to go to it again, and I do wish you would.

Simon will be thinking that to be so near Peacehaven is good enough for anyone though the rain beats and the wind howls. His dream must now be that Wilkinson's should be removed to Peacehaven, and no holidays.

I am very sorry Beb is retarded just when he had got to 'the gallop up the avenue' as they used to call the winding up of a novel. The more I think of his father's book[1] the more

[1]Biography of Lord Oxford.

I feel that he might be well out of it if the writing does not fall to him. Of course it is a filial duty to do it if he feels that otherwise it is likely to be badly done. No doubt he could do it better than anyone else, and I would put Violet[1] next, but it would interfere heavily with the books he has in his head.

I am going off now to the Scots Club. I told you of it. There are speeches, but nothing is reported to the outer world, and it is wonderful how newspaper men so greedy for news keep absolutely to this rule. I do hope you will sleep well and have sun at Brighton.

[To Peacehaven]   Californie Palace, Cannes 12 January '29

Well, here we are, and I sent you a wire though I am not absolutely sure that the Gables is the address and in any case I suppose they don't deliver on Sunday. 'C/o Simon' would probably have been judicious. In all material matters it is so far a great success, for the sun is certainly rather enchanting, and greatcoats, etc., are things of the past. I have a luxurious bed-sitting-room at present with bathroom attached and Frank opposite my door, and if I find I want a sitting-room it can be managed. Shields has one. He met me at the station, and has with him his wife and a son and a brother. I walked with him for an hour and watched them play tennis later, and will be rather an ingrate if I can't put in some hours daily in the open to my betterment. I certainly feel more fit already, though I couldn't sleep in the Blue train which is a bit pretentious and too condensed when made up for night. I spoke to Lady Alexander for a moment. She was going on to Mentone, and otherwise I hear of no one I know. I am above the town, a view rather like that from the flat touched up by paint and magic and demons. Immediately opposite is the island you bathed at and in my mind's eye I see you all on your rafts rushing along. The Mediterranean looks as if you could bathe in it equally well in January though the hills are white with snow and there is some close to us, looking as if it might scorch you if you touched it. I lunched with the Shields but go down to dinner to a table for one. I may get some games with Shields of some kind as he is so keen thereat and if only I can sleep tolerably all should be well. I read the Stella Benson book for hours in the train and saw clearly that she is a brilliant

[1]Lady Violet Bonham-Carter.

person of much and many brains, but what is its aim or object or even subject I can't get hold of at all, I seem to be *deaf* to these writers and yet with the conviction that I should greatly admire them if I could hear them. Tonight I must have a fight with my central heating apparatus, Shields assisting. All this about myself, but the nicest thing was your coming to the station to see me off. Frank asked me if I noticed what the name of our railway carriage was. It was the 'Cynthia', so I started with good luck. Frank much more communicative about his war experiences, etc., than I have ever found him before.

To SIMON ASQUITH

[To Peacehaven]　　California Palace, Cannes, 18 January '29
My dear Simon

This place is 24 hours away from London, and it is blazing with sunshine till about 4 o'clock when all at once it gets cold and dark. Every morning I walk five miles in the sun with two or three other men, all among mountains, and it does me a lot of good, and there are gorgeous views of the Mediterranean, and some people are said to prefer Cannes to Peacehaven, but not me,—at any rate when you are there. Now you will be glad, especially as Michael is off to Winchester again, to go back to dear old Wilkinson's.

The waiter spilt a plate of soup all over me today at lunch. This is the brightest thing that has happened to me since I came.
　　　　　　　　　　　　　　With the love of James Matthew B.

To Lady CYNTHIA ASQUITH

[To Sussex Place]　　　　　　　　　　　　19 January '29

It is so odd to me that you have not had any of my letters but you must have by now at any rate. I had forgotten that *P.P.* ends tonight till I heard it from you today. I hope Simon and Nannie managed to get to the matinée and represent the author as you have to be away. My daily walk from 11 to 1 goes on determinedly and I am ever so much better of it. I am reconciled more to my lot because the half of it is already up, and I can see how delightful in a smaller abode it might be here if we were all together with Simon as the spirit of the place. Somebody like Dr Johnson said 'Don't bother me with the bill of fare; show me the bill of company'. I have read Blunden's book on the war with high admiration. Full of fine things—perhaps too much a literary effort but certainly an achievement. How we won the war seems more incredible than ever. We did, didn't we?

21 January '29

You seem to get my letters so slowly. I have written you every other day I feel sure since I came. I am so sorry Beb hasn't been well, and hope he is better now. Your letter about *P. Pan* came today, and I am glad all went well, though so far away I hardly feel any connection with it. I am very grateful to this place from the point of view of health and to Shields, etc., but there is no use denying the desire to get back and that the stepping into the dreadfully over-heated train will be a sort of savage delight. It does seem a shame that I should get all this when so many others would be heady with joy over it. Various invitations from the Duke of Connaught downwards but the only people I have seen are the Laverys whose villa is some miles away. We (not Laverys), meditate Monte Carlo on Wednesday as our only excursion, just to say I have been there. If you could go with me how easily it could be turned into a joyous affair. Evidently you have a ghastly pile of letters on your desk, while I have only to kill time, and I talk like an aggrieved person. No wonder I sometimes shudder at myself. I do, and then I get really afraid of the future. To keep oneself at arm's length becomes almost a profession with me. When telegrams come here (and a good number do) I shake like a leaf. I don't suppose you have any idea how much you are doing for me. Or perhaps you know and don't think I always know but indeed I do.

[To Elgin, Scotland]

Adelphi Terrace House 5 September '29

So you are going to —— after all. I don't think you have any idea what an unselfish person you are though you are exceptionally clear-headed; indeed the clearness of your head is what they all want you for, next to your sympathy. I am not in a position to blame them, having drawn on those two qualities so much myself, and I suppose we shall all go on imposing on you. As for that last week at Stanway it was delightful to me beyond words and I like to look back upon it as a time of sunny happiness, drawn out to its fullest extent. It is strange to think of you in a cold and wet land now for I assure you the heat here is almost dizzying. Last night I dined unexpectedly with Evan and I don't think I could have arrived if I had not boldly put on a soft collar. Evan's was stiff at the soup stage but as limp as mine before he produced his large cigar.

[To Preston Deanery Hall, Northampton]   18 November '29
. . . When we were having tea at No. 8 Nannie discovered that the biscuit I ate had not performed its function. She had put it in Simon's pocket between his letters merely to make him remember the letters but though he produced the biscuit it did not make him remember them. I laughed at this, but after I got back to the flat I found in my own pocket two letters which I had put there in order to ask you where I signed my name. They are of no importance, but evidently Simon and I are a pair. Or rather they are of importance as showing how dependent we are on you.

22 November '29
In case you worry about letters piling up here I send you the triumphant information that I have done the lot myself and that there is nothing whatever on your desk at present except receipted bills. Your learning of so much poetry is astounding, or would be from any one else; you are what they call an omnibus volume. An extraordinary success seems to have been made by those Scotch amateurs in *Old Lady Shows Medals* at Lyric Theatre, Hammersmith. The papers are raving about the man and woman giving a performance that no professionals in England could touch.

[To Aberlady, Scotland]
The Manor House, Mells, Frome 30 December '29
I am hoping Beb's cold is better and that you are now on the train for Gosford—with Simon deep in a new and still longer tale. I have been listening to much music, as the McKenna

family have become carol singers and not only performed last evening in the church, but are I understand going from house to house and singing at the windows quite as if they were out of *Under the Greenwood Tree*. This house however is very studious, with Helen[1] at one desk preparing for her summer exams and Quintin Hogg at another doing ditto, and as I have stolen one of the desks I feel I am again an undergraduate. You will be exchanging one tremendous mansion for another, and I expect it will be very cold up there, so I trust you are facing the elements in warm garments. I am still feeling well.

1 January '30

It seems a big milestone this time, but they are all that. We brought in the New Year here with a biggish party of McKennas, etc., including Freyberg, in the church tower, high up on it, in the place where they ring the bells, nine ringers, the bells in some sort of ecstasy and the tower itself rocking as if exalted. One felt they had only to go on pulling harder to bring it down. Before that we went in four cars into Frome, where the carol singers again carolled, in the middle this time of a cinema show, and heard later of that different and dreadful cinema scene at Paisley. I suppose you got my other letter, which had Longniddry on it instead of Aberlady. Your phrase in yours about —— with her arms full of goats and donkeys, and her eyes full of tears, sticks like something from a great poet, as your lines sometimes do. You are a one at times for hitting the nail on the head, and I listen or read with pride and know it is better than I have ever done. You then go on your way unconscious that you have done it, which is a blessed way to go. I'll try to get those seats for *P. Pan* when I return to London—on Friday, and we must also march upon the circus, of which the side shows are the most entertaining part. My love to your mother and all for the New Year.

[To Sussex Place]   Royal Albion Hotel, Brighton 24 March
It has been an astounding day here, as warm and sunny as July, and I felt I ought to sell my overcoat. This lasted till about 5, and now it is pleasantly cool. The only trouble so far is that they are re-building Brighton outside the hotel's

[1]Lady Helen Asquith.

door. However, I have got in some three hours' work. I was so glad to find your letter. Am now going down to face the evening-dress dinner in my neat tweeds.

[To Venice]   Adelphi Terrace House 10 September '30
No news of you yet except those first lines but I do hope you are well. I expect that the introduction of Michael to the glories of Venice occupies a good deal of your time. I remember a story of an American looking at a picture of Christ there and passing the remark 'Not my idea of the party'. We have been having a grand thunderstorm tonight but it now seems to be over. In any case I grow accustomed to noise as the building of the house behind my bedroom is clattering beyond belief and occasionally it sounds as if all they had put up had suddenly come rumbling down. A terrible rumour is also abroad that a rat (or the plural number) has escaped therefrom and got into the flat beneath me. You can imagine how this affects me and that I look under my bed, etc., like the old lady for the burglar.[1] I keep one eye open for it, even when I am reading in bed. At present I'm reading Priestley's new book, only in middle of it as yet, but it helps me along a road I have travelled some distance toward thinking that he is *the* man of those knocking at the door. There were some scraps in papers about the cricket dinner of Monday but I think it was meant to be private. I had a letter from Simon today and mean to rub it into him that I sat beside Woodfull and had talks with Bradman, Chapman, Ranji, etc. Good effect when I said of Bradman that I was very sorry for him as I couldn't doubt that he had meant to do better.[2] I also got in a local touch by saying that I hoped Woodfull felt he ought to give a handful of the Ashes to Gloucestershire. A sad thing that Faulkner the greatest of South African cricketers who was there was found dead this morning with the gas on.
An hour ago I knit my teeth and doggedly sat down to read 'Courage' which is the furthest I have got toward Edinburgh.[3] I trust I'll hear from you tomorrow with good news.

[1]Barrie had a special aversion to rats and would go out of the room if they were mentioned.
[2]Bradman had just made a record number of test-match centuries.
[3]His impending speech.

I was decidedly up and down yesterday and the day before but am feeling more like facing the world today.

It will be great to have you back permanently in London and will brighten me up. I fear I was very much dreary when you came up and should have fought better with the flatness that has come over me since I have ceased to be invalidish and could go out. Melancholy want of pluck in the author of 'Courage'. You have so much more, and I must try to borrow some of it.

What a lot of work seems to have fallen upon you since the quiet days of my week. If Simon's Romeo becomes sing-songy I expect you will get him out of it but it won't be easy for all my experience of 'child-actors' shows that they go through extraordinary phases and if they are amazing good one year may be amazing bad the next or vice versa. The ones who play placidly and don't think about it, like Mary Rose, are the most dependable, but of course Simon is thinking and planning fiercely, and the untoward may come out of it. The appearance before an audience is a thrill to him unspeakable, he is so anxious for a masterpiece. The magic of his Romeo words may easily go too much to his head. Probably commoner language would be better for him. As for your 'Impromptu' that you are all rehearsing I am very curious about it, and the only thing I feel rather sure of is that you had better rehearse it very thoroughly, or not at all. I don't know whether the Bennets have other scenery, but if not I think the Balcony scene should come first when it would have the enormous benefit of being new to the audience and the loveliness of the barn stage would be taken as part of the performance. I feel sure this would add greatly to the impression. Despite your labours there is one thing you are escaping that now faces me like an ogre, namely that work of sculpture. Did you see a bit about it in the *Times* today? Tomorrow the man appears and on Wednesday we get started, and I am feeling ignominious, as if, for Heaven knows no sensible reason, I am giving up all my rules of life. It doesn't matter of course but I do feel idiotic. I recall what Meredith said to me when they wanted to paint his picture. 'No one should be painted except beautiful women and great men, and I am neither the one nor the other.' It is obvious that I should have insisted on their sculpting you. Elizabeth has been in. I don't think she is at all well in health, but she is bright or at any rate contrives that appearance. On Wednesday I am going to dine alone with Wells at the flats from which that sad funeral so lately set forth.[1] I expect he is feeling very lonely.

[To Bude]   1 June '31
I hope the leafy month has begun with you as well as it has done here, but whether there are trees at Bude I know not ('As thick as thieves in Vallombrosa' is a new way I lately heard of putting an old saying). The leaves were very thick at —— those two days I was there; also there were a number of eminent botanists, and I felt rather out of it as you may imagine. The garden is the great sight and very lovely—a sort of wild garden all rocks and ponds where every rare flower grows, and they knew them not only by their learned names but could tell every variety of them and whether it was a No. 27 or a No. 28. After a time I found it good (but difficult) to find a spot where there were no flowers and there I walked up and down. It was a pleasant visit.

I suppose you have been living by the ocean and I daresay Beb has even lured you on to it if not into it. I got back after breakfast, and am anon to dress and go to the Literary Society where I have not been for many months. There are not very many letters but I'll look through them tomorrow and see if I should bother you with a selection. One amused me, from a medical gent, who had read that thing about 'The Greenwood Hat', and its statement that I had to write with my left hand because I had neuritis in my right. This he undertakes to cure for a consideration in two goes. I do hope your week will do you some good and that you are sleeping better.

                                                      6 July '31
Most gorgeous sunset from my window at this moment. I see an article in today's *Telegraph* about which is the finest outlook in London. Samuel Butler apparently said the view of St Paul's from Fleet Street was 'the finest in Europe' and almost equally extolled the view from the far end of Waterloo

[1]That of Catherine (Jane) Wells.

Bridge. But this is surely finer than the first at any rate. Sad if it all has soon to go. I think I have seen more magic skies from Stanway than anywhere else. I suppose you are again busy over your mother's book. Peter has just come in to dinner and to take away my tale[1] to be typed. It is terribly 'elusive' I fear and perhaps mad, but was I not dogged to go through with it! Wednesday I have to lunch out. I hope Simon had a good day at his match—I don't think you told me, if you knew. My love to your mother. I am tired today.

[To Zurich]   24 May '32
   Your news of Beb seems all very good but of course until it is confirmed by Vogt[2] himself one must not feel too sure. Mysterious man that he is, I feel no confidence that you have yet secured an interview with him though I don't see how he can delay it.
   Norman Forbes managed to lure me into going to a dress rehearsal of *Twelfth Night* yesterday. I sat in the dark for some time talking as I thought to Jean Forbes-Robertson, but she turned out to be Cathleen Nesbitt. You would have revelled in it much more than I, but it was an attractive production in most ways, with Jean as Viola and Phyllis Neilson Terry as Olivia. Jean's was a tender and fine performance of a timid boy alarmed at being loved by such a magnificent armful of a woman, but without the slightest gaiety. Of course the arch pantomime boy style would be unendurable in the part, but the play is a comedy, and I could see points when the comicality of the situation should come to her, not with the words but in silence as in some exits, etc. She spoke her lovely lines finely, but they are perhaps too beautiful for mortal to speak in public without something happening, such as their setting the scene on fire. There is a good deal that is jarring in such speeches being in juxtaposition with the huge amount of practical rough and tumble with which the piece is so laden.
   I was in the middle of these observations when to my delight another letter from you came in, dated yesterday, so perhaps your German letter to Vogt has now had its answer.
   What you say of the *Family Record* and yourself and Ego[3] is very engrossing to me. I think, though, that I could have written down for a long time what you say of your feelings

---

[1]*Farewell, Miss Julie Logan.*   [2]Oculist at Zürich.
[3]Lady Cynthia's brother, Lord Elcho, killed in the War.

for him, and the things you saw in those later days on the cricket field and indeed all over the house and grounds. What the book reveals to me, and the best reason of its existence to me, is that I know more of Ego himself. I had heard too much I think of his diffidence about himself which of course was part of him; I had not properly realised that he was of great parts. Now judging by what is said of him by his letters I see that he was a glorious young man of capacities that might have risen to high things and that life would not have smirched him, though it would often have hurt him. Somehow I never gathered from you what a delicious sense of humour he had and what a faculty for expressing it. Peter was wonderfully right in his estimate of those letters. I daresay it was rather horrible to you to hear them read aloud even in that good company, but her happiness in what she had accomplished was deserved.[1] You cannot but exult over the manner of his death. How passionately he would have liked to know that he could die like that. I should like you to break down your reticence and talk to me a great deal about him.

Now my dinner is ready. I have a letter today asking me to be godfather to the Priestley baby boy.

[To Sussex Place]   Edgerston, Jedburgh 22 September '32
It is grand weather up here and there is abundance of that Scotch air of which I have been prating. It must do me good I think and indeed I feel a touch of liveliness. As for Frank, though he certainly accompanied me hither I have not seen him since we parted on the door step. Arrangements of my garments however indicate that he is on the premises.

Scott's name is so much in the mouths of his countrymen that for this week they have forgotten Burns—though not quite, for I hear of a chairman being checked from proposing 'the immortal memory' on the grounds that those words applied only to Burns. Last night was the culmination of the celebrations, and was in this part glorified with beacons on the hills —a remarkable tribute. Oliver, Mrs O. and I drove in a car to watch, as did countless others, and it might have been that the lights were the warning that another English raid had started. Today I am going in with the O's to see Queen Mary's House again, as even it is adorned in honour of Sir

[1]cf. p. 246.

225

Walter. I am the only visitor at present. George Trevelyan has just left. Read his article in the *Times* on Scott—the best I have seen. I see the *Fortnightly Review* for July lying about with an article by Chesterton comparing W. de la Mare and me, which is also very good but bewildering. All these items from the north will seem rather small beer to you compared with Simon's hat, and I wish I could be with you to hear his account of his first day at Westminster. In the silence that now falls on No. 8 I seem to hear the Duchess of York emerging diffidently and saying 'There is still me'. How I wish you could do that book in your sleep and wake up with even the proofs corrected. I am writing at the table where Mary Rose 'came to me', so it is almost where you came too. Now for Q. Mary's house.

Edgerston, Jedburgh 26 September '32

It is rather woeful to have your tale of loss of will power. I have so much experience of the same and mine so long continued that it is no doubt now the chief part of me. Yours does not at any rate permeate your being, and you would spring back into something very different if the load of what you have to do were lifted like a knapsack off your shoulders. You seemed so lighthearted and merry at Brighton that it was sometimes difficult to believe it was a garment you were wearing to deceive. It showed plenty of will power, however, and often took me in. Among your many lovely virtues is certainly a noble strength of character, not so much natural to you as acquired by force of circumstances, and what I envy in you more perhaps than anything else, though I wish you could let it lie fallow at times for it exhausts you. I think that to be brave all the time is more than should be demanded of you, however gallantly you stand up to it and you are indeed a marvel at it.

Though so much writing becomes a scunner to you how deliciously you can express things as in your account of Simon's school adventures with hat, umbrella, etc. It makes a rich picture. If slipped into anyone's biography it would bring the book to life. If it could be twisted into an incident in the life of the Duchess it would be quoted over the English speaking world. A vast amount of money lies in the pursuit of Simon, and the giving of his sayings and doings to biographers. Anyone could turn him into monetary account in this way but of course no one in comparison with yourself. No doubt others have loved their children as much as you, but few indeed have your humorous insight into them, with the result that they have a similar humorous insight into you. It brings you and them extraordinarily close together and will I believe be a guard to them all their days.

My legs continue to remind me of their existence at times but are on the whole soon put to flight, and Edgerston is certainly doing me good though the rainy season seems to have set in. However I motor if rain is in the way of walking, and I walk a good deal. It would be lovely if I could find you on the hill sides or by the lake as the wild geese swing by.

[To Brighton]   2 February '33
It does seem such good news about Beb[1] and if it goes on (and one's hopes do get stronger and stronger) how happy we shall all be. Like summer breaking through. I am still getting on famously, which is as well, as today for instance I could scarcely dress owing to the stream of messages about a possible Abbey funeral, etc.[2] Apparently however that won't be. Of course I strongly supported. Yet how I should dislike anything of the kind myself. No words can express the depth of that feeling. I do hope Brighton will help Beb on.

[To Stanway]   Adelphi Terrace House 15 March '33
I do hope you are able to be up and about again, and not feeling sad, or feeling it as little as you can. I know it is more 'a house of the dead' to you than to any other of the family but passionately loved for that as well as for other reasons. I certainly love it too, and of course it is only for this time I seem to want to go to Scotland. If there are to be other times it would be my wish to return to dear Stanway. Wherever I go this time it would be hoping you and Beb and the boys were to be with me—otherwise I expect I should be a derelict, going up and down my lift. Even the light will be taken from me soon as I suppose another monster building will soon be going up. They are to be debating about it[3] in the House of

[1]After a serious illness.
[2]John Galsworthy had died on the last day of January.
[3]Demolition of Adelphi Terrace.

Lords tomorrow, but it is hardly conceivable that commerce will not carry the day. The new lighting which is partly installed over the bookshelves in this room makes it more weirdly romantic. I am not really depressed these days, or at any rate it is just over my own faults. I gloat many a time over my long unfair good fortune.

[To Tunbridge Wells]   27 March '33
    Reclining Cynthia, or She Takes a Rest at Last. It is the title or could be of your latest work. Or we might call it 'A Year in the Shafts, and so to Bed'. Few people can have gone off to bed more triumphantly or more exultantly or more deservingly or more lusciously. The golden prospect was what made you feel strong again after as hard a year as comes to most. Joy cometh in the morning (sometimes) and it is pleasant to think of you waking to that feeling. Perhaps the dead tired-ness that has been so long delayed is what you will wake up to, but even then it will be with the blissful consciousness that the deed is accomplished. I hope you have a south window letting in the maximum of sun and discovering our heroine (as indeed she is) surrounded by books which she is not so much reading as gloating over because she is not the person who has to add 10,000 words to each of them.[1]
    With the connivance of the book-salesman at Charing Cross I managed to secure a copy of the right magazine and I read your opening part with much approval and the hope that it tinkled with guineas.
    I like Algernon Cecil being here, and he is staying on for the rest of this week. If I ever felt I was helping him I must drop the claim for it is I who have been benefited instead of him, though I am glad to think the flat has been some comfort to him. I always liked him but I know him much better now and I find a vast deal to admire. First and foremost is the manliness with which he so unostentatiously faces his loss.[2] No one could feel it more, but he is really a lesson in fortitude. We have many long talks on matters men usually eschew as too intimate or heavy, and I find his conversation admirable, and his views whether I agree with them or not founded on sound thought or knowledge. He really is what is called a

[1]It had been necessary to add 10,000 words to her *Life of the Duchess of York*.
[2]His wife Lady Guendolen Cecil had just died.

228

full man and carries it lightly and is engaging and has a natural sense of humour. One can see how he enjoyed Guendolen's wit and that they were often merry together. It is good to me and for me to have him here.

The canary has conceived a passion for him and screams to get out of its cage as soon as he appears. This is the only thing in the flat that disturbs him, and I have to keep them apart.

I have seldom seen the outlook here so lovely as it is after sunset these nights. All the world a trembling light blue except for the lamps. Sad if one has to say good-bye to it.[1]

31 March '33

It is good to think of you wandering the gardens with pencil poised over nothing more strenuous than the crossword puzzle. Strenuous it would be to me all the same! That carelessness about your proofs was very discreditable but I daresay I was almost the only reader who minded the note of exclamation. Nearly all would take it as a friendly touch. Just think too how comfortable the use of them makes the lady (gent) with whom one goes in to dinner. Before one is at the foot of the stair she (he) knows you have a sense of humour and have perceived the like in her (him). Devoid of them, no one is a social success. I dined with the soldier Byng on Wednesday and must have sprinkled one or two to my lady, for a letter has arrived inviting me to another revel and to 'tell her that story again'. The people who look on me as funny are the ones who degrade me most.

Beb came in to lunch yesterday and none of the three of us found it necessary to be funny, so we had a good time. Proof thereof, he is coming to dinner again on Sunday. I have persuaded Algernon to stay another week, so he will still be here when you return. The Jedburgh portraits of me have come, and I must say your deadly remark anent them about the detectives in plays and films is so true that I feel the figure should give a jerk to the lapel of his coat and disclose his badge. On Sunday I shall probably conduct Beb and Co. to Sing-Sing prison.

Police Inspector, Tammany, U.S.A.

---

[1] Owing to the demolition of Adelphi Terrace.

[To Tunbridge Wells]   9 September '33

It is a lovely letter you send me today and I am much elated thereby. It just strikes me that this is pretty nearly my first letter to you with my right hand[1]—since making which observation I am struck with the delight of being able to give it such a beginning. I have not got by the pleasure of being able to use it again. I am so glad you did enjoy Glen Prosen; I had similar fears to yours about the experiment, but in a day or two I knew it was to be one of the happiest holidays of my life, and so without any doubt it proved. Fain would I have lingered. For the first time perhaps I was 'sweir' to return to the London that eternally thrills me and has been to me all the bright wishes of my youth conceived. I have often felt a wish that Branwell Brontë who yearned for it so much and never reached it had been plunged in as I was. In being able to live in London by my pen I achieved my one literary ambition; I never sought the popularity that is mostly fluke, I would have been as satisfied though I had remained in a nice two-pair-back to the end, quite unknown round the corner so long as it was a London corner. And now I am still best here, but nevertheless I do love my native parts with almost a ferocity of attachment. I could send my love even to all the side-boards in Balnaboth and indeed try to count them if that would warm their hearts. The house and its hills and little bridges over the burns had a very steadying effect on me. They were the only things that stood still. All else we saw as in a flashing cinema. I never showed you anything. We were always in cars and a mile in front of whatever I had to say. The only way to have shown you the boy[2] I was looking for of whom you write would have been to steal off in Michael's car in the night-time and to leave it hidden in Caddam wood while we wandered through a sleeping Kirriemuir. There is a window in one of the mills where I once thought I should have to live my life as a clerk, the window where my father sat for many years. There is the Lozie grounds I did most miserably frequent (and the Ben too) haunted (what would Michael think!) by the dread that there was nothing for it but to become a doctor. My chief memory of that birthplace is of playing with Maggie under a table upstairs on which stood the coffin

[1]He had returned to the use of his right hand.
[2]Himself.

containing my brother. I have no recollection of him but strangely enough 'Eugie' could tell me some things the other day. That other house in the south-muir opposite the window in Thrums is more full of me and I am more full of it than all else up there. Looking back I feel we might have made that night travail, and yet even then we might have been respectfully followed by figures in their nightgowns. An intruder you call yourself but you were far from that though perhaps some of us could not but be so. I expect I did go off and make those nocturnal searchings alone. I daresay it was not Michael I heard climbing back by my bathroom window but myself. If so and this was what disturbed my sleep, it was worth it for it brought serenity in the morning. The only thing that really did mar the sheer happiness of those days was not the rush of cars nor the forenoons lost to answering letters, nor the vagaries of young ladies, but that writing table in the dining-room and indeed all the writing-tables in the house, for you went from one to another till they were all covered with your far too heavy labours. The astounding thing was that you rose superior to them and somehow really were out a great deal, climbing and talking and playing and by far the gayest of the company. I wondered at it, but I exulted in it more, it was the same Cynthia I had known so long. Such are the views of my right hand which could always interpret me better than the left. I hope you are to have a good time in Cornwall or wherever you go.

[To Looe, Cornwall]   13 September '33
It was so nice to see you today that you were gone before I came to. I do hope you really are better and that the sun abides with you for another week. It has been shining here fitfully and may be ablaze at Cornwall. Looe must be near Polperro where I used to go sometimes with Quiller-Couch when I sojourned in Fowey. That was the time of R.L.S.'s death and the news reached us in the words that he had died making asalad. We could not think what asalad was but it turned out to be a salad. Couch and I had a sad walk by the sea that day.

[To Rottingdean]   4 April '34
Very late and I must take this out to post as Frank is gone and Mrs Stanley slumbereth. The play[1] seems to be moving
¹*The Boy David.*

forward I think, as far as people will allow, for they *will* come in and interrupt me and I have to hide the sheets like a conspirator. You see I can't tell them I am working at anything. It sounds so strange, that they would put me through an examination. A writer is everybody's fair game. I think I had better not go down to Rottingdean on Saturday, for though it would be very pleasant it would put me off my stride again if stride it can be called. I got a slight throat at Shields's but it is practically gone today and they were very kind. Shields and I got lost one day in Burnham Beeches.

I shall be so glad to see you on Saturday and the letters can easily wait as they don't seem to be important. Elizabeth Lucas is hoping to be able to come in tomorrow to dinner and I should not wonder if Miss Bergner came at tea time. If so I'll hear what she thought of the Trossachs. Frank and Mrs Stanley went to see her play last night, and Mrs Stanley was astounded at her being so good in such cheap garments.

I agree with you now about east winds. I had long hated them for your sake.

9 April '34

I trust you got past the cocktail by boldly not drinking it. There are few troubles you would not face more gamely than a glass of wine. Similarly did I in the long ago go to pieces when a formidable hostess gave me a cup of tea with milk in it. The room here is today presenting an appearance again that is to you familiar. Gilmour is sitting at my desk making up my Income Tax returns while I wander up and down grimly chewing my moustache. He is certainly a good bit better than he was but is going soon to Switzerland for a month, and of some such pick-me-up he is much in need. He is to stay the night, and tomorrow night I am to have Principal Irvine. Despite these distractions however I managed to slay Goliath[1] today at ten minutes past six. So far a relief. Thursday I suppose Miss Bergner will be in (about 6—7) to hear that news. Otherwise free all day, and also I should like you to meet her.

[To Peacehaven]   9 April '35

It was good to these eyes to see you able to go out into the open again; I was more happy of it than words can say, but

[1]In *The Boy David*.

of course I also saw how delicate you still are and rather like a leaf just now. I feel so crudely robustious by comparison and disgruntled with myself, and like a deserter to go away even for those few Welsh days. It makes me shiver when I think how little I do for you when you have done so much for me. I have a letter and a wire from Miss Bergner, saying she has not had any news from Mr Cochran but she has the play in bed with her and is 'in tears and joy and fears and rapture over it'. I have had another look at it myself and am this time rather in the doldrums over it. Mustn't bother with it any more, or I'll spoil it. Do be very extra careful of yourself when the nurse goes.

[To Sussex Place]   Hotel Royal Danieli, Venezia[1] 18 May '35
    Behold here we are, and were indeed in a gondola within five minutes of our arrival, personally conducted by Elisabeth Bergner who however looks frail and tired out. We shall stay here (to Frank's delight) till toward the end of the week when our address should be Palace Hotel Cristallo, Cortina, Dolomites, Italy. I expect we shall be away altogether about 10 days. The Danieli is an old palace of the great, and my windows are on the Grand Canal. The beauty of Venice is almost appalling, and so was Frank's knowledge of it as we stepped into it. He now has E.B. well in hand. I could not sleep in train but woke refreshed this morning. One would feel distressingly far from home were it not we are still in the land of Shakespeare, even all the Doges in his pocket. Just as much as if I were leaning over the gate by the barn at Stanway.

Palace Hotel and Cristallo,
Cortina d'Ampezzo, Dolomiti 25 May '35
After a masterly struggle with bewildered attendants I have contrived to get some note-paper and even ink, but blotting-paper—no; and as all the furniture here is white and bare it will probably be covered (as far as this table is concerned) with black blobs before I finish my letter. Outside, the world is as white as the furniture, heavy in snow and snowing as I write. We got here only last night owing to being kept in Venice and our journey by car was through the wildest mountain scenery I have been in, mostly shrouded by mist and night, but with magnificent peeps through that at moments. Cortina in its way

[1]Barrie had gone to meet Miss Bergner and her husband in Venice.

is as fine as Venice, a queer jump from the art of man to nature at its most primitive, and the panorama from my windows is superb. Nevertheless more sun and less rain and snow would add to the amenities. There is some central heating, and I shall never again call central heating opprobrious names. I look back on Venice as the world's loveliest toy. We shall be longer by some days in getting back to London than I thought, and I suppose it will be about the end of this week.

Of course I have long spells of inertia owing to my sluggish nature. The hotel advertisements speak of 'the international travelling world' but I evidently don't belong to it, while Frank does. He has gathered so much from our travels that I can see grand canals and churches, etc. etc. breaking out all over his face. It is indeed a considerable treat to see him at all.

[To Tunbridge Wells]

Adelphi Terrace House, 3 November '35

I am supposing this is about the hour—shortly after tea—when you proceed to the nursing home. After all it is comparatively a gay adventure to you to go to such a place—comparatively to the feelings that would be mine, for you are really looking forward to the rest and have earned it, while I would have no such justification. Also there is to you a dash of romance in setting forth to anything, which is one of your many qualities I envy. With that novel on your brain there cannot be so much rest as you really need, and I see you at the best resting one side of yourself while you hurry along with the other. The 'bundle of life'—if I may use the expression—is now dormant here, and I took an aspirin an hour ago just to make things more lively. I do hope you will sleep well, with shepherds around you and not a farmer to disturb your dreams. I have to confess that in a new search to confound you I can no longer find the word farmer in the Old Testament though the historical works I have consulted call Saul so.[1] In 1st Samuel Abigail says to David 'the soul of my lord shall be bound in the bundle of life,' etc. All your other queries were excellent (and the bundle is immaterial) and I wish you could tell me what is the matter with the daughters of Saul vision. I feel that something is.

[1]Barrie wanted to call his play *The Two Farmers*, and his correspondent had objected that farmer was not an Old Testament word.

As I expect you know, your telephone line is cut off and so it was in vain I tried to get on to you at Sherwood Park last night and today. It makes me feel so much further away. Even Mrs Stanley came to me to say mournfully that 'the flat is very depressing without Lady Cynthia'. Elizabeth Lucas came and had dinner with me last week and spoke cheerfully of herself but was not really fit. Suffering far more than myself,—indeed I am not suffering at all beyond inconvenience when I bend. The things women endure and make light of compared to men! And you are very much a woman in that as in other respects.

All you tell me of your novel sounds promising to me. At any rate, that taking of myriads of notes first has always been my way and occupied me longer than the actual writing of David. You are also on the right lines, for you, in being behind the heroine without her seeming to tell the story, and 'no scenes that she could not have been in' is very valuable for 'intimacy'.

I am sending you Dorothy Sayers's latest which I think a lot of. It suffers in a sense from being in two styles—one hand writing her usual detective and the other a bold (and successful) attempt at something much stronger and full of character and good dialogue.

Tomorrow I must be up and doing with Cochran and his people.

[To Redditch]   27 December '35

Maggie was brought up in ambulance this forenoon by William and a nurse and taken straight to No. 17. There was nothing unhappy for her in this as she took it as quite ordinary, and she accepts her bed at the home as naturally. Nevertheless there is certainly a little change in her since I was at Miss Bergner's, and it all seems for the better. She calls Sir Douglas by his name, and said she thought it good to have a change to London, and he says she is not in as bad a condition as we had led him to suppose. She knew me better than before, and with some faint quivers and smiles did this time have a slight expression in her face. When I took her hand she pressed and held it—mine—while at Medstead it might have been some foreign body. It was heart-rending when I came away. I said some endearing things to her and she looked at me steadily.

I won't say any more, but things look less cruel if perhaps

even more pathetic than they did. Should she recover one need not dread, they all say, her feeling alarmed at what she has gone through. William went back home this evening and returns on Sunday. I shall be glad when you come back on Thursday, but don't come London on Monday unless you must as it would be a pity to have all that travelling, and I feel more fit now.

[To Worthing]   13 May '36
I hope you are going strong with the novel, and yet have squeezed in some time to benefit from a sun that is so much to your liking. I meant to write yesterday from Sharpthorne but Miss Bergner would have us read the play together and talk about it so much that I seem to have done nothing else there. I got back for lunch today and you can't think what a state of squalid demolition the Adelphi has reached in these two days. All the opposite roofs in Robert Street are smashed. Roofs in tatters, windows gone, great holes in walls. At this rate one feels all will be gone in a week or two. Workmen are crawling everywhere with hammers and every blow brings down a chunk. The noise is not as deafening as you might expect. The chief feeling is that it is disreputable to be here. Elizabeth Lucas is coming to dinner tonight. There were a good many letters but nearly all could be destroyed unanswered, as they were the appeals the mention of one's name in the papers brings forth. I do hope you have got back your happiness in the writing and slinging sheet after sheet to the floor— the lovely experience.
I shall be so sorry if 'Jimmy' Thomas[1] is done for. It was for long I feel convinced a gallant life.

[To Longniddry, Scotland]   24 December '36
7 o'clock on Thursday p.m. at present, but when letters reach their destination at this festive time I have no notion. I trust it is being fairly festive for you and it has been so far at least quiet and comfortable for me and nurse, who is probably back from her cinema by now. I wrote out some suggestions for the Visions[2] last night which may possibly be acceptable. I said that none of them could be of any use unless the

[1]The Right Hon. J. H. Thomas.
[2]In The Boy David.

family of Jesse were visible on the floor during the dreams and did this because they were entirely invisible to me on Tuesday *though I knew to look for them*, but curious corroboration came today from Peter who came in to lunch and was astounded to hear that the family was supposed to be there. He had no idea of it. This sort of thing is hard to fight.

I must write some more letters but all I am thinking of is what a blessing you have been to me during the last five weeks. I don't conceive how I could have got through them without you. And you so overworked yourself too!

27 December '36

I hope Gosford does not seem as forlorn as the flat. I suppose you have not yet got my Thursday letter though there was one post here this morning (Sunday) and it was clever of Frank to manage to speak to Gosford House though he was not sure whom he spoke to. I hope this finds you as what I feel myself, pretty fair, and I have Saturday, 2nd, lunch to look forward to and Sunday, 3rd, dinner. Mrs Lucas came in to dinner last night and was very game though only by a brave struggle I fear.

Miss Bergner assures me that those changes in the third act have all now been made. The play goes straight from the Lament to the David and Goliath scene—the curtain falls only once in the Visions and in a day or two will not fall at all. The Jesse family are now clearly seen asleep during the Visions, the Death of Saul is cut out, and after the witch scene the Lament begins with Saul alone lying there dead,—each scene melts into the next and the pause from Lament to David and Goliath is very short. I'm going to the theatre in a day or two to go over all this and other things with Mr Parr the stage manager. The new Jonathan makes his start tomorrow. Miss Bergner says that on Wednesday evening she gave her first real performance as David, and enthused herself as well as the audience. So far despite the Press the monetary takings have been huge, but it is too early to know the future. All these things and others could have been done in Edinburgh.

[To Tunbridge Wells. Written in pencil]   19 January '37
All of importance going well as my wire had told you and I should have 'got into ink' if there ever was any in my bed-room, where Young wants me to stay for this day longer. He

237

won't be back unless I send for him. I always liked him personally very much and today was much impressed by his skill. He also had a look at Frank who returned this morning, though still pulled down.

The play alas will evidently be off in a fortnight or so, as, though profitable now, Cochran is insistent that it will soon be losing ground, i.e. after next Wednesday when the library deal ends. It would all have been incomprehensible in the old days and at ordinary theatres, but I daresay he is right about today and His Majesty's. The worst mistake was going there, but probably it is not what the great public cares for. I am not depressed for myself and know it is only one of the pin pricks, but I grieve for Miss Bergner. She is coming in to see me tonight and seems to be taking it in a wise spirit which is very nice of her.

Later. E.B. has just been in on way to theatre and has taken an oath against bitterness.

21 January '37

Such a dear letter from you about the play and all. This enclosure from tonight's *Evening Standard* explains its melancholy self and is poor reading. I have not a doubt that you could have helped me had you been here, but I don't think with any result other than adding one week to the run. I had already offered to give up my royalties and so I now learn had Elisabeth. I won't write any more about it but will tell you when you are back. It is a pity your having now to add so much to the Queen book.[1] Of course I'll do anything I can about the little princess. I have had a heavyish day today as up to now (nearly 8 p.m.) have taken no Veganin and so have stiffer pains. Just an experiment of my own, for which according to Young I have no need. At present am pretty comfortable.

Peter is bringing in Arthur Bryant after dinner tonight. B. is great about the play.[2]

About my trying Sherwood Park—we shall see how I am on your return.

[1] The Duchess of York having become Queen a new edition of her Life was in preparation. Barrie contributed the story of his first meeting with Princess Margaret Rose.
[2] *The Boy David.*

238

[To Stanway]   30 April '37
   It is the saddest of days to write to you.[1] Many think that
such a time is not quite so dire because it comes, to some extent
at any rate, expected, but in my experience that has always
been wrong. The over-whelmingness of it obliterates the small
things and a different world has come. Well, all these things
you know as well as or better than I. She was the sweetest lady
that ever was and I really do think the best loved because she
shed the finest light. 'Back to Stanway' you say, forgetting that
there is no such place now unless as yours. She and you were
certainly the Stanway of my days.
   Give my special love to the priest. Coley is coming in to
dinner tonight and I doubt not he was very useful in the last
days. I have not seen him yet. I have felt better today and
yesterday than for some time, and if you would like it I want
to go to Stanway if there the journey ends. I think I could
easily do it, with some little troubles perhaps.
   I do hope you will go on with all the things you have in hand.

[To 8 Sussex Place]   10 June '37
   I was just about proposing something of the kind,[2] and
indeed I should be miserable if you did not follow it out.
Furthermore though I miss you sore I can assure you that they
are doing everything here in exemplary way. The nurse is I
find excellent. And I find my greatest treasure of all is the
new doctor whom Horder (who has just left) has provided me
with instead of the other, and he will have complete charge of
me. Name of Macdonald and a blessing to me. He has a lovely
touch though a stalwart fellow, and seems to be accepted everywhere as the head of this department in these doings. I have
had hardly a touch of pain since he came on the scene.
   Paul[3] was in yesterday but had to go off to Cortina, but
nothing to do with illness—only business.
   I have been reading and smoking in bed and do wish there
had been such rest for you. I don't know whether Monday will
suit them as they may have to be doing things for my benefit,

   [1]Death of Lady Wemyss.
   [2]That Lady Cynthia should have a short Cornish holiday with her husband
and Simon. She was recalled from there after two days by telephone, and
travelling by car all night reached Barrie's bedside on the morning of June
14th. He died on the 19th.
   [3]Paul Czinner, film-director, husband of Elisabeth Bergner.

but all days I love the sight and thought of you, whatever befall at any time. But Shields thinks all is going well and I keep bright.

★

To the COUNTESS OF WEMYSS, mother of Lady CYNTHIA ASQUITH

Adelphi Terrace House 7 September '21

Dear Lady Wemyss

I was so much happier at Stanway than I could have been anywhere else[1]—indeed had not that lovely haven opened its portals to me I believe I should just have stayed on drearily in London. I do thank you from the bottom of my heart for letting me go there. I know of many kind things you have done and this is one of the kindest: it has certainly helped me to face the world again. It had no memories for me, and that in itself was helpful. I sometimes thought, though, how many it must have for you, and that the happiest of them must bring pain as well as pleasure to you now.

As for the tithe barn I revelled in it until I had to take the Australian team over it one at a time, and by the time I escorted the tenth man through it I wished it had been destroyed by William the Conqueror (who by the way I told them had been shown over it just as they were, and probably made the same remarks. They were so dazed that I fancy they thought it was I who showed him over it, and I am beginning to think that myself).

Yours, J. M. Barrie

To the EARL OF WEMYSS

10 January '22

My dear Wemyss

It was rather a triumph to draw such a good letter out of you. The only lady who has read it (and I won't particularise her farther than by saying I saw you acting a sort of charade with her lately) was mostly astounded by its length, but I applaud it for higher reasons. It is very difficult not to say

[1]This was the first year Barrie 'took' Stanway for the summer.

240

to you 'I thank you heartily for your letter and the kind thought that prompted it'. I have written this a number of times lately, but I should scorn to say it to you. I hand it on to you however as a useful formula. 'I thank you heartily for your letter' is too short in itself, but to say it again in such entirely different words is masterly. I was very sorry not to see you again before I left Stanway where I had a truly happy time. R. L. Stevenson once wrote me that two men who had used the dreadful lavatory at Edinburgh University, though they never met, could never quite be strangers. It seems to me that we have a higher bond in eye-drops. I shall not soon forget your wistful appeals for them outside my door. I see you restlessly roaming the passage. Man wants but little here below but when he wants eye-drops he does want them. I have got a good detective story for you though the cover is better than the contents. All good wishes to you for the New Year.

Yours very sincerely, J. M. Barrie

To the COUNTESS OF WEMYSS

6 January '23

I feel I am writing this to you from the little room, last door on right as one proceedeth down a certain passage at Stanway. When I die a complete picture of that chamber will probably be found engraved on my heart, all lit up by an admirable arrangement of the electrical installation. I shall also carry away with me a cinema picture of you emptying the drawing room of furniture in record time.[1] You might do it to the music of that band, and be shown dancing the heavy pieces off. I could come on constantly as a policeman arresting you for over-doing it. This sort of picture would be much more popular than the out of date family portraits. Think how attractive a portrait gallery would become if all the figures did something characteristic under the influence of the cinema machine.

Translated into bald English what I am saying is that English houses are the pleasantest in the world and the Gloucestershire houses the pleasantest of English houses and Stanway the pleasantest of Gloucestershire houses, and the hostess of Stanway the dearest anywhere.

[1] Lady Wemyss was famous for violent re-arrangement of furniture, particularly when tired!

To the EARL OF WEMYSS
Stanway 4 September '25

Everything going on well here but for my sister's accident, and so far as can be known yet she is progressing very favourably. She is in the library where she holds a salon, including musical instruments. There are also other salons and more musical instruments in various rooms of the house, and when I seek to avoid them, if I am not careful I run into literary circles. At dinner various youths discuss wine, woman, the future, with a certainty I do not find in older blades. Here for instance is a sample from last night when we were sitting over the walnuts, the subject being selfishness and the lad referred to twenty-one last birthday—

A I call Finchley a very selfish chap.
B I don't think so at all.
A Why don't you?
B Well, I don't.
C How do you mean he is selfish?
A I call any man selfish who ruins five homes every night.

It does seem as if Finchley was a rather selfish chap, but quite a personality.

Cricket going strong. On Monday Stanway were badly beaten in the first innings and went in for the second with 170 to make in an hour and a half, which they did, Nicholas and another O.E. making 120 of them nearly all in sixes. (Finchley is not here. He is doubtless otherwise engaged.)

Competitions at the shovel board. We get worse and worse, with spasms of incredible brilliancy.

My sister liked your wire about her.

To the COUNTESS OF WEMYSS
Adelphi Terrace House 19 September '25

My dear Mary

I enjoyed your letter immensely, but alas did not get it till I returned here yesterday as my correspondence was not forwarded. I am so sorry. As for that house building scheme, though fair it sounds, I must say 'Na na' like Queen Victoria when they showed her the crown of Scotland and she begged them (all monarchs do this) to put it on her head. I mean the others said Na na. Then she said if they wouldn't put it on

242

her head, would they at least let her hold it in her hands, but they said 'Na na' again and just put it away. I dare not even hold your fine idea in my hands, for I am past the time when I care to own things, indeed it is a pleasure to me to own as little as possible. But it was very delightful of you to think of me in this connection and of course its one great attraction would have been being near you. I don't like being near golf and the sea for any length of time. The mountains and the streams draw me—or did. We had one fierce day on the Beauly when the cattle, 100 of them, swam a brawling river and dashed down the glen like a torrent to get to their calves which were bellowing for them some miles away. It was as wild as though they had been Highlandmen rushing to the standard of Prince Charlie. My sister seems to be getting on as well as can be expected. She got back by ambulance to her home on Monday. She loves Stanway as much as I do, which is putting it pretty strong.

Always yours, J.M.B.

16 February '26
This here is just to say that what Walter Raleigh quotes as your observation about Julian and the war[1] is as pretty and witty as anything that ever dropped from the mouth of woman. I exclaim with pride 'I know her'.

6 September '26
Once again for me is over the great glory of being at Stanway. To the house itself with its many memories of more importance this is a small matter—just one leaf fallen from the tulip tree, let us say, though I question whether I loom as large, but to me it is august and sad for I was again very happy there and very conscious how much I am beholden to you for letting me go. My warmest thanks. We did very much the same things as of yore and were very much the same people. I think my only novelty (and occasionally I regretted the starting of it!)

[1]'My Lady Elcho, who is now Lady Wemyss, said rather a delicious thing about Julian Grenfell. I said that he, and perhaps two others, were all that I had ever heard of who liked this war, just as it is,—to whom it was bread and meat and wine and father and mother and betrothed. She said "Yes, of course it was Julian's war. We don't want to be horrid about it, and we're glad he had it; still, perhaps some of us—it does seem very expensive for dear Julian's treat." I love that, partly because it's a noble tribute to Julian.' From *The Letters of Sir Walter Raleigh*.

243

was telling a continuous story on Simon's bed to four boys with an occasional intrusion by their mothers. It was about their own adventures on a desert isle where they were wrecked and did prodigies of valour, including some slaughter and Simon was radiant every time he sent an enemy to Davy Jones's locker. I left Cynthia, Beb and Michael to go from Oxford to the Wharf by rowing boat, and I think Beb must at this moment be feeling rather hot.

Stanway 2 August '28

I have found a delicious place[1] in which to spend the month of August, named as above and situated among the far-famed Cotswolds. I feel sure you would like it, and if you could come this way on your Scottish adventure you could cut across north thereafter. Please consider it. I have a special desire to entertain you here. The grounds are lovely and the house is after your own heart. It belongs to a Scottish peer who I conclude is a hot Liberal in politics as he has put a bust of Lord Oxford[2] in the place of honour in the hall.

It sounds to me as if your treatment was terribly severe, though of course the good of it may lie in that. To pop into mud-baths in any circumstances must need a nerve, but a close study of your letter shows that your procedure is unusually drastic. First you took two mud baths running, then three running and you were contemplating four and even six running. Merely to lie in them or stand up in them must be tiring, but to run in them sounds like something that would daunt the stoutest hearts of our representatives now engaged in the Olympic games.

You make me jump (as if the door panel between the dining room and kitchen had suddenly opened with a whop) when you ask when my Scottish *lecture* is to be. None of that. Don't frighten me. I am merely opening a bazaar which I am assured is only a ten minutes affair, and it is at Jedburgh on Thursday, Oct. 11. It is for the benefit of a namesake of yours, Mary Queen of Scots, who I understand is now in needy circumstances. An unfortunate marriage, I believe. I shall be staying near there with one F. S. Oliver, whom you may know but it would be good to go on to Harestanes if I survive the bazaar

[1] Lady Wemyss's own Stanway, of course.
[2] A bust of Oliver Cromwell with a remarkable likeness to Lord Oxford.

stalls. Mary of course was a naughty lady like the heroine of that Willa Cather book whom I am glad you liked as I did also; they are often so much better and truer than their detractors.

It has been middling wet here for some days (greatly to the benefit of the country) but is fine today, and everyone is in good health and there is much bathing in the Stanton pool. For the Bank holiday which begins tomorrow Beb comes down and Mr Coles and Scribner (American publisher) and his wife and Sir Donald Maclean. After that, names which are more familiar to you. I met Lord Balfour (and his Rolls-Royce) at Lady Desborough's the other day, and he looked very well, was in gay spirits, and remains I should say without doubt the most charming figure in the world. I know the doctors are averse to his making speeches on account of his throat but in every other way I think he can both work and play. Like you I didn't go to Eton v. Harrow (though it turned out to be a glorious game equally creditable to both sides though Eton won). Think of it, there is not now a boy at Harrow who was born when last Harrow won. I was also absent from the Garden Party but Cynthia was there looking a vision with Brenda Dufferin.

Adelphi Terrace House 12 April '31
It now approaches your lunch time, and I see you appearing down stairs and making all Stanway different at once—or in a sense what it has been for so many years always the same because of your beloved (and fearfully strong) personality. I often think down there that the way you carry on at Stanway where so many have come and gone is one of the finest personal triumphs I know and am so glad that it brings you its own reward of happiness. It certainly creates much happiness in others and in none I think more than in myself, particularly when I sit on your right hand at meals which you may have noticed I always do unless there is a little card to put me elsewhere. I hear from a safe source that His Lordship has returned and I send him my warm greetings and hope that on his voyages he encountered some draughts champions whom he floored and then assured that the only person who was his master at the game was your ever grateful and affectionate

J.M.B.

Yours is the 'wite' (as I hope they would still put it at Gosford) if I have been slow in writing to thank you for our happy time at Stanway, as I have instead been engrossed in your book[1]. It really is a beauty, and all the time and loving care you have given to it are amply rewarded. Its outstanding figure to me is Ego whom I only saw once for an hour at Knebworth and in circumstances that prevented my even knowing who he was. I have of course heard much of him since then, but the other evening when you read some of his letters to us he came alive to me for the first time, and I seemed to know him as well as I know any other listener on that to me memorable occasion. In the last few days I have of course got to know him still better from the rest of the letters and the rest of the book. I had a general idea of his reticence and chivalry and have pictured him on that cricket ground and known his lovableness but now I think of him as the finest of you all. What humour he had, and with what delicious phraseology he gives expression to it. The one right way of saying a thing shows again and again in those letters. Peter had told me he thought them the best the war had produced and I certainly think with him. In your own work there are many delights and many from other hands, but for the moment I think only of him, and how he must have graced that house.

To the EARL OF WEMYSS

Adelphi Terrace House 6 May '37

I grieve indeed for this sad loss that has come to you,[2] a sad loss assuredly to the many who loved her, of whom I was one, and by our own sorrow we can have some closer sympathy with yours which is so much deeper. So great the merriment used to be at Stanway and I used to think it specially so when you were both in good form and having playful sallies up and down the dining table. For much joy I thank you and happy days, and I wish you were in better health, and indeed rather wish it for myself as well.

★

[1] A privately-issued family record.
[2] The death of Lady Wemyss.

To The Lady MARY STRICKLAND, daughter of Lord and Lady WEMYSS

Adelphi Terrace House 17 March '26

Dear Lady Mary

Though I have not written to you about the appearance on the scene of Sarah I have been applauding both of you and 'wish you very happy'. I hope by the way you spell her correctly—at least that is the way in Scotland where of course they ought to know. Tell her I am thinking out a way of getting her into the Stanway play. 'Enter Sarah, C' would bring the house down and Sarah too. May you bring great joy to each other.   Yours, J. M. Barrie

22 March '26

My dear Mary

As long as I can spell you this way (and it is the condition of my joining the family) I shall keep an open mind about the spelling of Sara. After all she is English and may as well begin at once dropping her h's. I am mighty pleased to be asked to be her godfather, and it is an honour I accept with alacrity. Yes, there is one other condition, that you now learn how to spell my name, or at least how to pronounce it.

Yours affectionately, J. M.

5 July '26

It is very nice of you to remember me for the Eton and Harrow match, but flown away are now all the birds, and I suppose I shall no more grace that festive scene. Caught, bowled and run out for ever. I am so glad that Sara smiles a lot—another thing she takes from me.

Stanway, Cheltenham 14 April '28

You will be thinking ha ha, a letter from Stanway—delicious —who is it that is breaking in on my loneliness. Then turning to the name at the end you will get a sad disappointment and two tears will roll down your dear face.

Here am I for a day or two at Stanway with many of yours gathered together and you not one of them which is a melancholy state of affairs. They are not the only persons who miss you. I understand that in a week or two you will be able to go to a hotel, and after your time of seclusion this will probably seem bliss to you. This will be a chance for hotels to come out strong such as they are seldom given. I was in a Cannes one not so long ago, and was so weary of it that when a waiter spilt a plate of soup over me I could have thanked him publicly for the diversion. I must often have tobogganed through Glion with Nicholas on my back when he was about five as we were at Caux for a month just above you. My chief duty however was to wait for them at the foot of the run laden with their coats, waterproofs, leggings, etc.

Stanway at the moment contains your mother, Cynthia, Letty, David and Martin, Guy and his three maids and son, Beb resting from his novel which will be out this week, Bibs and Lady Desborough. I won't swear that there are not one or two more. I now record any changes I see in them since about the time I last saw you. Your mother now rules us like a rod of iron except when she forgets to do so. The voices of David and Martin have broken, so that when they speak one looks around for elderly gentlemen. Laura startles me by her resemblance to a grown-up young lady. You will be interested to hear what we wore last night at dinner. Lady D was in a dark claret velvet with many graceful thingamebobs on it. Bibs I swear was in the same but without the thingamebobs. Cynthia shone in soft armour, and I was in unrelieved black and white, giving me that distingué effect which is the despair of Beb and Guy. Everybody except myself has a dog or dogs, and every owner thereof takes me aside to express their surprise at the way the other owners bring up their dogs. I have not been bitten yet but I stay till Tuesday.

Do get better quickly and come back to brighten the hearts of the deserving and undeserving.

To SARA STRICKLAND

Stanway, Cheltenham 27 December '33

My Dere Sara

it was LOvely 2 C U again and i thot u was nicerer than effer i lov u trulie. When the uther KOMONER ones waS DANsing U and I SHAred a SWEET secret i Hop u will not bother lerning lessons and pianos but will come and B my Houskeeper that will Be ~~sipers raping~~ ripping

FROM ure Loving Godfavver

248

Adelphi Terrace House 26 July '35

Your letter to me was quite the nicest one I have had for a long time and I keep it for safety in my pocket. Also I love the beautiful scroll round the paper, and if I could do anything as pretty I would do it round this sheet. When I was a boy I meant to become an artist but I always lost my paint-box so I had to give that game up and take to pen-nibs. If you lose your nib you can always get another one, and I hope you will get another one and write to me again, and put a scroll on it and pictures. I think the picture on your letter I liked best of all is the one of the 'very queer fish'. You have the art of making it look very queer indeed. It made me wonder whether baby scorpions have god-fathers, and I think I should have felt a shudder if I had had to hold it up at the baptismal font. How proud you must have been to catch the 22 shrimps in your net. Of course it is rather sad to think you ate them at tea-time, but I expect they know that this is what they are for and took it all as a compliment as they went romping down. I am often rather lonely here in my flat and I wish I could catch you in a net. Then I would bring you to my flat, and when I looked up from my work, behold I should have the happiness of seeing Sara sitting near me. From this you will see that I do love having you for my god-daughter.

★

To Professor A. E. HOUSMAN, poet, after the only occasion on which they met

Adelphi Terrace House [1922]

Dear Professor Houseman

I am sorry about last night, when I sat next to you and did not say a word. You must have thought I was a very rude man: I am really a very shy man.

Sincerely yours, J. M. Barrie

[Housman replied:
Dear Sir James Barrie
   I am sorry about last night, when I sat next to you and did not say a word. You must have thought I was a very rude man; I am really a very shy man.
                                   Sincerely yours, A. T. Housman.
P.S. And now you've made it worse for you have spelt my name wrong.]

To the husband of a Dead Friend

Adelphi Terrace House

It is a woeful thing to many and certainly so to me, which makes one have some understanding of what desolation it is to you. To intrude on you may be a shame. This at any rate is only a hand to clutch yours. For myself I can truly say that she was one of the delights of my life. The quality of her was such that she can never be repeated. Our gatherings at Stanway, so happy, owed more to her than to any other visitor.

I wish you to know that I consider you were worthy of her. She gave of her abundance to you but you gave as much to her. I cannot think, looking back through a long stretch, or any woman who ever had a better husband. I grew to care for you almost as much as for her, than which one cannot go much further. The talks you and I used to have when we were alone were among my chief delights and I am proud to know that we are friends for always.

To Miss ROSALINE MASSON, of Edinburgh

[Miss Masson compiled a book called *I can Remember Robert Louis Stevenson*, to which Barrie was one of the contributors. 'As I never saw Stevenson face to face,' he wrote, 'I have no right to be in this volume; but I should like to step into some obscure corner of it so that I may cheer and cheer as the procession of him goes by . . . When I came to London there was a blank spot in it; Stevenson had gone. It could not be filled till he came back, and he never came back. I saw it again in Edinburgh the other day. It is not necessarily that he was the greatest, I don't think he was the greatest, but of the men we might have seen he is the one we would like best to come back. Had he lived another year I should have seen him. All plans arranged for a visit to Vailima, "to settle on those shores for ever," he wrote, or something to that effect, "and if my wife likes you what a time you will have, and if she does not, how I shall pity you."'
On the publication of Miss Masson's book Barrie wrote her a letter which she subsequently obtained his permission to add to a new edition in 1925.]

Adelphi Terrace House 4 December '22

Dear Miss Masson

I am depressed to read my own fell admission that I never saw or spoke to him. Such a galaxy you have found, who even in the 'Seventies (Scotch canniness) were qualifying for future admission to your pages, while I kept hitting my forehead in vain, to recall some occasion when I touched the velvet coat. Why did I not, for instance, hang about the Fleeming Jenkins's door? If only I had this much to go upon we should soon have got started.

Even without it? Why not?

It is a lasting regret to me that I met R.L.S. but once. This was in the winter of '79 when I was in Edinburgh, my first year at the University, Masson my great man. One snowy afternoon, cold to the marrow, I was hieing me to my Humanities, and was crossing Princes Street, nigh the Register House, my head sunk in my cravat, when suddenly I became aware, by striking against him, of another wayfarer. Glancing up I saw a velvet coat, a lean figure with long hair (going black) and stooping shoulders, the face young and rather pinched but extraordinarily mobile, the manner doggedly debonair. He apologised charmingly for what was probably my fault, but I regarded him with stern disapproval. My glowering look was meant less for the chevalier himself than for his coat and hair, which marked him dandiacally as one of a class I had read about as having dinner every day. When he had passed he turned round to survey me, and I was still standing there, indicating in silence my disapproval of his existence. He went on, stopped and looked again. I had not moved. He then returned and, addressing me with exquisite reasonableness, said, 'After all, God made me.' To which I replied, 'He is getting careless.' He raised his cane (an elegant affair) and then there crossed his face a smile more winning than I had ever before seen on mortal. I capitulated at that moment. 'Do I know you?' he enquired.

'No,' I replied with a sigh, 'but I wish you did.'

At that he laughed outright, and was for moving on, when perhaps struck by my dejection, he said, 'I say, let us pretend that I do.' We gripped hands, and then taking me by the arm (I had never walked thus before) he led me away from the Humanities to something that he assured me was more humane, a howff called Rutherford's where we sat and talked by the solid hour. I had never been in this auberge (as he called it) before, nor have I been since, but I am sure it was a house of call of d'Artagnan and company in the days when they visited Newcastle and found it on the Scottish border. I associate that night indeed (for the afternoon wandered into night) with the four musketeers for various reasons, one being that we drank burgundy, and Chambertin at that, he reminding me that it was the favourite drink of Athos, and therefore the only drink for us, and when he ordered it he always said 'a few more bottles' in the haughty Athos way. It was served in tankards and there was froth on the top, but we drank on the understanding that it was Chambertin. As for his talk, it was the most copious and exhilarating that I ever heard come from man's lips, and ranged over every variety of subject. You will be interested to learn that I was not one of those who let great talk pass on unheeded like a spate, to regret afterwards that I took no notes. I could write shorthand in those days, and I 'took him down' in my class note-book (holding it beneath the table) till I had filled that bulky book. Alas that this record of wonderful hours should be lost. I lost it that night before we rose from the table. I had a vague recollection next morning that he had sold it to the waiter for a few more bottles of Chambertin. The waiter had proved to be a university student of my year, who valued, not the pages of talk, but other pages about the Differential Calculus.

I say that the work was lost before we rose, but I have a notion that we rose more than once. The first time was the result of his discovery that someone in Edinburgh had said in public that he considered the works of Robert Burns to have an immoral tendency. Who this person was he had no idea; but my companion's proposal was that we should go out into the streets and ring every door-bell until we found him. The intention was then to argue with him. We did go out (I think) and ring many bells, but without success, and the snow was still falling heavily, so I agreed with alacrity when he proposed that we should return to Rutherford's.

We had no more money (I had had none from the start) but he sold them his velvet coat for a few more bottles of Chambertin. As the hours sped we seem to have become quarrelsome, just as Athos and his friends sometimes did. I think the reason was that one of us maintained that he was a 'braw singer' (I am not sure which one) and insisted on putting it to the proof with inharmonious results. I am certain that I left Rutherford's pursued through the blinding snow by my erstwhile friend, who kept shouting 'stop thief!' and describing me (happily incorrectly) as a man with a wooden leg and a face like a ham. Long after all the rest of Edinburgh was a-bed he was chasing me through the white empty streets of the New Town and the Old Town, and I was panting hard when I at last reached my lodging in Frederick Street.

I had no idea of his name, nor would it have conveyed much to me, but I always longed to meet him again however risky it might have been, and I searched for him and for a velvet coat (for I suppose he had more than one). I remembered him as The man in the velvet coat until years afterwards, when I saw his portrait in a newspaper, and discovered that my friend of a night had been no other than Robert Louis Stevenson.

Alas.

Heigho.
It might have been.   Yours sincerely, J. M. Barrie

[From Vailima in 1892 Stevenson had written to Henry James: 'Hurry up with another book of stories. I am now reduced to two of my contemporaries, you and Barrie—O, and Kipling—you and Barrie and Kipling are now my Muses Three. And with Kipling, as you know, there are reservations to be made . . . But Barrie is a beauty, the *Little Minister* and *The Window in Thrums*, eh? Stuff in that young man; but he must see and not be too funny. Genius in him, but there's a journalist at his elbow—there's the risk.']

To Lady GWENDELINE CHURCHILL

Adelphi Terrace House 13 February '23
Dear Lady Gwendeline
On my way home tonight I remembered a little thing of long ago that it strikes me might interest your husband. Just this, that the first person who wrote to me about my first book[1] was Lord Randolph Churchill. A very small book, price one shilling, that has shot down the horizon long ago, but I carried it in my pocket for a week with peeps at it to see that it had not evaporated, which is much more than I have done with any of my books since. It was a very nice letter, that led to my knowing him in days when I must have been about the loneliest man in London, and he was very kind to me. I told Lady Randolph about it long after.
Why don't I tell this to your husband instead of to you? Answer, because though I like him well I like you better. You weren't born at the time, else I feel you would have written me a nice letter too. Therefore excused.
                                    Yours sincerely, J. M. Barrie

★

To the COUNTESS OF LYTTON

Glan Hafren, near Newtown, Montgomeryshire
My dear Pamela   12 September '19
Please to remember that you are booked to go to a matinée next Tuesday with Antony[2] and as many others as are on the

[1] *Better Dead* (once to have been called 'The Society for Doing Without Some People'), published at Barrie's expense in 1887.
[2] Viscount Knebworth, the Lyttons' son, at Eton with Nicholas Llewelyn Davies.

253

spot. 189 hours till Eton begins, Nicholas came in to tell me a moment ago. This is a very Welsh place, and if one calls out 'Davies', Michael comes, and the gardener, and the stable boy, and the Member for the district, and half of the school children, and the dogs prick up their ears, and the poachers hide. It was dear of you to come to the first night of the old play and made such a difference to me.

I have a better scheme for you at Eton than Mr Ramsay's. He with his pedagogic limitations only invited you for a night, but as you were taken for a little girl at *Crichton* I suggest your going to Ramsay's house for the first half as a little boy instead. Antony would be your major and you would be his minor, but you could look after him in secret, and when I came down and saw you in a tall hat or in flannels I wouldn't give you away. There seems to be an idea in this for a comedy or a tragedy, and I pause to think it out.

Yours, J. M. B.

Eilean Shona, Acharacle, Argyll-shire 15 August '20

I have paused in sheer admiration of the way in which I have written the address. It recalls the days in which I got a prize for hand-writing at school. It makes me hope that outsiders (but not you) on seeing it would exclaim 'If thus with his left hand, how superbly he could write with his right'.

We came up here three or four days ago and have got settled down for a month. It is the wildest sort of an island—10 miles round with only this house on it, which Lord Howard de Walden has lent us in a grand spirit of generosity. Nothing could be more beautiful—in the heart of the Prince Charlie country. You blow horns from miles away when you want anything—an engaging way of telephoning that would please Davina. We have mountains and lochs and boats and tennis and billiards, and most of the Western islands of Scotland lying at our feet. Lovely weather till today when it is coming down in blankets.

I hope you are all having a good time at Knebworth and having picnics and getting lost in the woods. I was really touched to think I was missed at the children's party. The fact is I am very self-conscious with children nowadays. I am no longer any good with them, and the nicer they are with me the more melancholy I feel over a lost accomplishment.

We see papers so late here that yesterday's has not arrived

though it is now evening. The world may be afire again already without our knowing it. I don't suppose so, but it will go on smouldering this many a year, with lots of people to encourage it and some to warm their hands at it.

Adelphi Terrace House 29 May '22

All hail, your Excellency.[1] I feel that I have to speak very loud to be heard. If this new contrivance that is the talk of London, 'Broadcasting', turns out to be the wonderful thing they say, all we shall have to do is to get a box apiece and then we can talk as easily as if I was on my telephone and you were on yours at Buckingham Street. I was taken through that street by my taxi on my way from Victoria on that mournful day—the only time I ever have been taken that way—as if to sharpen the barb—and there was the house crying to me to take down the boards. I bolted before the end came—it was too sad, you smiling so bravely. Well, but there is evidently a deal of happiness to be got out of it now you are there, and as they say in *Quality Street* I am happy of that. Which reminds me that during the Easter holidays I always knew when the cash of Antony, Nicholas and Co. was running low by their having at such times to go to my plays. They had evidently a colossal time at Knebworth in Antony's house where five or six of them had several days together. At present their chief excitement is who is to get into the XI. None of them will know probably till a day or two before the paralysing affair at Lords. I saw to the matter of the cinema machine and got one the same as Nicholas's, which was sent off some days ago, so it should, I presume, reach Calcutta as soon as this. It is not however an affair of yours to pay for as it is a present from me to the children. I had been wondering when you set off what I could give them, and this seems the right article. With my love. Very full instructions are on the inside. Also there are doubtless cinema people in Calcutta who can explain it all, and my own idea is that you will find you can hire films easiest through them. I wish I could get hold of a film done at St Andrew's when I was Lord Rectoring there lately. It has been exhibited in London but I missed it. Fine if I could send it to you. We had a great time in which I delivered an address that lasted an hour and thirty-seven minutes (the time is what

[1] Lady Lytton was thus addressed because Lord Lytton was now Governor of Bengal.

I am proudest of). When your picture arrived of the entrance into Calcutta *I took for granted* that it was Haig and myself arriving at St A or Dundee, and looked for my face everywhere until with sudden rapture I saw yours. It is a delightful photograph. I have however another score over you, viz. that Antony and Nicholas had both to write essays at Eton on my address. I can picture their scowling faces! I can also picture you prone on that journey from Bombay among the blocks of ice and 'biting at the air' (a good phrase). Lots of good phrases in your letter, especially about your guarded life. You tell me enough to make me able to write a romance about it with realistic details, but indeed that is one of the reasons why you are missed so much here, that you have taken away some of the romance of London. I do miss you enormously. The only remedy now seems to be that surprise visit, and I don't see why it should not be accomplished yet if Providence is helpful. We should evidently have to bring weapons with us to fight our way through to you in the final bout of the journey. Nicholas and Antony may come disguised as dervishes while I sell rugs in picturesque rags, drawing cunningly nearer and nearer. Then at last we see a face at a window, looking on to the scene in which she may not wander and simultaneously we shout 'Pamela'. Nico and I are immediately put to the torture, but Antony gets in, and some hours elapse before you say to him, 'By the way, who were your companions?'

19 November '22

You need not be afraid that Brown's successor 'won't let you in'. I can see him becoming your servant at once. In short he is a connisseur—and knows how to spell it, too, better than I do. There are however certain p's and q's you will have to attend to, for he is in his way quite as much a character as Brown. Very different. I have not yet found out what it is he does not know—yet there must be something. For instance, he is much better educated than if he had been to Eton. The other day Nico was having a cut finger bandaged by the cook, and exclaimed 'Think'st, madam, that I fear the sight of blood'. Through the wall from the pantry came Frank's timid voice, 'If such a man there be then trust him not', followed by 'This day is called the feast of Crispian'. Fortunately Nico was able to take him up, and they fired the whole scene through the wall at each other. He waited on them all at Stanway and could also have superintended their Greek and Latin studies (he reads Latin in the pantry for a diversion), and is very much at home in French and Spanish. When you come to stay here you may take a frivolous novel to bed but you must hide it between a Chaucer and the newest theory of Ethics.

Stanway and its week! I have a fear I never wrote you about that, but you will have heard from other performers. They played all day and danced all night, and one could see a terrific yawn taking possession of their faces as they bowled or batted. Antony was very gay, and I think enamoured for one brief night of a fair maid, as he constantly kept coming into my room to look for her, and finding only me constantly withdrew. The affair however seemed to be of the briefest. He also made the biggest hit of the cricket—a lovely drive over the bowler's head and out of the field. They all made speeches on the last night, and most of them afterwards took me aside to ask which I thought did best. I haven't seen Antony since they went to Oxford, but he spent a day (and possibly nominally a night) here on the way, accompanied by his new dog, which is the most forlorn looking creature I ever beheld. They seem to like their lodgings, and I am very glad they are together.

Politics! You will have been sharing in the excitement too. Queer turns of the wheel! It gives to think that Labour had nearly as many votes as the Conservatives, and they also seem to have the only distinct policy in the house. The Liberals will go permanently to bits if they don't combine and quickly into one party. But I am only a looker-on. I shouldn't wonder though the week at present celebrated for the meeting at the Carlton Club is better remembered in the future as the week in which the new volume of Housman came out. In any case—— But you would really rather I returned to Antony. It is extraordinary, happy though they are at Oxford, how Eton still grips them with both hands. They think of it and talk of it and revisit it both awake and in dreams. That last year makes the real world a difficult place to sit down in. Something I suppose like losing your seat in the H. of C.

Stanway, Winchcombe 26 December '22

Hie, hie, hoy, I am shouting at the top of my voice in the hope that you may hear me across the oceans—a merry Christmas to you all. I wonder what it is like, so far away, and hope you are drinking to absent friends, as I do. They are mostly a family party here. We went to church and the waits have been round. I wonder if you have waits, or anything corresponding thereto. I remember once writing a newspaper article about the waits and how they interrupted me at work in my lonely London lodgings, so I went out and knocked them all on the head with a spade and buried them beneath my window, and always henceforth when Christmas came round I thought of them with gentle melancholy. Various readers took it all seriously and wrote to the editor that it was one of the cruellest most callous murders of modern times and that they hoped I would swing for it.

As for Stanway I think every one in it is writing a book except myself. I hear therefore lots of literary talk and pick up information about how the thing is done. So long as all are together I fear not, but I become shy if left alone with one, having all my life had a dread lest authors should read their works to me.

Adelphi Terrace House 27 July '24

So glad to have your letter, but I can see you are very downcast at not being able to come and meet John. However when 'early next year' comes you will be rejoicing that the reunion lies before instead of behind you, so please find some comfort in that. I gave your message about John to Nico with my urgent request that it be carried into effect, but whether it will I know not, for he and all of them are very sniffy about 'youngsters' being present—none of them apparently being aware that they are just a gathering of infants themselves. Their week is in the end of August, and there is some talk (which may not come to fruit) of having the cinema man down again. Nico fancies a lady's face becoming so large that a melting photograph of himself is seen in both her eyes. Others want to emerge from roses. I don't think any of them have any special lady in view, indeed I am not certain who are coming, except that with the callousness of youth they are choosing new ones. Hermione and you will probably be pleased to hear this as you cannot come yourselves, which I do and do wish you could. Your healths will be proposed and drunk, and if I am cinema'd at the moment and enlarged I expect one of you will be found in each eye. I am alone in the flat at present, Peter and Nico having gone off on a continental fishing excursion. Nico was only seven when we were last in Sutherland, that lovely part of it which must be like a dream now to you as it is to me. Have seen some politicians lately, but bless you, you know as much at Darjeeling of what they are up to as we do if we are in the next seat. My own idea in a nutshell is that if an election comes within a year Labour will be stronger than ever though still without an actual majority. Probably the Conservatives would overtop them if they really dropped Protection, but they are carrying it about with them hidden in their pockets. Winston dined with me alone here the other night and is full of fight. He would be a great asset to them, but after drawing nigh they turn and run.

And now to my solitary meal. *P. Pan* is to be done in the Movies when we can find a Peter. If you had played him I should of course have changed the title to 'Peter Pam'.

1 May '27

I have only now heard, Pamela, that you are back. May 1! what a capital day for such good news. *May One* rejoice? Yes, *One May*. I hope you are happy and well, and that all the others are also. Here am I longing to see you again, so please be quick about it.

24 September '33

You have been very often in my thoughts since that dire day befell you and I have talked to you as it were and with distress for you though I have not seen you. Your woe is the one kind of human suffering that can get no alleviation from the lips or pens of friends however deeply wrung their hearts may be for you, or at least that is how I have felt at some times of my life. It is not we who can help—indeed the only earthly thing that can help, if it can be called earthly, is Time's soft finger. It does not in the crude way take away from pain, but leaves a feeling that breeds some composure, some happiness, the feeling —the indeed grateful knowledge—that some part of ourselves died with the loved one. I know that so much of you died with Antony that what is left of you can be ill able to cope with life as it must be faced, but that is the hard road through which you can come to any serenity. If you had cared for him less, if he had been less worth caring for, the road would be less

259

heavy going. Joy has to be paid for. He had a wonderfully happy life, and he owed it chiefly to you. As I saw him he was often ecstatically happy, and already they were probably the best years that can be. So much that he was not deprived of. What suddenly made me write you this note was that his laugh came back to me, the most glorious laugh I can remember in his bright circle.

Stanway 10 January '37

I am just enough of an invalid to ask you to excuse pencil. Also Cynthia is writing so many books simultaneously that all the inkpots are in use in other parts of the house. It was dear of you to write me a letter almost as pretty as yourself at a time when I consider I needed it, which is a time that frequently occurs. I read your words about the Lament to Miss Bergner and she was very pleased though she insists that she is shocking in it. I saw the play[1] for the first time a week ago, had not even seen a rehearsal for two months owing to a slight attack of something or other called neuritis, slight but persistent. I went to Edinburgh to rehearse it for three weeks and was never out of my hotel except to be x-rayed.

To be done with myself, I am now much better though this is my first venture from the flat. You must have been having a time of trouble and anxiety too with both Hermione and Davina prostrate in the throes of flu and I do hope that like David they will be able soon to carry their beds into the open though the weather hardly seems to invite it. W. S. Morrison[2] and his wife are coming in to dinner tonight. I expect you know them. I think mighty highly of him. I also liked a talk I had with her lately:—

Mrs. M. I should like so much to be in Edinburgh some time and show you round.

J.M.B. That would be delightful for me but of course I do know Edinburgh a bit.

She. But not the place I want to show you.

He. Do tell me.

She. I want to show you the very spot in Princes Street where W. S. and I first met.

My love to all.

[1]*The Boy David.*
[2]Now Postmaster General.

260

Adelphi Terrace House 30 May '37

My dearest Pamela,—I am gloomy about it but alas if the weather and my health remain hostile to me I must go away in a week or two for a month or so. The weather indeed looks all right but not for me it isn't, and though I can dissemble you would all find me out. May there be a happy time for me with you in the nearest by and by.

The writing shows that I have even ceased to be able to make words.

★

To Mrs W. S. MORRISON

15 August '32

Dear Mrs Morrison

How pleasant it is here, with no pack of boys running round the table as steam engines, and another one already I expect giving promise of being the worst of the clanjamfry. Compare your unhappy lot with mine but expect no further sympathy. Twins would have been more worth boasting of, and would also have helped me out of a difficulty (but not a thought did you give to me), because as you invited me to suggest a name and a lady writes me that she has sent me a Cardigan and a Spencer from —— we could have fixed on Cardigan and Spencer Morrison. As it is, though I suggested Hugh I now hear that a tiny voice from the blue begs for Neil, and whatever you, with your Ronalds, may say, I beg to intimate that to me Neil knocks Hugh out. Well, we can't have everything, not even you, but as far as I can see you two have all the best things of life and I am glad with you, and you must acknowledge your happiness daily on your knees, for whatever lies in store for you you can never be happier than now.

Always yours, J. M. Barrie

★

To Principal (later Sir JAMES) IRVINE, of the University, St Andrews, Fife

Adelphi Terrace House 10 February '22

My dear Principal

I have your letter and the enclosures. I hope the date[1] will

[1] For Barrie's rectorial address, 'Courage'.

suit the Chancellor, as it is evidently a good plan to combine the functions. So far as I am concerned, if another date about the same time was better for him it will be all right for me. Also I don't see why you should limit him to five minutes! The more of him the less of me strikes me as a very fine working arrangement.[1]

I trust the hall is not a large place, else I don't see how I can be heard. The smaller the better, I beg of you. (I conceive a deadly hatred of any outsiders who have applied for tickets.)

The Town Council want me to attend their function on the previous day.

I shall make out a small list of people as you propose and send them for the consideration of the Senators. I mean for the hon. degree.

Thank you again heartily for the kind invitation to your house.

Yours sincerely, J. M. Barrie

25 February '22

Your letter and the accompanying information received and digested—not that I am quite sure of the digestion. Many thanks to you however. My best plan seems to be to stay till the Friday and come back that night, and it is most kind of you to be prepared to suffer me so long.

I have been thinking over names, as you suggest, to propose for possible honorary degrees, and here they are. This may be too many but they are only suggestions.

Mr Thomas Hardy, Max Gate, Dorchester.

Mr John Galsworthy, Athenaeum, London.

Mr Charles Whibley, C/o Macmillans, Publishers.

Mr A. E. Housman, author of *The Shropshire Lad*, Cambridge University.

Sir Sidney Colvin, so much the friend of R. L. Stevenson, Athenaeum.

Sir Douglas Shields, the surgeon, 17 Park Lane, London (to my mind the best here).

E. V. Lucas, author of *Life of Ch. Lamb*, etc., Athenaeum.

Col. Freyberg, V.C., etc., Grenadier Guards, Guards

---

[1]Sir Douglas Haig, who was admitted as Chancellor on the same day, had suggested that his own speech should be limited to five minutes.

Club, Brook Street, W. (He had an extraordinary record in the war. Haig will know of it.)

Miss Ellen Terry (I am not sure of her address but C/o myself would find her).

I don't know whether you ever give the LL.D. to ladies. This would be rather fine, I think. If you don't, I propose (to have one person from the theatre) Sir Squire Bancroft, Athenaeum.

Hardy couldn't go north, I'm afraid, too old and frail, but if an exception could be made on account thereof, he is certainly in my opinion the chief man of letters living.

I don't know how many names you wanted, but consult me of course if you wish to.

16 March '22

It was beyond my hopes that the Senators should look with favour on that long list of mine and I am delighted. I have heard from several of them of their having already written accepting and that Sir S. Colvin is in too poor health. I know however that he is very appreciative of the honour. Miss Terry has not had the invitation as yet, and as I gave you 'care of me' as her address I am wondering whether it has miscarried. I suppose it is too late to add another name. I should have suggested Sir W. Robertson Nicoll who did much for me in my early days. I had a great letter from your household which I am immensely pleased with. Oh that the address was over and I could get at them.

I think my boy, now in his last year at Eton, will manage to get up with me.

Galsworthy is in Sweden for the next ten days or so, and may not hear until his return.

To VERONICA and NIGEL IRVINE

7 April '22

My dear Veronica and Nigel

What times we shall have when that address is over. Not that it ever will be over, but let's pretend.

Don't you go and like Miss Terry better than me. Every one else does. Mr Galsworthy is also rather hefty with the young. Be coldish to him—not sniffy you know, but on the cool side. Please tell your mother that I'm afraid my boy won't be able to come as Eton begins again on May 4. Also could she find two seats at the fearsome function (and address them here) for Lady Cynthia Asquith who is my secretary.

Be good but not too good else I won't feel at home with you. Besides, I shall probably say such noble things in the hall that I'll need to be rather naughty with you the moment I get out.

Your loving friend, J. M. Barrie

To Mrs IRVINE

3 January '23

Dear Mrs Irvine

I have just got back here from the country and got your letter. I am so sorry to hear you have those anxieties about the children, and your picture of Felicity by the fire in her eiderdown is almost more than I can bear. When you have a moment, please send me a line about her, and I do hope all is well again.

Yours sincerely, J. M. Barrie

To Principal IRVINE

2 December '25

I was hoping you might have remained over and come in tonight, but it waxeth late and you are evidently not coming. I was in Glo'stershire, else should have turned up to cheer you for I am proud of your Davy Medal. I might have followed the custom of further-north and helped to brighten the proceedings by passing eminent blokes down the hall over the heads of their fellows. Bravo at any rate for a fine thing right amply earned, and I have a cheer left for St A. for beating Glasgow at the desperate game.[1]

2 May '26

Very sorry but needs must. I see I can't get off for the rectorial ceremonies and have had to acquaint the Secretary with my disability. I am uncommonly disappointed. I feel sure Nansen is to be worth a much longer journey, and there is the opportunity lost of revisiting a loved place and people.

16 May '26

Good for the red gowns of St Andrews. I am very glad to hear of their sporting behaviour but not surprised.[2] One good

[1]Rugby.　[2]In the General Strike.

thing out of the darkness is the exhilaration of feeling that youth can turn from its own jobs when need be and run the country. With a little guidance they ought probably to take it on permanently. (Of course they would have to strike first.)

Balnaboth, Kirriemuir, Angus 17 August '33

Well-a-day! There is a story which seems to apply to us of a son writing to his mother 'Dear mother, I am in prison,' and getting a reply 'Dear Son, so am I,' for I too have been in the wars and had two recent bouts of bronchitis lasting about two months each. We might evidently have had a double-bedded room in the nursing home I frequent. I am very glad you are better and I am also pretty fit again, though not able (I wish I was) to go a-galloping with Felicity on a charger.

This is a pleasant glen, very familiar to me once upon a time, and I shall probably remain into the first week of Sept. If you are to be back about the 4th thereof I should like to bear down upon you at St A. In any case I shall hope to dab you on the head in the back end of Oct.[1]

To Lady IRVINE

Adelphi Terrace House, 9 September '33

Dear Mabel

(You need not expect me to let you off with anything less than that, especially with the right hand.) I waved you all good-bye with infinite regret, and then turning to my *Scotsman* was a bit cheered to find I was again with the Principal. He is a grand fellow that, and how well you know it and how glad I am to know that you know it. And how devoted he is to you. No truer pair have ever come within my ken. I love all that household including the aunt, the sister and the fascinating Williams.

I have sent out a demand for Emily Shore,[2] who completes our circle.

23 September '33

Your letter delighted but did not surprise me. The absence

[1] At a forthcoming graduation in Edinburgh when the LL.D. degree was conferred on Irvine by Barrie in his capacity as Chancellor.
[2] *The Journal of Emily Shore.* (See Chapter in de la Mare's *Early One Morning*.)

265

of surprise was because though I had not hitherto known you well I always did know in my bones what you were in yours. Your Jim is a man who (as far as it can be said of mortals) makes no mistakes, and it was unlikely (though there are precedents) that he should blunder in the greatest of his adventures. Well, at any rate he didn't. I think you have made for him as happy a home as I know in this world. As for Veronica I hope you don't need to be told that she will be received here with open arms. I shall rout her out. Of course her departure must leave anxiety behind it, but the bird of today is stronger in the wing than the young birds of yester year—at least the females are, and have a reserve of grit that may be almost called a new thing in life; it is not acquired, it is not necessarily their upbringing, it is in some inexplicable way born with them; it is a sort of sturdy little twin carrying a light; it is perhaps, who knows, the only light lit by the war. You need have no fear that any special danger lies in the R.A.D.A.; there are doubtless all kinds there as elsewhere but from my experience of them they are mostly hard workers and valiant souls. Many are too hard up and have to live too hardly in poor rooms, but are worth Veronica's knowing for all that, and her living with friends takes away the one anxiety. Besides, as a brave girl she must try those wings. Courage, didn't some one say (who did not have much of it himself).

11 October '33

Your letter was a shock to me. I evidently had not understood the gravity of Jim's symptoms from your previous letter and am vexed with myself. Things seem to be so much better now that thankfulness is the first note but nevertheless he is not out of the wood and I see he must be prostrate for a bit yet even before he becomes a convalescent. As for you what thorns of anxiety you must have endured. Joy cometh in the morning and now it is at least breaking through. I wish I had you all in my flat. The one thing I am good at is at being a nurse to those I love. I have a wonderful professional nurse[1] who hies to me when I am low and the last time she got much bowled over, far more than I, and I arose to nurse her and felt gloriously happy at being of some use again though it was a

[1]Miss Mildred Thomlinson.

266

fairly grim time as we were handicapped in a monster Margate hotel. It was in a faint way as if old days were back and my mother alive again and I was creeping out and into her bedroom to lay coals on the fire without waking her. If I can't have the lot of you here I could at almost any time have Veronica if she fell ill or troubled in any way. A moment's notice and I would bring her along and get that nurse, and in no time the three of us would be drinking ginger beer. You will please to take note of this. I have just polished off a boy in this manner who hardly knows my name and sent him off to his preparatory school. I don't want to trouble you but further communications about progress would be a relief to me however short. My love to all and not least to you who I am sure are running the ship heroically.

23 October '33

Veronica and I have sworn together that her visit has been a grand success, and as she has promised to come back soon I have the lovely feeling that she means it as sincerely as I do. She is as engaging as she is personally alluring, and we talked heaps on all sorts of subjects except the one for which times are not yet ripe, though we even skirted that, each wondering how much, if anything, the other knew.

I go to Edinburgh by Friday morning train, and propose St Andrews for two nights if all is well on the Monday. It fits best for me to stay over Sunday in Edinburgh to make some private visits.

19 December '33

I am knocking at your door or getting in by a window or any nefarious manner necessary to join your Christmas party. Nefarious entrance is suggested by our having had a burglary on our stair three nights ago, of which the unburgled flats are naturally a little proud.

I suppose you are at home and that we are having a glorious time twixt drawing-room and study. There could not be a nicer home for Christmas time, nor for the other months of the year. As things are I am here in my own study, sitting into the fire and refusing to go out of doors lest the east winds make up on my bronchial tubes which are in the condition of being all right but open to offers. I shall probably go to Stanway and Somerset before the week is out.

I had a nice present the other day of a tiny miniature of my mother, unknown to exist, and done many years before I was born. So young and so pretty, it seems to me. I should like to show it to you. It was found in an old box of fragments that had been put aside ages ago.

Well, I just set out to write to send my love, at this season of the year, to all you dear ones.

15 August '34

Established again in London for the nonce but it's rather close here, and I am hoping the nonce will only last till Friday when I may go into Somerset for a little. I had verily a grand time at Greenfield,[1] and I think rain may say it never saw itself more contemptuously treated.

My love to you all including the yellow ball—and tell your Jim I am so sorry the red and the yellow gave the blue and the black such a hammering, but of course we were obviously too good for them. Blessings on you and yours.

To Sir JAMES IRVINE

5 October '34

You would be plunging me into woe were I to accept your proposal. St Andrews is the one place where I cannot make a speech again. The last time was the occasion of my only real appearance in public, when I somehow managed to reveal myself instead of to conceal myself, and I want it to stand alone in St Andrews with none of the rest of me beside it. Don't spoil my 'lucky day'. I think you will understand, and Mabel also. So kindly get another man for the University speech and leave me out of speech-making altogether. It will make all the difference to my happiness. Possibly at some unofficial moment I might 'greet' the students in a word or two somewhere or other, but not in any arranged way. Do forgive me. It is not of course a matter of being a trouble—far from that.

31 March '35

You are slow in reappearing on this scene. I don't know when your graduation ceremony is, but I drop this line to say

[1]Radnorshire.

268

that you will find Priestley (I forget if you know him) full of
interest and more particularly to say that I believe Mabel will
find in Mrs Priestley (whom he tells me he is taking with him)
a woman after her own heart. This is meant as a very big
compliment to Mrs P., and I shall be curious to know if I
prove right.

To Lady IRVINE

17 April '35

If you don't know that you have the lovely gift of intimacy
in epistles something will have to be done about it. Not only
in epistles, for it was undoubtedly your faculty in this way that
first drew me to you. Your Jim is much more quick to be
known, he disarms at once, but suddenly one (this one please)
knows you more than that subtle one because either your bars
remain up or you throw the door open with both hands. How
sad to me if the man of whom I am so fond had taken to wife
a woman of the kind you often pretend to be. I am reminded
of Louis Stevenson's invitation to me to Samoa, 'You will have
a grand time if my wife likes you, and if she doesn't, O my
Gord.' What all this really means is that I know you like me
and so reveal yourself unto me, of which I am mighty proud.

I hope to see you some time this summer at any rate and
to cut across with no delay to that studio, where indeed I am
visiting now. No I will not sit down by that fire till I have
looked round at the pictures on the walls and even poked
among the canvases behind that sheet, and chuckled over the
coloured splashes on your smock, and the glee on your face,
and your general abandon to all restraint thrown off. As you
enter and close that door behind I see a sense of freedom come
over you as if you were Robinson Crusoe in his hut.

Yours always, Friday

12 May '35

A recent visitor[1] now returned to St Andrews told me you
were off to Ireland, but no matter—I must write. He and I
had such a fine time together that we pretty nearly got to think
that the Jubilee was ours, especially after the arrival of the
cake which is quite the prettiest of its kind I have ever seen.
I think it must have been made in the studio by fairy hands

[1]Sir James Irvine.

and that it should have been sent to the Royal Academy and hung on the line.

The woman you pretend to be should read pretended to be. It means I suppose that you deceived me into thinking that you fitted into your multitudinous duties so admirably that this was the whole of you instead of merely a little artificial part of you. You see you are so anxiously good at this part of discharging functions which are certainly of great importance that I thought thus were you made instead of thus had you made yourself, to help a big man in a big life's work. All honour to you for it certainly, but it is just a job victoriously carried out—the real you begins when the doors are shut on it and you emerge as the imaginative artistic dreamer of dreams, far from sure of yourself, indeed very humble, but nevertheless conscious that you are not as the women among whom your life is mainly cast. I ought to have seen it in the first hour, for I now consider you transparent as the day.

Jim did me a remarkable service when he was here, as I read him my play.[1] He made such an acute suggestion that I adopted it at once—an important cut that makes him a sort of part author. It had been running thro' my own head but no-one else had seen its wisdom. Cut it now is. Tomorrow I go off for a week to Venice and the Dolomites and I beg to inform you that my tie (and also Frank) goes with me.

4 February '36

Jim has told you of how things are here. They are not happy, as my sister is so ill, but I assure you it was a blessed thing to me to have him with me for that too short time and gave me some hours of brightness. He went off in good spirits but obviously desperately in need of the rest the voyage will force upon him. My sister, who is the last of us except myself, was so much to me that you can't know me well without having known her. She has always been delicate but this illness began about six weeks ago with a general breakdown and for two weeks her heart has been so weak that she has just slept all the time, and the doctors think the end may be near. She is in the nursing home of Sir Douglas Shields here and I am thankful to say has had no pain, and has none.

I don't know now whether I shall go to Edinburgh for the

[1] *The Boy David.*

270

play but I have Jim's message, and if I can do anything about seats you may be sure I will. The trouble is that they had all been disposed of before the postponement, or so I am told, but surely I can get two at any rate. You must have had a grim time over all that treatment he had to undergo—and how loath to let him out of your hands! I am all right myself now.

10 April '36

It is long since I heard from you and I am sad about it. I fear you can say the same of me, but I have been going through a bad time and was not even able to go to my sister's funeral. I am pretty right now but will not venture north for Lord Allenby's rectorial.

I miss my sister very much.

I heard from your Jim before he landed and now I suppose you are all in a tremble of delight at the prospect of soon having him back. I certainly join in that joy.

The postponement of the play caught me in bed and I would not have been able to get to Edinburgh. No dates for resumption can be fixed yet but probably the autumn. Miss Bergner is now making good progress but for a time the perforation made her case very very serious.

28 April '36

Hoity toity and O woman, woman—but I have said all that to you before. The reference for the moment is to your nonsense about fearing your letters are not as welcome as spring flowers because they entail an answer. Go to. Nevertheless I love your absurd side as well as all the others. I knew you were in Switzerland because Jim did turn up at the flat for an hour and never have I seen him look better or found him in more flaming spirits. This Indian business has freshened him grandly. Also he has promised to stay here for the nights of the 6th and 7th. Also he did not say you were to be here. (The hound! or probably he did not know at that time.)

I am glad you are having this holiday, and undoubtedly it was the right moment to choose while he must be so full up. And what fun for Veronica and Felicity.

Till we meet and always thereafter.

★

271

To Lord DESBOROUGH

Adelphi Terrace House 14 October '25

My dear Desborough

It is very good of you to send me that photograph of Denton Betty,[1] and you have sent it to a person who appreciates it. The portrait of the Bishop has now been removed from my walls, and Denton Betty takes his place. I am now so pat about her prizes that visitors think I am deserting literature for agriculture. With a slight shuffle of the cards she might be a charming young woman who got the prizes not at the shows but at Newnham. 'Lord Desborough,' says the *Times*, 'was at Cambridge yesterday, very proud of his Betty who has been awarded a First in classics.' 'Among the débutantes', says the *Morning Post*, 'was Lord Desborough's Betty, looking very charming in crêpe de chine and a rope of pearls.' 'We understand', says the *Daily Mail*, 'that Lord Desborough's so popular Betty has rejoined her husband at their place in Yorkshire.'

Yours sincerely, J. M. Barrie

31 May '27

I am glad to hear the good news of Panshanger Betty[2]. It will, I fear, have prevented her getting to London to see Lindbergh, but one can't have everything, and what she has got will probably prove to be the more lasting glory. When I think of her and her child at play I am almost unmanned.

To Lady DESBOROUGH

Stanway 10 January '37

My dear Ettie

I am very downcast to hear that Lord Desborough is ill. Please give him my love and hope that he will soon be well again. He is one of those divinely modest people who know

---

[1]A shorthorn belonging to Lord Desborough, female champion of all breeds at the Royal Agricultural Show. She was shown one Sunday at Panshanger to Barrie, who asked Lord Desborough to introduce him as the greatest shorthorn expert in Scotland. Barrie wrote a little play about Betty—an 'Elizabethan Drama'.

[2]Another shorthorn.

not how they are admired by their fellow-men. Here is one fellow-man to whom he is just about as fine and sterling a human being as I have ever known in my tolerably long pilgrimage. It is one of my greatest prides to know that he likes me. My love to you both,

J. M. B.

★

To Major J. J. ASTOR

Adelphi Terrace House

Dear Major Astor

If the enclosed suits your purpose for the Newsvendors' Benevolent and Provident Institution you are very welcome to it. To help in the smallest way a charity that was a favourite child of Charles Dickens—that is very pleasant to any author. Should this MS. find a purchaser,[1] please break the information to him that soon after *The Old Lady Shows Her Medals* was written my right hand (probably horrified at sight of my caligraphy) gave out, and I have ever since had to write with my left, to the joy of all my correspondents. Indeed, you had better present this note to him, to show him that in one way I write better now that I write worse. He will wish that my right hand had given out sooner.

Yours sincerely, J. M. Barrie

★

To Mrs RAYMOND ASQUITH

Adelphi Terrace House 12 April '25

My dear Katharine,

I went alone to Tenebrae at the Cathedral on Friday evening. Frank had lent me his breviary to read first, but I got the service in English at the door, which was good, for most of my Latin went whistling down the wind long ago. It was a tremendous experience and beautiful enough to keep this old world very still, or to do just the opposite—to shake it. The beginning seemed to me worthy of the end, and one can hardly say more. I have some understanding of what it means to you and am very glad of your faith. And I am very proud of your

---

[1] The manuscript of *The Old Lady Shows Her Medals*, knocked down to Mr Walter Spencer at 325 guineas.

letter. I won't write about other things just now. They wouldn't mix. So as soon as you got down you bathed. How like you! (But I forgot, I don't know you at all.)

I have sent the girls their tickets for Thursday. Their first 'first night', I suppose, but I won't be there to see them. I have had too many first nights, and would see more ghosts in front of the house than in the play itself[1]. I see lots of it rehearsing, though, and am just going off to the theatre for many hours, coughing on the way to cheer myself up. Nicholas unfortunately is in the Park Lane home again (tonsils) and the nurses recognised my cough and some of them hastened to it, which rather pleased me. The children acquitted themselves well at the Stanway performance which did take place at last and I did the break of the surf hauntingly with a drawer full of sago. Your friend Ronny Knox has created a furore by a burlesque message to 'listeners-in'. The press are full of it. It was quite a witty affair but the public took it seriously and believed that London was in the hands of the communists. I expect Trim[2] has been having great doings in the snow and that you have had to go rolling after.

Stanway 7 August '26
You can't really be enjoying 'northern latitudes' and toothache simultaneously and I am so sorry you have this worry. I hope by now that the humorous dentist has had his successful say. In my early days in London I used to drop into chemists' shops and get 'em to tug out a tooth for one bob. I once made a tooth for myself, with the thrilling career of which I won't detain you, but remark in passing that no one who doesn't know about that tooth really knows me. Of course no one really knows any one, which makes biographies such mockeries. Few people really know themselves (just as well), and one of them who doesn't know herself is you. Nor are you good at knowing other people, though I admit that to be in your secret circle of the liked is as good a certificate as I can think of. I am not referring to myself, being aware that if you like me at

[1] *Mary Rose.*
[2] Lord Oxford, Mrs Asquith's son.

all it is against your better judgment, but to this lucky Laura, for instance, with whom you are probably walking at this moment in that walled garden exchanging flowers, I mean confidences that I should like uncommonly to over-hear. Lovely talks I am sure and sometimes I think holy talks, souls really in communion. I like to so think of you together out of this world for a little time.

I wish I could take Trim into Inverness and buy him a kilt not of the Lovat but of the Ogilvy tartan, indeed I should like to put you into a kilt also and tramp the heather with you and lure the trout from the stream. However you have more attractive blades to squire you. This house is full of pretty women and wise men, including Lord and Lady Desborough and Lady Guendolen Cecil and Algernon, and some of the Australian cricketers come tonight. We had an afternoon visit from your Lord Oxford and your Margot and your Cis and your Cis's wife, and he said how clever Helen[1] was and I said how pretty she was.

Adelphi Terrace House 22 October '26

Are you really there in the rue de Miromesnil, which seems all the further away from me because never never dare I attempt to pronounce it. It is like an extra barrier, an additional intimation that you have burned your boats, a reminder that you are of those who don't do things by halves. Have you settled down now to the new piano and the French sticking-plaster for your brow (taffetas d'angleterre) which I fondly hope was the object of your first outing, and has the other girl[2] gone to classes where she is known not as Perspicacity but as *Perdreux*—I mean *Perdreur*—no I mean *Perdreau* (it's dogged as does it). The remainder of this letter had better be written in English, which you cannot yet have quite forgotten. Periodigue (there I go again) will soon forget it if you and she don't firmly devote half an hour a day to recalling old times when you lived in the *place d'Oxford*. Well, well in all the languages of Europe I hope you are happy and finding it worth while as I expect it is. I have no doubt too that a certain Father told you of a particular place of worship and that

[1]Lady Helen Asquith, Mrs Asquith's daughter.
[2]Lady Perdita Asquith, Mrs Asquith's other daughter, with whom she had gone to Paris.

you have been oftener to it than anywhere else and I like to think you sometimes remember me there, and so help me along.

An odd thing, I find his name where I never expected to see it, in the Fashion column of tonight's evening paper. I didn't know he frequented gilded salons, but it was the 'beautiful Moonlight music room of Sir Philip Sassoon's house, a marble-lined mansion', and Lady Lovat was 'tall, slight and wistful' and 'Father Vincent McNab was in white serge beneath a black cassock-like garment.'

To descend to more trivial things I am wondering what cigarettes you find in Paris. My attempt to have them sent failed ignominiously, but there is a tobacconist's near you (just opposite the Grand Hotel) where they have various kinds of English tobacco (as we call it). I hope all your news of Mells and the children is of the best. I wrote to Helen today and I expect she is glorying in the use of her wings though she must often long, and Trim too, for your loving arms. A dreary letter but I seem to be like that of late. I am very well though, but still a stagnant pool into which you should throw a stone. And of course I have heaps to be thankful for, and indeed am.

27 October '26

I have no doubt Chartres is rather magical (and I should have been clever enough to guess that you had it in your mind to go there promptly) but I think less divinely of it than you do as it has given you a cold. I love your rhapsody but I do hope the cold has gone. When I was at Hatfield I got a cold which I put down to reading the Casket Letters below ground and decided Queen Mary had had a cold when she wrote them which she thus passed on to me. This rather gratified me, but as it would have meant that she did write the letters I nobly surrender my point. I daresay it is more worth while to get colded by Chartres than by Mary of Scots, but never shall I admit it if Elizabeth is within hearing.

This is not the first time our letters have crossed. Is it because just when I think you are beyond hearing you have the same thought about me? At any rate yours was a very dear letter, and the only earthly touch in it consisted of your commas and semi-colons. I *was* clever enough to suspect you as capable of retorting thus, but please to understand that you must now

276

drop them, they don't go with the rest of you. You have had your revenge. I am so glad you are comfortable in the flat and that you had Hilary and Mrs Herbert to soften the change. It is inevitable that little qualms should sometimes come to you about your children being divided from you by the channel, but though I may have basely pressed this before you left, there is no real need for worry. I suppose it is all owing to your being an islander that you feel further away there than you are. If any of them was ill you would be wired about it at once, so the connection is really almost as close as when you were here. The only real difference is that you would be going to see them now and again, and that indeed is something to be deprived of, but with all well you must try to keep serene. I have a fear that days may seem long to you, with not so much definitely to do, but of course with Helen gone there would have been less to do here also.

It is odd to think of you amongst someone else's cushions and photographs. Will you gradually come to think of Mr Fairbanks as your valued friend? Will you remember him in after days as the man who made Paris pleasant for you and took you to the Café de Paris and leapt over houses to divert you when you fell into a sombre mood? I see him smiling terribly on you from every mantelshelf.

I have a letter from Helen of a quite grand character. She moans naturally over being separated from you, and undoubtedly it is harder for her not having had the boarding-school experience, but otherwise she admits to enjoying the new life hugely. One little touch showing the difference between the male and female undergrad—she begins to tell me of her tutor but the account rapidly goes off into a description of the lady's garments, eyes and the colour of her hair. She also encloses at the end a number of Xs, the middle one with a circle round it which much exercises me but I hope it is what the waiters call 'special' when they order your coffee. She also informs me that you have not discovered how many stamps to put on home letters and that she has to fork out. Which reminds me of my schooldays when a boy friend went to Paris and kept sending me French comic papers with the jokes translated into English in his own writing, for which I had to pay a penny per word. I didn't know his address so couldn't stop him. I used to fly at sight of postmen.

I have Michael Asquith with me for a week as one of the epidemics has broken out near his school though not in it, and he must be kept away from Simon for a week in case. He is all right and exults in the unexpected holiday.

Here I paused to ring up your mother so as to be able to tell you that all is well at Mells, which it is. I shall try one of these evenings to ring up you. It is nearly 10 P.M. and I am going to the Speaker's to meet colonial premiers—not like me, but I was rather pressed about it. My first outing since you fled.

15 November '26

I daresay you have heard from your mother that we had an evening together last Sunday and I hope we shall have another next week. Your father evidently stood the journey very well, and all the children are in good health. Here's a thing you must not misunderstand. I think it would be wise for you to let the head at Trim's school know that if there was the slightest thing the matter with him or with the school he should let your mother or me know at once and at the same time give us the right to act for you. I say this because you are far enough away to make it just possible for him to be less ready to apprize you. The same thing holds about Helen. I think it best to mention this because at Broadstairs where Michael was, and this curious epidemic of infantile paralysis broke out, it was useful to get the boy away at once. (There was no case in his school but bad in one other.) Now it has occurred at Uppingham and they are sent down. There is nothing of the kind—not a trace —within a hundred miles or so of Worthing, so that is not in it ət all, but just in case of anything else occurring, such a precaution is an added safeguard. There is nothing in this to worry you, it is just common sense and applies to the two of you in Paris just as much as to those here. Those books I sent were publications of Peter's who is producing a good class of book, mostly reprints. In the *Cruise on Wheels* (try Per on it— it would be good to read aloud) Mrs Pinchhold was really the author's wife—a daughter of Dickens. Haydon's autobiography seems to me as a picture of the times to be worth putting beside Boswell and Pepys. He was a bad painter, but my word, he could paint in words. There are two or three pages in which he dines Wordsworth, Keats, Lamb and a 'stamp comptroller' that seem to me a complete masterpiece. Lord Oxford (!),

278

Lord Grey and Birrell were dining with me here the other night and all agreed with me on that point. It was interesting to find that Grey knew the whole passage off by heart—nothing if it had been verse but remarkable for prose. We had a good evening—talked of nothing but literature for several hours while the bottles went round, and they were all very gay. I have been a lot in the papers lately, but not a word has Katharine seen, and she will also miss my obituary.

I wish I were with you of an evening when Per's diary is read out, I have no doubt it is uncommon good. And now to the post. My love. Yours,

Dull Dog

6 July '27

I am so sorry you can't dine this week but of course it is right and good that everything should give way to the beloved Helena. If I could cut myself this way and elongate myself that way and remove the crows-feet and bring back the smile and generally drop half a century I would with much joyous perturbation ask her for her one vacant dance. Do you remember that night I danced with you on your 18th birthday at Lady de Poppery's rout, and I thought we were getting on so well until you threw yourself into all the other dancers' arms exclaiming 'Take, oh take me back to Mamma.'

Alas, I won't be here tomorrow between six and seven as I have to be at an Eton function and it was only by some sharp practice that I had planned out to be back by eight and to await you quarter of an hour later. Sic transit. I had a nice time at Taplow though was not given as much time alone with your mother as I should have liked. She seemed to me to look a bit better but there is a delicacy about her face of a kind that only comes from suffering. Anything bad happening to her now would hurt her more than in former days, she is less capable of standing up against rough-shod things; I am sure none of her pluck has left her but some of her high spirits; none of her pride but she is more sensitive, she is in need of all the love that can be given her but would only be hurt by any well-intended pretence of it. Her talk though was very acute and indeed I think she was seeing into life and people with a penetration greater than I had ever noticed before. Well, you know those things and most other things better than I do. I have been reading *The Orchard Floor* and am so glad you sent it to me. The preacher is a poet and so wise. How good, and I believe never said before, 'Human pain is such a boon that if it did not exist it would be the instinct of a perfect soul to create it.' There are some fine thoughts about Confession. I have just read a little of it. Catholics seem to me to know almost too much. I used to think the smile on the Monna Lisa meant that she knew some one thing that is only known to the dead. You are sometimes suddenly a little like that to me. This is very dull on my part. You have no fears that the soul when it leaves the body perhaps just starts across the seas rudderless. Perhaps some do and some don't. It is difficult to know which to be sorriest for.

8 September '27

I am thinking of tomorrow—your birthday, and hoping that nothing will come to you but what is good. 'Those who bring happiness into the lives of others cannot keep it from themselves.' There must be something wrong with this for it is a quotation from myself. Besides, you are not one who clamours for happiness. But nevertheless I hope it will be a day of happiness for you long drawn out and among your dear ones. There is nothing much wrong with me, I think—something to do with my head, and I have to lie here a little longer but the doctor is excellent and I'm well looked after and my only visitor, Peter, is very kind. It will be great if I can come up to you all. I hope no troubles in your journey but a gay company.

8 April '28

I do love those long gossipy letters[1] of yours, and they have kept me from missing you too much. I am so glad you are having such a good time.

Life here of course is not so gay. I am the only man in London, quite a common experience of mine at Easter. There are it is true a few visitors wandering the streets and longing wearily for the trains that will take them back to their homes. The silence is so great that all sorts of sounds become audible that are not heard at normal times, such as a stick falling in the fire or a dog pattering along a distant street or a clock (or a heart) ticking. If the postman had knocked on Good Friday

[1] Ironic.

how we should all have jumped. There has been a church bell at long intervals which made me stare at your cathedral (of which though you may not know it there is a fine view from some of my windows); I felt it was calling to me but I didn't go, I don't know why or perhaps I do. Now I must stop and let you go and take your extract of malt. Not of course that you are doing it. You are getting thinner and thinner.

I had hoped to be seeing your mother but she is away till Tuesday, they tell me on the telephone. I'll be away a little myself, but hope to see her very soon.

I hope you pray for me still.

1 September '28

It all sounds very good at La Croix though I am sure it is not the bathing nor the lights nor the enchanting fishing villages that make it good half so much as the heart you put into your forethought for everybody. If I were there, and I wish I were, I should just be another for you to keep in good care and no doubt the most selfish one. I picture you scattering largesse among the family. I see now that it is a good thing your mother is away at this time, though it would not have been a good thing without your being with her. The things she says about you in the note you enclosed make good reading. It is mentioned in the papers that Lord Haldane leaves in his will (not of course published yet) £1000 to his old German university, which strikes me as highly honourable. I search the papers in vain for pictures of the Earl of Oxford bathing with four ladies inset. The newspapers seem to exist chiefly on such just now, and it is very clever of you to elude them. But Shaw in the nude is their great catch, and he looks adorable. I came back to London town yesterday and so the season may be said to be at an end. I notice in a newspaper that I have been spending August in a shooting lodge which I have rented for the summer and have been having magnificent sport. Otherwise there seems to be no news unless you will accept as such that the canary, which I left here with housekeeper, has been rather seedy, this being the moulting season. It however burst into brief song at sight of me, after having been silent for days. This is boasting, but I make no pretence that I was not top-heavy with elation, though on reflection I see I had to get a canary to do this. I am wondering whether I could not dress it up beautifully and take it to share a table with me at the Devonshire. In honesty I must now spoil everything by admitting that it is of the male sex. But that you no doubt guessed as soon as you heard how it greeted me. And here is another item of news. Tunny is in London. I don't suppose you know who he is, the mighty boxer, and (almost as flattering as the canary) he has expressed a wish to meet me. Little you thrill with pride in me on account thereof, but the news is not meant for your consumption, but to be passed on to Trim that he may think more highly of me. You have amazed as well as delighted me by your letters and I am very proud to have them even though there might be a jag here and there.

11 July '29

Things have been going better with Mr Winter[1] so far than I had dared to expect when I last saw you. I did not expect him to recover from the shock itself, but so far as that is concerned he has stood it excellently. He has been for a fortnight now in Sir Douglas Shields's Home and the other surgeon Monahan has also examined him, and they think there is quite a hopeful chance of his complete recovery, or nearly so. So many bones are broken that outsiders can hardly believe that possible, and it must be a good long time before one knows, but at any rate he is now comfortable and bright and there is no immediate cause for anxiety. I am with him a lot and very thankful that things are even as they are. I am glad you had such a good time with Trim, and can see him getting ninety minutes into the hour, but you evidently had a disturbing day over your mother. Of course she always will tend to do too much but if she did too little she would suffer also, and there is no one who can keep her between extremes so well as yourself, nor care for and love her as you do, as it has often been my intense pleasure to see. My love to you all and to the garden.

30 July '29

I loved your letter for the good things that are in it. If I am too egotistical (I don't know that I am but I was) you are too little so, and seem to me rather to starve yourself about yourself. Give the lady more thought, I assure you she is worth it. We could make a compact—you to go further in that direc-

[1] Barrie's brother-in-law had broken his leg.

tion and I to be more bridled. As for letting your children
see all sides of life, what you have to accept is that they must
inevitably do so—not only that, but they have already seen
many sides and are making their choice for themselves. In a
sense, though Helen and Per are gorgeously unworldly, it is
not because they don't already have a great deal of knowledge.
Their natural goodness is what protects them and will go on
doing it. Still, to be flung unnecessarily into mundane ways
of living must be dust to the finest eyes. The moral currency
must suffer with too much tolerance. I expect I am gibbering,
and you had much better be off with Trim than reading this
(and off with him you are in any case). I wish so much I could
get to Mells before I go to Stanway, but evidently I can't. I
must hang on over some publishing worries and to settle a cast
of the revival of *Dear Brutus*. If only Winter's leg would heal
it means more to me than a score of plays, and they still give
some hope. I shall come to London occasionally to see him,
and some time you may be there.

12 January '30

It was indeed good of you to send me your fairy tale, and
well I know that it gnawed you to do so, which of course makes
me value it the more. I don't want your humility ever to grow
less, so I won't smile at you therefor, but I do think it delightfully told in the choicest because the simplest words. I wish
I could have heard your voice as you told it at Mells and still
more as you told it 'to your children when they were small'.
When I speak my voice is as raucous as a broken bell, and no
one wants to get away from it more than I do. It is a mercy
for all concerned that they did not get the little mump instead
of the little prince but I shall always think now that the mump
wanders solitary through Somerset knocking vainly for admit-
tance at lighted windows. I must find who Mrs Hardy meant.
I thought she said you were at the wedding with the girls. I
want still more to know which of the Hardy heroines you would
care to be. I see you on Bathsheba's horse, that vivid scene,
yes, and in a good deal of her contrariness that you think you
haven't got, but there are others better even than Bathsheba
for you.—Already two years ago yesterday since Hardy died.

Poor Mascot.[1] She is really a little bit of yourself gone.

[1]Dog.

Makes one think of Walt Whitman's lines about—

> *I think I could turn and live with animals, they are so placid and*
> *self-contained,*
> *They do not sweat and whine about their condition,*
> *They do not lie awake in the dark and weep for their sins.*
> *Not one is dissatisfied—not one is dominated with the mania of*
> *owning things.*
> *Not one kneels to another nor to his kind that lived thousands of*
> *years ago.*
> *Not one is respectable or industrious over the whole earth.*

This torn picture [reproduction enclosed] is Sir Walter Scott's first love of whom when she married another. (and afterwards so did he happily) he said 'the crack will remain to my dying day'. Looks like a boarding-house keeper to the eyes of today but I suppose it is the head piece and the apparel. Helen was the belle of Mary Herbert's ball according to Davina. With her at Oxford, and Trim soon going back to school, you will soon be alas scattered again. I wish you had somebody you liked in London.

Now I am off for a lonely meal at a pub as it's Sunday and the flat empty save for me and the canary and a roaring wind.

26 January '30

I hope it was all different from your expectations and that you had a happy time at the ball and that it was Peradventure who had to drag you away in the small hours, leaving one slipper behind you. I feel sure also that Trim is enjoying Ampleforth, else would you have had a much worse time at the station where I so wretchedly failed you. The going back at the beginning of the second half is usually the grimmest, there is no novelty to help, and not enough of the camaraderie that comes later; the worst bit of leaving home is now past and those three were probably rollicking by the time you tottered back to loneliness. As for my little cold it had nothing to do with Olympia where I enjoyed everything immensely, though I know I was stupider than ever. The previous fog was what did for me, and already I'm all right and up today.

It was dear of you to write—just got it last post, and I am so glad of its good news which truth to tell I had rung up Per for earlier in the day. My own opinion is that you should not come away before Saturday if even then, as that temperature or something might fluctuate a little, and in any case now that you are there the knowledge thereof will be a big fillip to Trim every time he wakes up. His whispers and the bandage would begin to assume proportions in your mind before you reached King's Cross. It is however very reassuring that you like the nurse so much and the general arrangements in the hospital—this will make for your peace of mind here.

I dined at No. 16 on Sunday and dropped Per on my way back. She was very touching, she looked so like an angel. She really did. We had the A. P. Herberts, very nice and merry. He gave an amusing account of his first book's publication. He went to the publishing office in a glory because they had written they wanted it, was ushered into a room where a serene man said 'Your book? Ha! Herbert? Ho. Of course we are sure to drop a lot of money on it. Do you know what the price of paper is nowadays? No? (whistles down tube) What is the price of paper just now Mr Brown? Mr Brown tells me the price of paper is 70s. the so and so. Do you know what the price of bookbinding is Mr Herbert? No. (whistles) What is the price of bookbinding at present, Mr Jones? Mr Jones says the price of bookbinding is etc. Do you know Mr Herbert what we have to spend on advertising? No? (whistles) What have we to spend on advertising, Mr Robinson? He says we spend £0000 on advertising Mr Herbert'—and so on.

I'm all right but I do take a time to go to sleep. Another grand go at it tonight—oil stove to heat milk, a powder to put in it, then watch myself for results.

The thing I've set off writing[1] is badgering me, as I meant it to be six pages and it is now six and twenty and I question whether I have reached the middle. A spate, but I'm afraid of muddy water. A heroine arrived this evening, and there should be no women in the thing at all.

That book, being out of print, hasn't arrived yet. I'm sending you one called *Fathers*, much of which I think quite fine and a few of them nasty. Afraid it can't go off till tomorrow

[1] *Farewell, Miss Julie Logan.*

285

morning. If you are a good girl you were in bed some time ago. Now for the post—and my kettle, which is pretty sure to capsize.

To Lady HORNER (the mother of Mrs Asquith), at Mells
Adelphi Terrace House 7 January '35

My dear Frances

I still have a melancholy conviction that I was a boorish visitor for you all at the festive season but however I failed it was just because some dreamy fit was on me, for you were as triumphant a hostess as ever and I loved and envied your victorious ways. Dick has shot down the horizon and we shall probably hear no more of him for a long time but you made him blissfully happy and in his dreams I have no doubt he is ringing you all up with invitations to the racquets court. Mells may be now or next day as snowy as a Christmas card for it seems that winter has now arrived, very cold here and white flakes falling. My sister is with me and a piano I got in for her has knocked the back out of the lift. My love to you,

J. M.

★

To BRIGADIER ————

[The Brigadier wrote to *The Times* a letter lamenting that his cricketing days were over, and describing his failure in his last match. Barrie replied to him also in *The Times*.]

29 April '30

Dear Brigadier

Though I don't know you I wish I did, and that is the only excuse I can offer for my presumption in begging you to dine with me at any time or place that is seemly to you. It is today's confession in the *Times* about your last cricket exploit that makes me long to see you opposite me sitting at a table for two.

Though I am not a brigadier (through no fault of my own) I, too, can look back upon days when I led my men into the tented field, and to the last match of all when I performed so differently from you that ordinary civility prevents my stating at this early period of our acquaintance what I did, though it may come out at our little dinner. You will, I am sure, pardon me for pointing out that on the great occasion you

286

made a regrettable mistake in going in last. I gather indeed that it was your practice to be tenth man or so. You were no doubt influenced by the reflection that with a little luck you might carry out your bat, though you should have known that when the ninth wicket falls there are always four more balls to that over. You were playing for the glory of the moment when you should have been thinking of posterity. No one seeing you go in last, or hearing that you go in last, or noticing in the *Times* that you went in last, will ever credit you with being a batsman, not even if you get into double figures. Now, having thought the matter out profoundly, I always as captain went in first. This did not deceive the onlookers, and still less my side, as to my prowess, but I was intentionally playing a waiting game. Readers of the local weekly seeing that I opened the innings, same as Hobbs does, took for granted that I was an accomplished bat who on this occasion happened to be 'unfortunate'.

The things we can talk about if you will only come to dinner! The Australians, for instance. I must admit that I have a leaning to them, being such a young side and having, all the time they are batting or holding out their hands for a catch, to remember the 67 rules they have sworn not to break about wives and autographs. I daresay when you were a captain (I mean a real captain, not a military one) you had my experience about tossing? The opposing captain, after looking me over, always told me to toss, and he called 'The Bird', and then, whether the coin came down head or tail, he said, 'The Bird it is; we shall go in'. I often felt there was something wrong about this, but could never quite see what it was. Now do you think that, as the Australians are such a young side and have so many things to remember, I would be justified in dropping a line to Mr Woodfull putting him up to calling 'The Bird'?

Another thing, ought I to give him or Mr Hornibrook a tip about slow left-hand bowling? Mr Hornibrook I understand is their only slow left-hand bowler, and I am a slow left-hand bowler myself. I was elated to read of Mr J. C. White's success in Australia, and as soon as he came back I hurried to Lord's to see him. To my horror I discovered that he did not know what slow left-hand bowling is. I would have called it (and did so) fast left-hand bowling. You say nothing of bowling in the *Times* except that you were out first ball, so that perhaps you find all bowling alike and inclined to be fast. Now my left-hand bowling is so slow that it exasperates the batsman, who has gone through all his flourishes by the time the ball reaches the middle of the pitch. My bowling does not so much take the wickets as lie against them. If I think I have sent down a bad delivery I can pursue the ball, recapture it, and send it down again. Ought I to tell Mr Hornibrook about this, or would it be more patriotic to tell Mr White?

Perhaps wisest to give them no tips. A side that can leave out Macartney needs them not or is mad. Did you ever see a swallow with a sense of humour chased by dogs? It would come down close to them to tempt them, then soar, then down again and soar again, and so round and round the lawn. That was Macartney with his bowlers. They say Jackson is such another. How splendid! I mean, Oh, dear! Such a talk we shall have if you will dine with me.

J. M. Barrie

To the Hon. MAURICE BARING, writer
Adelphi Terrace House 14 July '31

My dear Maurice

It is a beautiful book.[1] I have read it with intense enjoyment, and I think it will live long.

Yours, J. M. Barrie

To WILLIAM YEAMAN, of Edinburgh
25 July '31

Dear Mr Yeaman

I am uncommonly obliged to you for writing me about Mr Haggart.[2] Certainly we must try to get him up to Kirriemuir. I have written to him and mentioned that I was also writing to you. The enclosed little cheque is to help him in our plot, but I did not speak of it to him. He ought, if he goes, to be

---

[1] *In My End is My Beginning*.

[2] Alexander Haggart, a boyhood friend of Barrie's. He was a near neighbour in the tenements at Kirriemuir, and taught Barrie the use of a bat. He became a tailor in Kirriemuir and a member of the Cricket Club, subsequently disappeared for over thirty years, and turned up again in Edinburgh.

received warmly, and if I knew the time I could write to some people there. You are doing a capital thing and I repeat I feel beholden to you.

Yours sincerely, J. M. Barrie

★

To the Children of Mr and Mrs J. B. PRIESTLEY

Adelphi Terrace House 13 December '31

Dearest Angela, Darling Barbara, Sweet Sylvia, Precious Mary, Beloved Rachel, I thought you had forgotten your Uncle Bigley and I had a sad heart, but now I leap with joy, and as soon as you said you wanted me to write another story I banged one off and it is to cost only Tuppence (so as to try to beat your father's circulation) and it might be called 'Five for Tenpence', and so might you perhaps, but I would give more. So that is an offer.

With Uncle Bigley's love

To Mrs PRIESTLEY

24 May '32

Dear Mrs Priestley

Yes I shall be both pleased and proud to be godfather to your 'little son', as you call him with a casual effrontery that does not take me in. I want further to tell you though it may seem over-bold that I had hoped you would take this step, no light offer to make nor lightly accepted. I accept it because from the first my arms wanted to enclose the whole clanjamfry of you, and I consider that you have now merely made the natural response. Of course I shall be at the christening in your village [Highgate Village] and we shall have five bridesmaids.

Yours affectionately, J. M. Barrie

Tell the five that clanjamfry means Rag tag and bob-tail, which is all they are.

3 June '32

June 19th is duly noted down as the red-letter Sunday. I look forward most uncommon to the gay and trembling affair for it will be both. I put it to you that in the circumstances (by which I mean the bridesmaids) the marriage-service should perhaps be used. Or a line could be inserted for them 'Do you take this boy to love honour and bully you?' If the clergyman is inclined to the historical he might mention that here Barbara and J.M.B. met face to face for the first time. If at the last moment you find you have forgotten the christening-robe *you can have mine.* Somehow I have it. I consider it rather a fine affair, made by my mother for me, and among my earliest recollections is people knocking at the door and asking for the loan of the christening gown. Anything else that may have been overlooked refer to me.

15 June '32

The christening robe was sent off to be beautified as soon as I got your message this morning and will be forwarded to you by messenger on Friday, or latest Saturday when you must decide whether it is right. It may not be fit for present times as it is 72 years old, and though I love your being willing you must also be wise. I must admit that I offered it to various relations and others and none of them would have it. I shall be with you in good time on Sunday. I hardly know what I am writing as I have just been rung up and told of the death of one of my greatest friends.[1]

26 June '32

I have been reading those two booklets, and with what you say yourself it is obvious to me that Father Jellicoe's work is a splendid affair. Whether the country is coming to crash or not there is much more being done for children than ever before, and in the end they may be the ones to set things right, led by Thomas with a trumpet. Speaking of him I have not felt so pleased with myself for a long time as when I carried him home from the christening—a bold (but determined) step, for I was not oblivious to your mortal terror. The robe arrived back safely, and I beg to inform you that it was my housekeeper who had it starched. If she had consulted me I think (or at least hope) that I should have known better. I daresay you made fun of me to the five for having starched it. That is where the canker gnaws. My love to the whole clanjamfry.

[1]Sir Donald Maclean, M.P.

To J. B. PRIESTLEY, writer

9 July '32

My dear Priestley

There is no doubt at all about *Faraway*, it is a beauty. I have come to the conclusion that you have invented a new art of writing, which is to include fiction, biography and travels, for this is all of them in one and obviously the best way. I certainly never knew the South Seas as I do now in all their glamour and corruption, and any intention of visiting them is on my part cancelled; it would be too much like your three musketeers setting forth a second time. A subject in this flat has become 'Whether do you like William or Ramsbottom or the Commander best?' Ramsbottom seems to be the favourite but I knew there would be something like him in your book (and in your next book) and that you can do him on your head. He belongs to your specialty department. The Commander is finer and rarer work, not rarer in one sense for many a writer has had a shot at him while Ramsbottom is unique, but because 'the fine old name of gentleman' fading from sight is here held for permanence. Having said which my vote is (tonight) for William.

I trust Thomas is flourishing like a green bay tree. What a happy household.

Yours, J. M. Barrie

To Mrs PRIESTLEY

22 December '34

The little picture of Rachel and Thomas is terrific and sums up childhood. At least it would were there not such a grand row of names on the *English Journey* J. B. P. so kindly sends me. What a good name for the lot would be *English Journey*. My love to you at this time and all times. I don't neglect you in my mind, however contemptible in my actions, and at a word I would adopt the whole clanjamfry.

To J. B. PRIESTLEY

6 August '36

I have read *They Walk in the City* with a long delight. Nobody else could have written it. You face the woes of life without

any flinching and some others can do that but not I think with
your sanity and your great saving grace of seeing the good and
giving it a dwelling-place in your pages and so being a heartening writer because you are a heartening being. The sensa-
tionalism of the end is certainly thrilling but I don't like it as
well as the rest, it seems hardly to belong; it set one wondering
(an end being so troublesome in this case) whether your mind
had ever played with the idea of the two wanderers missing
each other in London till almost the last page. Your two sailors
in *Bees on the Boat Deck* are glorious figures. I read the play
but did not see it.

I hope you had all a great time in U.S.A. and are also happy
to be back. The picture-card I got of the family in their
sombreros was grand and I wished I could be dashing about
with them in a solemn or at any rate grave ecstasy. They have
probably the best time in the world. They would have brought
me out of my shell in which I now seem permanently to abide.

10 October '36

Herewith the note for the Wells dinner.

You must both have felt pretty white when you turned away
from the child in Paris. I hope the novelty of it saved her. I
daresay you considered waiting a year and sending Barbara
with her and damn the increase of loneliness to yourselves. It
will seem a rather empty house to you but I have no doubt,
sir, that it was a right step to take. What I like best about you
both is that it makes you feel forlorn. Go to! I shall be uncommon glad to see you when you can come in, and want to
descend on you also. I have to begin play-rehearsing now but
could easily get away some evening before the left-overs go
to bed.

[Enclosure]

10 October '36

I regret much my inability to be at the dinner in honour of
Wells, regret it personally and also officially as President of the
Society of Authors. He is of course one of our chiefest glories,
one of the two angels left to us, and I should have loved to be
with you and have a go at him.

★

To 'EDDIE' (Sir EDWARD) MARSH
Adelphi Terrace House 5 April '32

Dear Eddie Marsh

I am very sorry you have had this bad bout. I had the same thing long ago, and know how out of spirits one is even (and indeed more) after the convalescing time arrives, which I understand is what you have now reached. The occasion prompts me to say what I have often wanted to say to you, though we have never seen much of each other, that there are few men of letters who in our time have so abundantly earned the affections of our calling. One can trace your helping hand here, there and everywhere, you never seem to give a thought to self when there are others whom you can encourage along the way. So many know this, and I just want you to understand that I know it also, and have long had a deep regard for you.

Yours sincerely, J. M. Barrie

To Sir KENNETH BARNES, Principal of the Royal Academy of Dramatic Art
10 November '32

Dear Kenneth

I don't have a bust. Yet I should like to be on one of those walls. Would a photograph be any use? If so I could get one enlarged in my grand garments as Chancellor of Edinburgh University.

Yours, J. M. B.

To Miss DEUCHAR
Balnaboth, Kirriemuir, Angus 25 August '33

Dear Miss Deuchar

My telegram on Wednesday had let you know of the safe arrival of the Clarinet and Flute, and various papers. My very hearty thanks. The Clarinet is without a reed, but that is easily being supplied, and I mean to buy the Clarinet tomorrow at the sale, and present it to the town in perpetuity. Though I think the flute is of almost equal interest, I feel we shall get better effect at the moment by confining our attentions to one object, so I am returning the flute to you, registered, with the suggestion that if you care to do so, you should offer it to the town at a later date. This should be done through the Provost (Mr Peacock), and I also advise you sending through him some such interesting note about the Clarinet as you mention. Your kindness in the whole matter will help me much in getting through tomorrow's ordeal,[1] and I feel greatly beholden to you.

Yours sincerely, J. M. Barrie

To JOSEPH ALEXANDER, of Kirriemuir

Adelphi Terrace House 24 October '33

Dear Mr Alexander

You are a good spokesman for them, and the Club have my permission to play *Quality Street* at Kirrie free of royalty.

Thank you also for your very interesting letter, with so many familiar names in it—your uncle, the volunteers on march to Logie, and above all what you speak of doing for the proposed Museum. It is a most generous proposal and will make all of us much beholden to you.

Yours sincerely, J. M. Barrie

To Miss EUPHAN CRICHTON, of Edinburgh

[On the occasion of the 350th Anniversary of Edinburgh University in October 1933 Barrie was principal guest and speech-maker at civic celebrations. Going down the stairs, escorted by the University mace-bearer, at the Music Hall, George Street, he was about to pass Miss Crichton when on an impulse he stopped, saying: 'I don't know who you are but I would like to shake hands with you.']

5 November '33

Dear Miss Crichton

You would have 'spoilt it' a little if you had *not* written—

[1] Barrie opened a bazaar at Kirriemuir on August 26th, 1933 in aid of the Town Band, and auctioned the clarinet, bestowed by Miss Deuchar, on which her father, Mr George Deuchar, had played at the inauguration of the band in 1861. Barrie pretended that his canary had accompanied him to Kirriemuir and was perched in the roof of the hall; and whenever the bidding flagged, he took a bid from the canary, to whom the clarinet was finally knocked down at £50. Barrie then presented it to Kirriemuir in perpetuity.

and such a nice letter too. That was an odd meeting on the stair; why did I stop and speak? something in your face made me do it—the only incident of the kind too while I was in Edinburgh. A ship passing in the night that I felt a drawing to. This is to wish you all the best kind of happiness.

Yours sincerely, J. M. Barrie

To Miss MILDRED THOMLINSON, Barrie's Nurse in sickness

28 January '34

Dear Mildred

How delightful is your clear handwriting after the almost impossible scrawls with impossible signatures that are often my portion—the signatures especially of business men . . .

I have been getting on peacefully in health, no new colds; and your chest-quilts, for which my hearty thanks, defy ingress of wind or fog. I still have a fight to get into them in the right direction but usually rise triumphant from the fray. An artist[1] has been doing a little picture of my fireplace with me on the settle, and has been asked by the sitter to allow for the Mildred-quilt.

Yours, J. M. Barrie

10 May '34

Dear Mildred

It is grand of you to take note of my birthday in such a heartening floral display. I celebrated it myself by taking an aspirin (five grains), not that I needed it but I felt I must do something. Also I attended the first-birthday-party of Ruthven Barrie Llewelyn Davies[2] and ate of his cake, on the top of which was one lovely candle, surrounded by my 74 at the base. When Peter blew out the candles, R.B.L.D. (who thought they were the ballet) had to be removed yelling. You seem to have settled down permanently with this lady and this babe, so it is a blessing for me that I am in stalwart health.

J. M. B.

[1]Peter Scott.
[2]Son of Peter Llewelyn Davies and his wife Margaret, and born on Barrie's seventy-third birthday.

To *JOHN T. EWEN, of Forfar*

24 March '11

Dear Mr Ewen

I have pleasure in answer to your letter in sending you £1 towards the Brodie Memorial.[1] I can't say however that I referred to him in my book.[2] That was to another school. I think I had my arithmetic from him and writing. If he had continued to keep his eye on me this letter would not be as it is now.

Yours sincerely, J. M. Barrie

7 April '35

Na, na, not for me to engage myself for anything nowadays except the very few jobs where I am tied. I could not in any case be north about that time. It is uncommon nice of you to ask me[3], and the kind invitation to your home would be an added incentive, but I am not built for any functions that can be avoided. I have pleasant memories of Forfar, and Canmore Street and the Academy and that place where clothes were washed in the open, and also of dear friends now gone, and am glad to hear that I am not quite forgotten there.

To *R. T. SKINNER, of Edinburgh*

18 April '35

Dear Mr Skinner

It was indeed a kind thought of yours to let me know of the little repair the memorial to my well-loved old landlady, Mrs Edwards, stands in need of, and I shall be still more beholden to you if you will ask the firm you mention to do the repair, and to send the bill to me.

I am further indebted for the delightful sketch of you by Mr J. M. Bulloch, which I much enjoyed.

Yours sincerely, J. M. Barrie

[1] In response to a request for a subscription to a memorial in Forfar Academy to an old mathematics and writing master of Barrie's and Mr Ewen's in that school.

[2] In *An Edinburgh Eleven.*

[3] To open the Forfar flower-show.

8 May '35

I am glad to hear that the renovation work on Mrs Edwards's stone is being completed. I am trusting to you to send me the account when it comes in, and in this connection I may add that I am on the eve of going off to the continent for about a fortnight.

I was interested to hear of your visit to Dr Daniell[1] though saddened by what you say of his condition. I think (but am not sure) that Viewforth Gardens was the address where I had tea with him six or eight years ago, and then his landlady, with whom I had some talk, was a cantie woman, looking after him well and proud of having such a distinguished lodger. As you say, one could not dare to offend him. I have, however, written to him just a friendly letter, mentioning a delightful nurse (who had nursed Mrs Edwards) who was his other guest at the tea party. If he gives me her name and address (I have asked him for this) I might get to know more about the state of affairs without his being aware of it.

To The *MARCHIONESS OF SALISBURY*

13 November '35

Dear Lady Salisbury

I had a right good time at Hatfield—as ever. Have not been well this last week (all right now) else would you have been informed earlier, though of course it must have been obvious. I am now fully prepared for the election, having found out who is my man for this division (he very kindly sent me a card to tell me). I looked him up in *Who's Who* and found he said 'Recreations—None,' which at less strenuous times might have made me pause. I have also hired a wireless set for the one night. My grateful thanks to you.

Yours, J. M. Barrie

[1] A Welshman, barrister and scientist, who in succession to Barrie had lodged with Mrs Edwards at 3 Great King Street, Edinburgh.

297

To Miss *PAULINE FOLLETT*[1]

10 November '35

My dear Pauline

You write me a very nice letter which makes me think more of you than ever, and indeed, behind you, of your mother and father. I have not heard from the theatre or Mr Bright though I suppose I shall tomorrow, but must accept your news as definite, as I am still not quite well enough to take the responsibility on myself, and I see that without my being at the rehearsals to rehearse you, it would probably be done in the wrong way. But be sure that my interest in you is greater than ever and that I believe in you and look forward to your being Peter etc. etc. etc. in the future.

Yours affectionately, J. M. Barrie

11 May '36

What a delightful little present to send me—it almost makes amends for having a birthday. I wish I had been there standing ready to gaff the salmon you caught. So many times I have had that comparatively humble part to play with my boys, who were most enthusiastic anglers. It will be great to see you in November bringing the house down as Dick Whittington.

To Sir *EWEN MACLEAN*, M.D.

28 April '36

Dear Sir Ewen

I think it a happy idea of yours to keep in the lamp-stand drawer a few words about your brother Donald[2] from favoured friends, and I am proud to be considered one of them. I may safely say that I never knew a better man. I miss him sore for I loved him much, and my visits to him at the House of Commons brightened my days as did his visits here to me. My windows look out upon Westminster, and many a night still, just before going bed-wards, I am saying good-night to the light over the clock feeling that it is Donald on guard.

Yours sincerely, J. M. Barrie

[1]Barrie had met her on a cruise; she had stage-ambitions and was fourteen years old, and Barrie, who had always wished to see the part played by one as young, thought she looked an ideal Peter Pan. The producers considered her youth and inexperience an objection.
[2]Sir Donald Maclean, M.P.

To Major JOHN ROSS, of Glasgow

7 October '36

Dear Major Ross

I learn from C. E. Lawrence[1] that you want to dedicate your book on Royal Scotland to me. This to say I am beholden to you for the thought and will be made proud if you do so. May you have much success with it and happiness from it.

Yours sincerely, J. M. Barrie

To Mrs J. W. HERRIES, of Edinburgh

[in Edinburgh] 22 November '36

Dear Mrs Herries

Thank you very heartily for the flowers. It is kind of you. I thought your husband's piece in yesterday's *Scotsman* an astonishingly correct interpretation of the words I had said to him about my play.[2] You will be sorry to lose him but he will have a fine holiday. I am a little better and hope to get to the Scottish Arts Club dinner or other meal before I go, but I wish he had been to be there.

Yours sincerely, J. M. Barrie

To C. B. COCHRAN, theatrical-manager

Adelphi Terrace House 16 August '34

Dear Mr Cochran

Thank you for letter. I send you along with this in another cover a copy of the *David* play.[3] The visions in it, as you will see, are now real figures. I have also been working out in my own copy how to give David more time to change. Very interested to read what you say of the possibilities of an earlier production and will be delighted if they succeed. If not it

[1]Of the firm of John Murray, publishers.
[2]*The Boy David.*
[3]Barrie had seen Elisabeth Bergner in *Escape Me Never* and had been introduced to her in her dressing-room by Peter Scott. Barrie later told her he wished to write a play for her and she herself chose the part of David as a boy. Barrie, who had not written a play for fourteen years, set to work with infinite zest on *The Boy David*. C. B. Cochran was to be manager.

can't be helped. You have scored over me in having those talks with Elisabeth [Bergner] but I am promised one this evening. I did enjoy our supper that night, and between you and me I liked Mrs Cochran.

Yours sincerely, J. M. Barrie

13 April '35

This Desmond Tester seems a possible boy. Let us have a talk about best way of judging him. Also Wilfrid Walter sounds to me right. He is a good actor and I believe tall enough (with additions at any rate). You see a real giant would tend to seem comic, which would be all wrong.

15 September '35

Miss Bergner has sent me a letter she had received from Mr Halevy who produced the Old Testament plays a good many months ago at the Scala. He speaks in it of having seen you and of wanting to be in production of my play, and those productions of his certainly much impressed me, indeed I think he could work the crowds and make suggestions about clothes and scenery in a way that probably no one else could do. I am wondering whether he could be brought in to *help* the producer, Mr Komisarjevsky or whoever it may be. Could two men work amicably on the same job? His letter is in English but is probably in another's hand, but you will know if he speaks English. Don't you think also we should be meeting soon about the casting?

16 September '35

I am going tonight to see Banks in his play and to the Old Vic on Saturday to see William Devlin in *Peer Gynt* as he seems to be a man to consider. This will make such a week of playgoing as I have not experienced for many a year.

30 September '35

I thought William Devlin a decided possibility for Saul and I believe Ion Swinley in the same company would be first-class for Samuel, but of course your views and Miss Bergner's are what I want. I am delighted that the new piece is shaping so well but I don't really like first nights so with many thanks I had better defer seeing it till that is over. I hope you had a good time in Paris and brought a star or two back in your pocket.

300

30 March '36

I am truly grieved that your leg is giving you so much pain, and I do wish you could give it the long rest that I understand it cannot do without. On the other hand with so many irons in the fire and so many issues that you cannot depute to others one can see that rest is hard to come by as well as something contrary to your nature. At any rate save the leg to this extent by letting me come to you at any time instead of your coming here. I can do this easily and I like your house as the house of friends of mine. Certainly one of the happiest things in connection with the play is the affection for you that has grown up within me.

Caledonian Hotel, Edinburgh[1] 1 December '36
[in pencil from his sick-bed]

In case you should be making any alteration in the last scene (David and Jonathan) my idea is as in enclosed sketch, though as I can't draw it may carry little meaning to you. I am not pressing you for this, and I don't really understand properly what the arrangement of the scene is at present. Probably quite good. I conceived one of those sky-cloths (which have probably a technical name) that go round the stage in a half-circle from left to right. A suggestion of Bethlehem painted on it, and also painted on it some of the grass and barley which are 'practical' in front.

The only important 'practical' thing in the scene is the 'mound' within which is David's little cave. I fancy that neither Komisarjevsky nor Stearn quite understand my mound. It is just a lump in the ground, nearly C, and covered with the grass growing on it. I conceive it of the shape in my sketch (very important this). David drags spear with both hands to the lower end of mound and then (himself at side of mound) draws it up in ferocious jerks as very heavy and at first the audience is puzzled as to his object. When he gets the head-piece of spear over the high end of mound (which should here be about 4 ft. 6 in. in height) he gets beneath this heavy projecting end which now becomes balanced on his shoulder and

[1] *The Boy David* after a number of unprecedented and disastrous delays, was having a preliminary run at the King's Theatre in Edinburgh, where Barrie himself was ill in bed at his hotel during all rehearsals and performances. The play was produced a fortnight later in London at His Majesty's Theatre on December 14th and was withdrawn on January 30th.

moves away, thus having shown the Lord that he can do something 'all by himself'. He looks upward twice with rapturous delight at his success in thus outwitting the Lord (who may be imagined to be amused at the little rogue's exploit) and exits triumphantly. The other end of the mound is so low that it is practically on the ground.

As I say, don't worry about the sky background if it is new trouble or much expense, but get the mound right. Godfrey Tearle understands about how the mound should be.

All going well here, but I am not equal to a performance . . .

17 February '37

Many thanks for sending me those charming letters. Some of them are very good reading and would be better if it were not that I am still in the hands of the doctor and rather forgetful of plays. But I might be much worse and think I am a little better. What a channel journey Miss Bergner and Paul must have had. Excuse what looks to me shaky handwriting.

★

[Barrie's last letter, written from a nursing-home, where he died on June 19th]

To FRANK THURSTON (*Barrie's man-servant*)

[June '37]

My dear Frank

. . . This is for your guidance[1] Consult anyone you like. Don't of course publish a word of it before you are certain I am gone, and I suppose even the doctors are not sure how far spent I am. I feel a certain strength at present. I have been quite comfortable here though it would be better of course to die in one's own home. No one could have done more for me than you and Mrs Stanley, and I bless your names. I want you besides the monetary bequest to pick for yourself a hundred of my books and anything else you like. Few persons who have entered that loved flat have done more honour to books.

J. M. Barrie

Come and see me tomorrow.

[1]The first part of the letter refers to another enclosed with it which was cut up and sent to the various friends concerned.

302

INDEX

Pages in bold figures indicate Letters

304

307